GETTING IT DONE

GETTING IT DONE

How Obama and Congress Finally Broke
the Stalemate to Make Way for
Health Care Reform

———

SENATOR TOM DASCHLE
with David Nather

THOMAS DUNNE BOOKS
St. Martin's Press
New York

THOMAS DUNNE BOOKS.
An imprint of St. Martin's Press.

GETTING IT DONE. Copyright © 2010 by Tom Daschle. All rights reserved. Printed in the United States of America. For information, address St. Martin's Press, 175 Fifth Avenue, New York, N.Y. 10010.

www.thomasdunnebooks.com
www.stmartins.com

Library of Congress Cataloging-in-Publication Data available upon request.

ISBN: 978-0-312-64378-2

First Edition: October 2010

10 9 8 7 6 5 4 3 2 1

To my brother Greg,
whose life reminds us every day
of the importance of good health

Contents

Introduction

I will never forget the feeling of shock when I read the message. On the morning of January 13, 2009, I received an e-mail from my younger brother, Greg. He had been teaching English in Sapporo, Japan, for a number of years, and he had just gone to a doctor after becoming ill as he was working with one of his students. He had a seizure in the doctor's office, so an ambulance took him to a hospital in Otaru City. To his horror, they found a brain tumor. The doctor believed it was a malignant glioma—the most common kind of primary brain tumor, but also the most lethal. Specifically, after running more tests, his doctors thought it was probably a glioblastoma multiforme, the most aggressive kind.

The same kind Ted Kennedy had.

Immediately, my priorities changed. Until that morning, I had been completely immersed in my preparations for two important jobs in the new administration. I was to be the next secretary of the Department of Health and Human Services, but I would also be the director of the new White House Office of Health Reform. It would be my job to help Barack Obama set the strategy for doing what no president had been able to do in one hundred years: win passage of a health care reform bill that would cover all Americans. This would be one of the biggest challenges of my career, but so far, we were off to a good start, laying the groundwork for passage through the hard work of the transition team.

Now, my family had to be my first priority. I dropped my work, and my plans to attend the new president's inauguration, to join my brother for his surgery at Duke University Medical Center in Durham, North Carolina. Vicki Kennedy—who had more than enough on her hands with Ted's illness—was a treasured voice of sympathy when I told her the news. She was kind enough to put me in touch with Dr. Larry Horowitz, Ted's former chief of staff, who had advised them on his care and now put me in touch with Ted's team of doctors at Duke.

On January 19, the day before the inauguration, the doctors successfully removed most of Greg's brain tumor in a five-hour operation. The next day, the family gathered in Greg's hospital room—my wife, Linda, my mother, my two other brothers, and me—along with Dr. Lorraine Hale, a dear family friend. We watched the inauguration on television. And we all toasted the new president with champagne in plastic glasses.

Most everyone knows about the troubles that ultimately forced me to withdraw from consideration for my health care role in the administration. Those troubles were just beginning to surface around that time, as the Senate Finance Committee staff pressed me for more and more details on my tax records. But not a lot of people know about the personal drama I was going through at the same time. The irony of it was almost too much to believe. Here I was, preparing to help the new president lead the most promising health care reform effort we had seen in decades, and I had been temporarily sidelined by my own brother's crisis. It was a reminder to all of us that health care is an issue that affects all of us in an intensely personal, emotional way.

It was also a reminder of why it has been so hard to have a rational debate over how to fix the problems. Every president who has proposed health coverage for all Americans—from Theodore Roosevelt to Harry Truman to Bill Clinton—has been shouted down with cries of "socialism" or "government-run health care." It is not just the power of all of the health care and business interests who would be affected. It is also the deep-seated anxiety people naturally feel about changing a health care sector that affects them so personally. They want to solve the problems, but health care is so complex, with so many moving parts, that they are easily misled by opponents who want them to fear the changes that might make our medical care work better.

So when members of Congress faced shouting, frightened audience members at town hall meetings in August 2009, and had to force their way through angry protesters at the Capitol as the debate neared its end, no one should have been surprised. Health care is too important to people, at a raw emotional level, to lend itself easily to a rational debate. And yet, a rational debate is exactly what we had to have, if we wanted a health care system that would spend our money more wisely and prevent millions of Americans from falling through the cracks. Only a rational debate could give us a system that works on an economic level and treats people with basic human decency.

That is what the health care reform effort was all about.

This book tries to capture the rational side of the debate and the story of how we arrived at this moment in history. So much was at stake, with so much incomplete and sometimes outright false information about the new law, that it takes a book to sort through it all. But there also were some compelling personal stories, from a new president's determination to push for comprehensive reform—against the advice of much of his inner circle—to the race against the clock to rescue the bill after the window for passage seemed to have closed.

The political side and the policy side of health care reform are very different stories to tell, but it is important to understand both, because both shaped the comprehensive reform bill that is now the law of the land. So the book is structured in a way that I hope will help you understand both stories. At times, it is necessary to move back and forth between the political narrative and the explanation of the policies. This way, you will have the background you need about how Congress tried to solve the most serious health care problems. And this background will, in turn, give you a greater appreciation of the political dramas that affected how much Obama and Congress could actually do to pursue those solutions.

Along the way, I draw on my own experiences in the story to provide insight into what was happening at different times. I was, of course, a participant in the early health care discussions of the new administration. After my withdrawal, I was fortunate enough to stay involved in the reform efforts as a senior policy adviser at the law firm of Alston & Bird, and later at DLA Piper. Together with my roles at the Center for American Progress and the Bipartisan Policy Center, two organizations that have contributed greatly to this debate, these unique opportunities have broadened my perspective and greatly enhanced my understanding of the health care industry and our policies involving it.

However, this is not a memoir. It is a book about the accomplishments of others. Against the odds, and in the face of constant and willful distortion of their true goals, Obama and Congress broke through the seemingly endless deadlock and gave us the comprehensive health care reform the nation sorely needed. They did not let raw emotions stand in their way. The rational side of the debate won.

Many people may wonder why Obama and the Democratic leadership insisted on passing such a massive health care reform bill so early, even as the nation was already spending hundreds of billions of dollars to pull the nation out of the worst economic disaster since the Great Depression. The answer, as you will see, is that the problems with our health care were so serious that we had to address them to make our economic recovery complete. The law was also written to pay for itself—not simply to spend more billions of dollars. And politically, there would be no better time to attempt reform than at the beginning of Obama's presidency. If it did not happen now, it would be another generation before we could try again.

How close did we come? Remarkably, we now have a law that will attempt to address all three of the most serious problems: the rising costs, the uneven quality, and the access problems that have left millions of Americans with either no health insurance or major gaps in their coverage. The law is not perfect by any means. It does far more to improve coverage than it does to control costs or improve quality. But that is, in large part, because we are still learning how to control costs and improve quality in the right way. The law will test many different ways of addressing these issues. As we learn which ways work, we will be able to expand them throughout the country.

The goal of health care reform is clear. No matter how much we disagree on how to get there, we all want the same thing: high-performance, high-value health care with better coverage, improved quality, and lower costs. We have not reached the goal yet, and even with the new law in place, we will have to work for years to get there. There will be problems along the way, and we will have to be ready to fix them. But there are many good things that can happen because of the new law—far more than most Americans realize. All we have to do is give it a chance.

Ted Kennedy did not live to see the signing ceremony for comprehensive health care reform. But he knew that the time was as good as it would ever get for the issue he called "the cause of my life." It was the message he carried to Denver in August 2008 for his final convention speech, at the Democratic convention that officially nominated Barack Obama for the presidency.

The emotion in the Pepsi Center that night was as high as it ever gets at a political convention. As convention organizers passed out "Kennedy" signs, people crowded onto the convention floor, snarled in a huge traffic jam in front of the Massachusetts delegation, wondering if the ailing Kennedy was actually capable of giving a speech. Even his own family and friends were not sure he could pull it off. Already struggling to recover from his brain surgery, he was now also suffering from a painful kidney stone, and he was so groggy from pain medication that he could barely stand.

Yet somehow, he made it to the podium, to cheers so loud and intense the floor seemed to shake under the audience's feet. He had enthusiastic fans and harsh critics during his lifetime, but on this night, they all knew this would be the last time they would see him on a convention stage. They listened in rapt attention as he declared that, through the best and worst days of his political life, "we have never lost our belief that we are all called to a better country and a newer world." And they cheered wildly once again when he promised that, before long, every American would have "decent, quality health care as a fundamental right and not a privilege."

And he had one more promise to make. His most memorable speech had been the one at the Democratic convention in 1980, when he ended his own campaign for the presidency. The spirit of that speech was eloquently captured in its final line: "For all those whose cares have been our concern, the work goes on, the cause endures, the hope still lives, and the dream shall never die."

Now, Ted Kennedy ended his last convention speech with a new twist on that line, a final note full of hope and optimism: "The work begins anew. The hope rises again. And the dream lives on."

On that night, the raw emotion of the health care debate did not seem insurmountable anymore. This time, emotion just might bring out the best in us.

Part One

THE STAKES

———

1 | THE GREAT DIVIDE

Of all the stories from the summer of 2009, when town hall meetings across the country erupted in fiery protests against health care reform, there was one story that quickly made the rounds among Democrats on Capitol Hill. It was the perfect illustration of just how deeply some people's distrust of government had affected their views of the health care debate.

It took place on Monday, August 3, right at the beginning of the month-long August recess that Congress traditionally takes. Gene Green, a moderate House Democrat, was facing a rowdy crowd of constituents in his hometown of Houston, Texas. Already, they were unhappy with his recent vote for the House climate-change bill. Now, they let him know they were equally unhappy with what they'd heard about the health care reform bill.

One man in the audience shouted out to the rest of the crowd, "How many people, by a show of hands, oppose any form of socialized or government-run health care?"

Almost everyone in the room raised their hands. There was lots of cheering, whooping, and hollering. Someone yelled out, "Yes, sir!"

So Green turned the question on its head. "How many of you have Medicare?" he asked. Medicare, of course, is the government-run health care program that pays for medical care for 45 million people, including 37 million seniors and 7 million people with disabilities. It is the program that provides the crucial safety net for our nation's elderly, regardless of whether they are rich or poor, sick or healthy. About half of the people in their crowd raised their hands.[1]

The discussion quickly moved on, so it's not clear how many of those people understood the irony. Green didn't ask the natural follow-up: "Are you aware that Medicare is a government-run program?" Instead, he let a man in the audience raise his concerns about how Medicare is working in practice—with doctors refusing to accept Medicare patients because the federal government is cutting their payments. That's a valid concern, and it deserved to be dealt with on its own. But it's one thing to address problems in the Medicare system. It's another to oppose, on its face, any kind of health care safety net that involves the government in any way.

Should we get rid of Medicare and let senior citizens fend for themselves? Should we eliminate the Medicaid program for the poor and people with disabilities? What about the State Children's Health Insurance Program, which helps low-income families get health coverage for their kids? Some people might, in fact, be happy to end all of those programs on principle. But it wouldn't be a widely held view.

And yet, that moment in Gene Green's town hall meeting went a long way toward explaining the forces that have kept health care reform out of reach for nearly a century. Why has it been so difficult for the United States to do what the rest of the world's industrialized nations have already done—build a complete health care safety net that protects everyone in his or her greatest time of need? Some nations have done it through a government system, others have done it through the private sector, but our nation has always stood out for its inability to help the millions of Americans who fall through the cracks.

There are plenty of reasons for that, and to some extent they reinforce each other. The issues in the health care debate are complex and often poorly explained; people want to preserve what they have, even if what they have is less secure than they might think; and the nation has become so politically polarized that different groups of Americans see the same reality in different ways. But it's hard to miss the one factor that truly drives the intensity of the opposition. Health care has become a symbol of the deep divide in Americans' feelings about the role government should play in solving our social problems.

Even for the majority of us who are fortunate enough to have health coverage, what we have is so fragile that one bad turn of events can end in disaster. Six out of ten personal bankruptcies in the United States are directly related to people's medical bills—and of that group, three out of four piled up unaffordable debts even though they had health insurance.[2] Medical crises have caused as many as half of all home foreclosures.[3] And more than a third of all Americans who tried to buy health insurance on their own couldn't get the coverage they needed because they had preexisting conditions.[4] But for many Americans, the distrust of government runs so deep that they'll resist anything that might expand the government's role in solving the problems.

There is a bit of a disconnect here, because many Americans seem to believe that our medical care is run completely by the private sector. That just isn't the case. What we actually have is a public-private hybrid. As of 2007, public programs such as Medicare, Medicaid, and the State Children's Health Insurance Program accounted for about 46 percent of all national health care spending. That leaves a little more than half to private spending, mostly insurance coverage and some out-of-pocket costs.[5] What we are really arguing about, then, is what the proper mix should be. Should it be closer to half and half? Mostly private spending? Mostly public spending? Other countries have had this same argument, as we will see later, and it is usually an ongoing debate, never completely resolved. We can continue to debate the question, too. But it should not stop us from fixing what we have so it does not continue to let millions of Americans fall through the cracks.

Many of my former Republican colleagues, I'm sorry to say, have fed Americans' distrust of government with speeches and public comments that greatly exaggerated the role Washington would play in a reformed health care sector. House Minority Leader John Boehner of Ohio regularly warned that the bills in Congress would lead to "a big, government-run health care system."[6] Senator Jim DeMint of South Carolina—the same senator who predicted that health care would be Obama's "Waterloo" and that a defeat would "break him"—predicted that health care reform would "eventually crowd out quality private insurance and force Americans into a government-run health care system."[7] Even Senator Orrin Hatch of Utah, who worked closely with lawmakers from both parties to create the State Children's Health Insurance Program in the 1990s, argued that Democrats were really trying to create a single-payer health care system like Canada's. "If they can't do it automatically, they'll do it in increments," Hatch said, and "that means we're going to have a one-size-fits-all government-run health care program right out of Washington."[8]

I never have understood why so many Republicans make this argument. It is basically an admission that Americans might like a public option if they got to try it—because if they didn't, how could it ever lead to a single-payer system? The larger point, however, is that the critics of the public option misread how Americans truly feel about government-run health care. When they actually experience it, they are fine with it. Medicare is so popular with seniors that they resist anything they think will threaten it. The economically disadvantaged may not love Medicaid, but they understand its vital role in their lives. The Department of Veterans Affairs health care system is more popular with veterans than private insurance is with other Americans.[9] And TRICARE, the health care program for the armed forces, keeps topping the customer satisfaction lists in surveys that include all of the major private insurers.[10]

Still, the fear of government-run health care has been easily exploited by opponents of reform for decades. There's nothing new about the charges of "socialized medicine." It's the label the powerful American Medical Association (AMA) used to use as a weapon against the earliest national health care efforts. In 1934, the committee that drafted Franklin D. Roosevelt's original Social Security bill threw in one line about the need to study national health insurance and make recommendations to Congress. Lawmakers received so many angry telegrams in protest that the House Ways and Means Committee removed the line from the bill.[11] That year, the AMA blasted a more specialized group, the American College of Surgeons, for endorsing national health insurance, condemning "this apparent attempt to dominate and control the nature of medical practice."[12] When Harry Truman asked Congress to pass national health insurance in 1949, the AMA's charges of "socialized medicine" helped unseat some of the plan's strongest supporters in the Senate.[13]

It was only after the Lyndon B. Johnson's landslide election in 1964, which gave him strong Democratic majorities in Congress, that the political environment was right to create Medicare and Medicaid—a more incremental strategy that provided special protections for the elderly and the poor. But every attempt since then to expand those protections to all Americans has bogged down, largely because of the fear that a bigger government role in health care would take away the freedom most people have to obtain the health care they think they need. When our efforts to pass Bill Clinton's health care plan failed in 1994, it was partly because it was too complicated for most people to understand. But it also failed because that complexity allowed its opponents to portray the plan as a threat to their ability to choose their health plans and their doctors.

This time, many of the old foes of health care reform had turned to supporters, thanks to the growing recognition that skyrocketing costs and serious gaps in people's coverage had made it impossible to defend what was happening. Even the AMA became an ally of the reformers, at least in principle. In June 2009, J. James Rohack, the association's president at the time, declared "our dedication to provide affordable, quality health insurance coverage not just for some, but for everyone."[14]

But the old skepticism of government had not completely disappeared. Instead, the distance between the ideological camps seemed greater than ever.

As Barack Obama began his presidency, Democrats became more hopeful about the role of government, and Republicans became more deeply pessimistic—a direct reflection of voters' happiness with who was in the White House. In May 2009, four months after Obama took office, the Pew Research Center for the People and the Press found that 74 percent of Republicans agreed with the statement, "When something is run by the government, it is usually inefficient and wasteful"—a view shared by only 42 percent of Democrats. Two years earlier, there had been almost no gap between Republicans and Democrats, largely because Republicans were happier and Democrats were unhappier during George W. Bush's presidency.[15]

How deep is the public's distrust of the government's ability to solve problems? Andrew Kohut, the president of the Pew center, concluded that Medicare would face just as much opposition as the current health care reform effort if it were proposed today.[16] In January 1965, as the momentum to create Medicare reached its peak, Gallup found that more than six out of ten Americans supported the idea. But in the May 2009 survey, as Congress prepared to start its work on the health care reform bills, the Pew center found outright confusion and hostility toward government. The vast majority of Americans, 86 percent, said the government "needs to do more to make health care affordable and accessible." Yet 46 percent were also "concerned that the government is becoming too involved in health care"—meaning a substantial number of Americans held conflicting views about what Obama and Congress were about to take on.[17]

It was also clear, though, that the distrust was lopsided, and that Democrats and Republicans had almost nothing in common in their views of the health care debate. Sixty-eight percent of Republicans thought the government was "becoming too involved in health care"—a view shared by only 29 percent of Democrats and 44 percent of independents. Still, it was sobering that the numbers were that high among independents, and that so many Democrats were so skeptical. Democrats have a lot of disagreements, and we have learned over the years that government can't solve all of our problems. But if there is any single core value we have always shared, it is the view that government is still the best forum we have to help each other in times of crisis. And when millions of Americans struggle to meet their basic health care needs, they are dealing with one of the most urgent crises anyone can face.

The great divide in our society, which keeps us bickering endlessly about the role of government in our health care, largely exists for people who have no direct experience with its shortcomings. For those who have been affected personally by those shortcomings, the divide disappears. Even Republicans who are deeply skeptical of government's ability to solve problems sometimes change their minds about health care when they have a direct experience with the failings of the private side.

Barry Keene, a Republican mechanical engineer and private consultant in Lafayette, Colorado, believes government handles a lot of things badly—but he no longer thinks health care is one of them. When his wife fell off a step stool in 2005 and broke her leg, the couple ended up more than $50,000 in debt, thanks to a health insurance policy that did not protect them from "balance billing"—where the providers charge more than the insurance company has agreed to pay, collect whatever they can from insurance, and then send the patient a bill for the rest. What truly astounded Keene, however, was what happened when his wife called the hospital about its $42,000 share of their bill. Within five minutes, she had negotiated a 50 percent discount—over the phone. "That captured my attention," Keene recalls. "To be able to negotiate a fifty percent reduction in five minutes, that just doesn't happen in my world. What is the real cost? And who pays the list price? And what do the insurance companies really pay?" Keene is now a vocal supporter of single-payer health care and an advocate of greater transparency in our medical care.[18]

For decades, it has been easy to convince Americans that health care reform will lead us down the path toward greater government control over our lives and interference in our most personal medical decisions. That was the troubled political environment that greeted the Obama administration as it set out to break the health care deadlock. But if Obama and Congress could overcome those odds, they would transform the landscape of our national debates over health care. The great divide would no longer prevent us from solving our most urgent national problems. And Obama's place in history would be set.

2 | "LET ME TELL YOU WHAT YOU WANT TO HEAR"

There is a pattern with polls on health care reform. Early on, when it's just the idea of reform, most Americans say they're for it. They are even willing to sacrifice a bit for it. But unless they have had personal experience with the problems of our current health care sector, all of the issues at stake are abstract to them. Most Americans are happy with their health care, even if they are sympathetic to other people's problems. So when reform opponents try to tell them that reform might ruin what they like about their health care, the scare tactics often succeed.

This is a dynamic that can make it easy for Democrats to assume that the public is more enthusiastic about health care reform than it actually is. We want to believe that people support it, since health care for all Americans has been such an important cause for our party for so many years. But reform has always been a more urgent issue to Democrats than to Republicans and independents. Moreover, most people aren't experts on the health care sector and the trade-offs that take place when you change any particular piece of it. When they find out what the trade-offs are, their opinions can change dramatically. It happened when Bill Clinton tried to reform health care in the 1990s, and it happened again when Obama rose to the challenge.

Just after Clinton spoke to a joint session of Congress in September 1993 to issue his call for health coverage for all Americans, the public approved of the plan by a 32-point margin. Three weeks later, that margin had closed to 12 percentage points.[1] By the end of March 1994, most Americans opposed the plan.[2]

Some of that early drop in support was actually because the detailed plan wasn't ready yet—a fact that created its own set of doubts—and because Clinton got distracted by a foreign-policy crisis, the failed U.S. Army Rangers raid on warlords in Somalia. Still, by March 1994, when Clinton's 1,342-page plan had been well circulated on Capitol Hill and throughout Washington, opponents had had plenty of time to convince the public that the plan would take away their freedom to receive the health care they wanted. More and more Americans said the plan would hurt them rather than help them, and senior citizens turned against it in large numbers.[3]

By the time Obama took office, enough time had passed that Americans seemed, once again, to be ready for health care reform. But even at the height of public support for his efforts, some of the same warning signs about the shakiness of that support were apparent if you studied the polls closely enough. The Obama team was more successful than the Clinton team at reversing the drop in support once it happened. But once again, the critical question—"What's in it for me?"—became the source of fears that the president and Congress had to address throughout the entire process.

In March 2009, before Congress began working in detail on the health care bills, the Pew Research Center for the People and the Press found that there was actually less support for completely rebuilding the health care sector than there was in 1993—even among Democrats. Still, six out of ten Americans said the government should guarantee health insurance for everyone, even if that meant they would have to pay higher taxes.[4] Most polls around that time got similar results, though some found the public more conflicted than others. Barely half of all Americans in an NBC News–Wall Street Journal poll said they would pay higher taxes if it meant everyone could have health insurance.[5]

Still, the majority of Americans were saying—for the benefit of the pollsters, at least—that they were willing to make some sacrifices to provide health coverage for all. And yet, as Congress focused more intensely on the health care bills and the debate began to dominate the news, you could see the enthusiasm slipping away. Democrats remained pretty steady in their support for the effort. But between February and August, the share of Republicans who believed they and their families would be worse off under health care reform rose from two out of ten to an astonishing six out of ten, according to a tracking poll by the Henry J. Kaiser Family Foundation. And by August, more than a third of independents felt the same way—a loss of support that the Democratic major-ity could not afford.[6]

This was a problem that would only grow worse as the debate dragged on. Just as the Clinton health care effort lost momentum right after his speech to Congress, Obama's effort suffered greatly when Congress went on recess in Au-gust and gave up the stage to the opponents and their most outlandish charges. The slide stopped temporarily in September, when Obama made his critical speech to a joint session of Congress about what health care reform was really about—shooting down most of the scary, and untrue, charges that had bom-barded the media during the August recess. But even then, an ABC News–Washington Post poll found that 54 percent of Americans agreed with the statement: "The more I hear about the health care plan, the less I like it."[7] And after Obama's speech, the slide began again. By January, the Kaiser Family Foundation tracking poll found that, for the first time, the percentage of Amer-icans who expected to be worse off under health care reform was about the same as the share that expected to be better off.[8]

Some of the same factors were behind the drop in support that we saw during the Clinton effort. Once again, many Americans worried that they, personally, would not benefit from the changes being made to help other groups. And once again, senior citizens opposed the plan more strongly than any other group. A Gallup poll in September found they leaned against the plan by a 10-point margin.[9] That had to be a major concern for the administration and Congress. Seniors were generally happy with the health care they already had—through Medicare—and worried about what would happen if Congress started messing with a good thing. And who could blame them? When you deal with health care as frequently as our nation's senior citizens do, of course you're going to want it to work right.

The other factor, though, is that pollsters get very different answers depend-ing on how specific their questions are and how they're phrased. That shouldn't be a surprise, but it's particularly true on health care reform, where people don't necessarily recognize all of the ways they might be affected—and can easily be led to believe their sacrifices will be more severe than they actually will be. In September 2009, a USA Today–Gallup poll asked several pointed questions based on the charges critics were making against the reform plan. Not surprisingly, seven out of ten said they would oppose the plan if it would raise taxes on the middle class. Eight out of ten said they'd turn against the effort if middle-class Americans would have to pay more for health care, if they'd face more re-strictions on what doctors they could see and what treatments they could receive, and if the quality of their health care would get worse.[10] The use of the term *middle class* made a big difference, suggesting that average Americans could expect to be hurt by health care reform in numerous ways.

There was a real danger of a public backlash on some issues, and this was something the White House and congressional leaders had to worry about—particularly on the proposals to tax the benefits on generous health care plans to help pay for reform. At the same time, though, some of the public's fears were absolutely groundless, especially the concern that Americans would end up with fewer choices of doctors and rationed medical care. The point of bringing down health care costs was to get rid of the wasteful treatments and procedures that don't work, not to deny people the best doctors and the care they truly need. The problem, though, is that perception is everything in politics, which is why the opponents of reform encouraged those fears as much as possible. Their tactics were especially effective among seniors, who were naturally worried about the vague reports that some of the cost savings were going to come from Medicare—assuming that these would be cuts in services to them, rather than in payments to providers and private-plan contractors.

Everybody understands health care at a personal level, from whatever experiences we or our family members have had with it. But not everyone understands the consequences of different reform ideas—or the consequences of leaving things alone. So people's opinions of health care reform can shift wildly when they hear more about the implications. One Kaiser poll found that nearly seven out of ten Americans supported the idea of requiring everyone to have health insurance—until they heard that such a rule could force people to buy coverage they couldn't afford. When they heard that, six out of ten people who supported the idea turned against it.[11] And as for those who opposed the idea from the beginning, when they heard that insurance companies would still be able to deny coverage to sick people unless everyone was required to have coverage, three quarters of them changed their minds and endorsed the idea.

From the beginning, the Obama administration had to convince Americans that they all had a stake in health care reform—that it wasn't just about help-ing unfortunate people they might not know, but about fixing major problems that affect everybody. Those challenges fall into three broad categories: the cost problems that are making it harder for people to get and keep the coverage they need; the quality problems that give unnecessary care to some and expose oth-ers to dangerous mistakes; and the access problems that affect not just the un-insured, but a rapidly growing group of Americans who find out they don't have the coverage they thought they had. Each of these problems prevents American health care from truly being the best in the world, despite what we've all been led to believe. And the solutions to each of these problems involve their own political risks.

And yet, somehow, these problems must be solved.

3 | THE COST PROBLEM

One of the most important decisions Obama made, right from the beginning, was to focus his health care reform plan on controlling health care costs as much as helping the uninsured. It was a good strategic decision, because it acknowledged that the fate of health care reform would depend on how it was viewed by people who have health insurance. He had made a campaign promise to lower a typical family's health care costs by up to $2,500 a year—a promise he took seriously enough that he asked the transition team for "hard numbers" on how he could keep it.

But it wasn't just about campaign messages and promises. On a policy level, Obama saw that slowing down the rise of health care costs would be the critical factor in determining the failure or success of the effort, long after he had signed the reform bill into law. "If we don't control costs," he told the transition team, "we will have failed at health reform regardless of whatever else we do."

The out-of-control rise in health care costs is the key to so many of the other problems. We're simply spending too much, without asking whether we're spending wisely or what price we're paying as a society for spending so freely. The United States spent about $2.2 trillion on health care in 2007, about $7,400 a person—compared to just $4,100 a person ten years earlier, in 1997.[1] Our health care costs have grown faster than the economy in each of the last four decades.[2] We spend 16 percent of our gross domestic product on health care—compared to only about 7 percent in 1970[3]—and we'll be spending twice that much in the next quarter century if the trend isn't reversed.[4]

Most industrialized nations are seeing their health care costs go up as well, but the United States stands out because we are spending so much more than the rest. In 2005, we spent nearly twice as much as Canada, Germany, and France and two and a half times as much as the United Kingdom, Italy, and Japan.[5] You may have heard the story that Starbucks spends more on its employees' health care than it does on coffee.[6] When that happens, our nation has reached the point where, as difficult as the solutions might be, the most painful option would be to do nothing at all.

The root of the problem is not complicated, but it is hard for our political system to address. When insurance covers nearly everything, there is no incentive to hold down costs, because neither providers nor their patients have to ask tough questions about what medical care is truly necessary. So our health care spending continues to rise, well beyond any value we are getting for it. This is especially true with the number one driver of health care costs: the advances in medical technology and the increasing availability of it. In 2008, the Robert Wood Johnson Foundation concluded that "medical technology is the driving force behind the growth in U.S. health care spending."[7]

We are spending more on technology than most other countries. Some of it clearly makes our medical care better, but it is not always necessary or even the best solution. The Organization for Economic Cooperation and Development found that the United States uses MRI and CT scans far more than any other OECD country—about twice the average. Such widespread use of new technology inevitably makes our health care more expensive, the organization concluded, because "no person or body is concerned with the overall cost level."[8]

Those costs, however, get passed on to all of us. One of the most direct ways is through the rapid rise of health care premiums. In 2009, family premiums rose 5 percent for Americans who got their health insurance through the workplace. That doesn't sound so bad, at first—except that inflation was actually falling. In what other industry would we accept rising prices when prices are going down everywhere else? In fact, though, 2009 was one of the better years for health care premiums in the last decade. At the beginning of George W. Bush's presidency, premiums had been increasing at double-digit rates.[9]

After the failure of the 1994 effort, we all knew that any successful campaign for health care reform had to speak to people's self-interest. The roughly

85 percent of Americans who have health insurance may worry about the 15 percent who are uninsured,[10] or they may not. But when health care costs are rising so quickly and so recklessly, that affects everybody. The political challenge, though, is that any real cost savings will have to come from the stakeholders, such as physicians, hospitals, and other health care providers. And the more specific we become about what costs we need to hold down, the more they fight back.

That is why the physicians, for example, have pressured Congress to eliminate scheduled cuts in their Medicare payments for years, and why the American Medical Association insisted that Congress cancel those reductions permanently as a condition for its support of health care reform. And that is why the issue of health care costs, more than quality and even access to coverage, is the biggest reason real health care reform has eluded us for so many years.

There is no real counterpressure from the public to cut down on specific costs, because the causes of rising costs aren't immediately obvious to most of us. If we're lucky enough to have decent health insurance, we go to the doctor, pay a small copayment for the visit, and then get the medication, the test, or the procedure the doctor recommends. We may ask questions about the safety of the medical care or discuss different options, but the cost isn't a big factor. That's because we usually don't know it, and we're protected from most of the costs anyway. As much as many Americans struggle with their medical bills, and while health spending overall is on the rise, consumers' out-of-pocket expenses actually fell from 47 percent of total health care costs in 1960 to 12 percent in 2006.[11] But once again, this is why the lack of transparency hurts all of us. Health care is the only sector of the economy where, when a purchase is made, we are not sure what the true cost is or who really pays. And yet, it will affect us in ways that only become clear much later.

All of us pay for health care in one of three ways. We pay through health insurance premiums, through out-of-pocket expenses, and through taxes. Over the last ten years, family health insurance premiums rose by 131 percent—far more than the 38 percent growth in workers' wages or the 28 percent increase in inflation during that same time.[12] Someone has to pay for those premium increases, and while employers shoulder some of it, a lot of it gets passed on to the employees—through lower wages, more unemployment, and more part-time work as opposed to full-time work with benefits.[13] Many companies are responding to the cost growth by making their employees pay a greater share of the premiums, increasing the amount they have to pay through deductibles and copayments for office visits, and making them pay more for prescription drugs.[14]

Even with all of the protections we have against out-of-pocket expenses, they're still not enough to shield many people from skipping health care because of the costs. More than half of Americans in early 2009 said they had gone without medical care they needed in some way—turning to home remedies or over-the-counter drugs, passing up dental care, canceling medical tests or treatments, or not filling prescriptions.[15] When costs are skyrocketing, and people discover the gaps in the coverage they do have, skipping health care may be the only option many of them have.

There is also the broader picture of the federal budget deficit, which will get far worse, thanks to the growth in Medicare and Medicaid spending, if nothing is done to rein in health care costs. Right now, Medicare and Medicaid costs are about 6 percent of our gross domestic product. By 2040, they'll rise to about 15 percent.[16] That's not just a crisis for our already exploding federal deficit—it's also a direct threat to the budgets of the states that share the costs of the Medicaid program.

So what's causing the runaway growth of our health care costs? The estimates vary, but research suggests that medical technology is the cause of anywhere from 38 percent to 65 percent of our growth in health care spending.[17] We are blessed with new technologies and therapies that can treat conditions we couldn't treat before—or simply improve on the way doctors used to treat certain conditions—and they're available to more people than ever before.[18] But what they're not designed to do is save money, and so they drive up spending instead, accounting for as much as half of the per capita spending growth on health care.[19] The technology is profitable, and that encourages hospitals, in particular, to stock up on expensive equipment such as CT and MRI machines.

Even when a new procedure does save money, particularly by making treatment possible in an outpatient setting, it can become popular because of its convenience, which means it ultimately drives up spending because so many more people use it. When hospitals started offering laparoscopic surgery to re-move people's gallbladders in the 1990s—a less invasive way to do the proce-dure than traditional surgery—it cost hospitals less money because the patients left more quickly, but total spending still went up because so many more people had the procedure.[20]

There are other important factors that help explain why health care is con-suming so much of our spending, and not all of them can be solved by policy changes alone. We have more chronic diseases—such as asthma, heart disease, and diabetes—and a health care industry that is getting better at treating them. We also have a well-documented obesity problem, and obesity leads to a variety of health problems that cost money to treat. The Robert Wood John-son Foundation found that obesity is a significant factor in our health care costs, contributing to 12 percent of spending growth in recent years.[21] So for all the time we spend debating the structure of health care, we also need to pay attention to broader issues in our society, such as nutrition and per-sonal behavior. And wealthier nations, in general, choose to spend more of their wealth on health care—a phenomenon that's not unique to the United States.[22]

We also shouldn't forget the out-of-date, paper-based recordkeeping sys-tems that continue even as information technology has become the standard throughout the rest of the economy. We have twenty-first-century operating rooms, with the most sophisticated technology anyone could ask for, but the rec-ords are all handled by nineteenth-century administrative rooms. David Cutler, an economics professor at Harvard University who was one of the Obama cam-paign's health care advisers, suggests that the federal government could save as much as $600 billion in spending over the next decade by modernizing our health care, including bringing it up-to-date on information technology through advances such as electronic medical records. With better information technol-ogy, doctors' offices probably wouldn't have to hire so many extra people to deal with numerous different insurance companies and to take care of the needs of the uninsured.[23]

And, of course, we spend far too much on prescription drugs. One study found that the United States spends more than twice as much for an "average" pill than other OECD countries.[24] That is partly because the drug companies have powerful lobbyists who have defeated our attempts to bring down costs in various ways, such as reimporting drugs from other countries—where they often cost less—and using the federal government's purchasing power to negotiate lower prices. The drug companies have also used advertising to drive up the demand for prescription drugs in general, and name-brand drugs in particular. And the industry itself has become less competitive in recent years, with the rise of agreements in which brand-name drug manufacturers pay generic competitors to delay entering the market.[25]

Ultimately, though, we have to take a hard look at the financial incentives in health care—which, when left unchecked, give doctors every reason to try to earn as much income as possible from patient care. In June 2009, Atul Gawande, a surgeon at Brigham and Women's Hospital in Boston and a staff writer at the *New Yorker,* caught the attention of Obama and many Democrats on the Hill with an article that brilliantly illustrated the problem. He compared the medical cultures of McAllen, Texas, which has one of the highest levels of health care spending in the nation, and El Paso, which has similar demographics but spends only half as much. In McAllen, patients simply got a little bit more of every kind of health care service, whether they needed it or not.

In trying to find out why, Gawande discovered that McAllen had more of the kinds of doctors who see their practice as a business, who owned surgical or imaging centers and had found creative ways to boost their revenues. By contrast, health systems such as the Mayo Clinic, which have achieved the highest quality at the lowest cost, have done it by paying their doctors a salary out of all the revenues collected by the doctors and the hospital, allowing everyone to collaborate on patient care rather than worrying about their incomes. The lesson, Gawande concluded, is that "someone has to be accountable for the totality of care. Otherwise, you get a system that has no brakes. You get McAllen."[26]

My own view is that there are at least five kinds of unnecessary health care spending. What Gawande described is a phenomenon I call "proprietary medicine," where doctors own medical facilities or diagnostic equipment, leading them to see health care as a business and encouraging overuse of medical care. There is the practice of volume-driven reimbursement, where providers get paid for each service rather than being rewarded for the most effective care. There is medical care performed without any real evidence of its effectiveness. And there is the care that patients receive to compensate for medical mistakes, which of course no one wants.

And somewhere in the mix is defensive medicine, in which physicians order tests or procedures that are only marginally useful, or even completely unnecessary, for fear of being sued if they don't and the patient turns out to have a serious condition. Most physicians insist this is a real problem, but it has turned into one of those typical partisan arguments on Capitol Hill, where Republicans use it to argue for limits on medical malpractice lawsuits and Democrats reply that those kinds of limits haven't had much effect on spending in the states where they've been tried. I believe defensive medicine probably does create unnecessary care, though it's hard to tell exactly how often it is the primary reason for ordering tests and how often it's really one of the other factors. The Robert Wood Johnson Foundation concluded that defensive medicine, along with the broader issue of medical malpractice, was not a major factor in the long-term growth of health care spending.[27]

It's hard to imagine a bigger political challenge than finding real ways to cut back on the health care spending that Americans take for granted, and that is why past administrations and Congress have failed to do it. Anyone who remembers the managed care debate of the 1990s knows how difficult it can be to contain costs in ways that don't deprive people of care they really need, or at least make it unnecessarily difficult for them to get it. One of my strongest causes in the Senate was the Patients' Bill of Rights, which would have cracked down on some of the worst bureaucratic abuses of the managed care companies. We never could get it through Congress and to the president's desk, largely because of opposition from Republicans who were concerned about the proposals to let patients sue the companies for delaying or denying treatment.

But the backlash against managed care forced the insurers to change a lot of their practices anyway, proving that, for all of the concern Americans say they have about government coming between their doctors and themselves, they don't like it any better when the interference is coming from insurance-company bureaucrats. There are ways to shift away from the current system of paying doctors for every service they provide—a system that rewards volume over value—and give doctors better incentives to hold down their costs, as we will see later. But we need to give doctors more freedom to decide how to do that, and show more concern for the patients' needs, than the insurance companies did at the height of the rebellion against managed care.

Whatever we did in this round to control costs, it couldn't be such a blunt instrument that it reduced necessary care along with the excess spending. It had to be targeted so that only the truly wasted spending would be questioned. And Americans had to believe it was only the wasted spending that was at risk.

4 | THE QUALITY PROBLEM

Here is one of the paradoxes of American health care: We're spending twice as much as other industrialized nations spend on health care, and yet we're not getting better care for our money. If any business tried to sell a product that cost twice as much as its competitors and didn't work as well, it wouldn't last long. If our tax dollars were going to any government program with such a lackluster track record, we wouldn't stand for it. So why do we tolerate it with health care?

We tolerate it because we are used to throwing money at procedures and treatments and hoping they work. In doing so, we have done more than just create the world's most expensive health care sector. We have also created health care that does not demand the quality that we deserve. There is too little transparency to allow us to see clearly which providers are contributing to the problems, and there is too little accountability for those problems when we do know about them. It is far easier to let that state of affairs continue than to risk the wrath of providers by putting their performance under tougher scrutiny. But if we don't hold them more accountable for the care they provide, we will never truly have the best health care in the world.

When we are sick or injured, most of us aren't in a position to second-guess our doctors. We depend on them to have the answers, and we have some level of trust that they do have the answers. But in reality, we don't know that much about how our doctor compares to others. We know far more about any sports figure than we do about a doctor, nurse, hospital, or the general quality of health care in any community. That is partly because our outdated, paper-driven administrative systems make it difficult to generate useful comparative information, but it is also because we are simply used to a health care sector with little openness. And when we do know the difference between what works and what has no real value, and doctors do not deliver the care that has been proven to work, we don't hold them accountable for their actions. A doctor who harms a patient might get sued, but a doctor who simply wastes money has nothing to worry about.

There are many different ways to measure the quality of our health care, but what we're looking for is nothing more than the simple and clear definition used by Carolyn M. Clancy, the director of the federal Agency for Healthcare Research and Quality. Health care quality, she says, is "getting the right care to the right patient at the right time—every time."[1] To do that, Clancy says, you need to satisfy a set of conditions: the structure has to be solid, with good doctors, hospitals, and clinics that have all the right supplies. The process has to be right, with doctors and hospitals treating patients with the most up-to-date knowledge of what works. And the outcomes have to be good—meaning, the patients got better.

But we also need to make sure that the right care is getting to patients throughout the country, aiming for results as consistent as we can possibly make them. Did people get the preventive care that might have headed off serious illnesses? Could they get doctors' appointments when they needed them? Did they get duplicate tests? Did they get the right discharge instructions to get better after they left the hospital? Did they have to go back to the hospital with infections or bad drug reactions? Did they get the right care regardless of their incomes or their racial or ethnic backgrounds? And most important of all, did patients die when proper medical care could have saved their lives?

Sadly, we know that the right care is not getting to patients throughout the country. The myth is that we have the best health care in the world, but that is not the case. The United States ranks twenty-ninth in the world in reducing infant mortality,[2] and a World Health Organization report in 2000 ranked our nation thirty-seventh in overall performance.[3] That's right behind Costa Rica and just above Slovenia. And in 2008, the United States came in last among nineteen industrialized nations in reducing "preventable mortality"— deaths that could have been avoided with the right medical care.[4]

What we really have is islands of excellence in a sea of mediocrity. We have

wild variations in how often hospitals throughout the country follow the recommended treatment standards, how often they give patients the right instructions to take care of themselves after leaving the hospital, and how often people
have to return to the hospital.[5] There is often little connection between how
much some regions spend and how well the patients do; with Medicare patients,
many of the regions that spent the least also had the lowest mortality rates.[6]
And the problems are compounded by the disorganized nature of our health
care. We have different rules for federal programs such as Medicare, federal-
state programs such as Medicaid, state health care regulatory agencies, and
thirteen hundred private health insurance plans, all of which were developed
with little regard for each other and are operated by authorities that don't communicate well with each other. It is not a formula for providing the best care in
the world.

Sorting out all of these quality problems might seem like a daunting task, so
let's start with one of the simplest. In 2009, the Institute of Medicine estimated
that $800 billion—a full one-third of the money we spend on health care—
goes to medical care that does not make us better.[7] If that's true, it means we're
all paying higher insurance premiums to help cover the costs of tests that didn't
need to be done, or surgeries or medications that don't really make people better.
It's astounding to think that, at a time when we spend $2 trillion a year on
health care, so much of the money might be wasted.

But it's not just a poor use of money. The overuse of medical care also puts
patients at that much more risk for being hurt by medical mistakes—a slipup
during a surgery, an infection that develops afterward, or bad drug reactions
that can happen when a patient receives medications that shouldn't be taken
together. In 1999, the Institute of Medicine stunned many of us in Congress with
a report that estimated at least 44,000 Americans, and maybe as many as 98,000,
die each year from medical errors.[8] We simply had no idea the problem was that
serious.

More recently, the Commonwealth Fund reported that one-third of adults
with health problems in 2007 said they had suffered mistakes in their care.[9]
That seems to be especially true in hospitals, which are still struggling with one
of their most basic and important tasks: preventing infections. According to
the Centers for Disease Control and Prevention, infections that patients develop

in hospitals while they're being treated for other conditions are one of the top ten causes of death in the United States.[10] And in 2006, the Institute of Medicine concluded that 1.5 million medication errors occur nationwide every year. Those errors add as much as $3.5 billion in costs to hospital stays alone—not to mention, of course, the unnecessary suffering of the patients.[11]

At the same time, while many people are getting unnecessary or error-prone care, many others are not receiving the preventive care that can head off major illnesses and even save their lives. According to one study, as many as 18,000 Americans die from heart attacks each year because they don't get preventive medications that are proven to work.[12] Another study found that people receive the recommended care—whether it's preventive care, acute care, or management of chronic illnesses—only a little more than half the time.[13]

And then there is the issue that ought to offend our basic sense of fairness: the differences in the health care people receive based on their incomes or their racial or ethnic backgrounds. The Commonwealth Fund found that minority, low-income, or uninsured patients were more likely than others to have to wait for medical treatment or go without it, be hospitalized unnecessarily, and have less access to preventive or primary care. A 2008 report by the Agency for Healthcare Research and Quality found that over a five-year period, roughly 60 percent of the quality disparities stayed the same or got worse for African-Americans, Asians, Hispanics, and low-income patients, compared to white patients and those with higher incomes.[14]

These are a lot of problems to tackle, and it would be unrealistic to think that any health care reform plan could do more than take first steps. Still, we know enough about the problems to have a good sense of what the first steps might be. For starters, we need to do a much better job of adopting best practices throughout the health care sector. It's not that doctors refuse to do what works best. In many cases, they are simply so overloaded that they do not have time to keep up with all of the latest research. It is also harder for them to find objective, peer-reviewed research than it should be; much of what comes their way is industry-funded research, which comes out faster than the truly valuable objective studies. And a lot of the scientific research that does exist is limited to one specific treatment or procedure. It can tell you how well that treatment or procedure works, but it cannot tell you how well it works compared to the alternatives.[15]

That's where comparative effectiveness research comes in. It is the study of which medical procedures and treatments work the best, comparing different approaches to help providers and patients determine which course is most likely to be effective. The problem is that comparative effectiveness research is expensive and takes a long time, which is why it needs federal funding to succeed—as well as a better method of being distributed so busy health care providers can keep up with it. It is often misunderstood, and was deliberately misrepresented during the health care debate, as a way of telling doctors what they can and cannot do. In fact, it is better understood as a way to give doctors and patients more reliable information and steer them away from medical care that is likely to be a waste of money and time.

The research has its limits, since not every patient responds in exactly the same way to the same medical care. But that problem can be overcome by giving priority to research that compares many different kinds of treatments and many different kinds of patients, as the Institute of Medicine has recommended.[16] If we had better research and a greater commitment throughout the health care industry to keeping up with it and following it, we could make a lot of progress in addressing our cost and quality problems.

Still, when half of all patients don't get the recommended care, it is clear that we are not doing enough to demand accountability when we do know what the best practices are and providers don't follow them. The best health care organizations are the ones where doctors have taken collective responsibility for doing the right thing. Using the example of the Mayo Clinic again, they took away the financial incentives to provide too much care and emphasized teamwork. In Grand Junction, Colorado, doctors teamed up with a local health maintenance organization to set up an electronic system for sharing notes and records.[17] These specific solutions may not work everywhere in the country, but the general lesson is one we should learn: the "islands of excellence" are the places that are the most dedicated to improving the quality of care.

We also haven't done enough to encourage better continuity of care, which simply means that you and your doctor (or doctors) stay in touch regularly to manage your care over a long time. That's the ideal, but what happens more often in reality is that patients, especially senior citizens, receive their care from many different doctors or facilities, and these don't communicate well enough to know what the last doctor did or what the overall plan of medical care is.

That's why one of the more promising innovations has been the experiments with patient-centered medical homes, where patients have twenty-four-hour access to primary and specialty care and the physicians and patients have access to electronic medical records. The use of electronic records is a simple step that can help prevent miscommunications and make it easier for patients to follow up on their own care, scheduling appointments and viewing lab results more easily and even e-mailing their providers. The medical homes have yet to become widespread throughout the country, but they are being used in well-regarded systems such as the Geisinger Health System in Pennsylvania, which serves patients who tend to have more health problems than average.[18]

On a deeper level, though, we need to think about why we don't know more about the causes of these problems. Think of what happens when a plane crashes. Within hours, a team of investigators from the National Transportation Safety Board is on the scene to examine the wreckage, talk to the pilots (if they survived) or recover the recording from the "black box" (if they didn't), interview anyone else with knowledge of the events that day, and piece together an elaborate record of why the crash happened and what might be done to prevent another accident like it. We pay that much attention, and demand that much transparency, because a plane crash is a traumatic event that can kill hundreds of people at a time.

The casualties of the quality problems in our health care aren't as visible to us. They are injured, or even killed, one at a time, and it's not always obvious that it was because of poor health care. But part of the reason it's not obvious is that we don't demand as much openness in the health care sector. Even though thousands more Americans die every year from poor health care than from plane crashes, we don't investigate their deaths with the same level of thoroughness, even though that might be exactly what is needed to make our medical care safer. If we want more than just islands of excellence, we have to build in more incentives to take health care quality more seriously.

5 | THE ACCESS PROBLEM

In October 2006, Judy Hodges sat down to read her family's new health insurance policy. Her husband, Tom, had just gotten a job as an assistant manager for a large retail store in Richmond, Virginia, largely so the family could get group health insurance to cover their medical bills. One of their daughters, Chelsea, had been diagnosed with Unverricht-Lundborg disease, a rare, progressive form of epilepsy that could only be controlled through medications that cost $1,000 a month. While Tom was self-employed, their insurance company was constantly raising their individual insurance premiums, to the point where they were paying nearly $1,800 a month—even though they were mostly paying for Chelsea's medications on their own, thanks to the limited drug coverage. So Tom went to work, hoping to keep Chelsea's care from bankrupting the family.

But as soon as Judy read the new work health insurance policy, she knew they were in trouble. It limited the coverage for each member of the family to $25,000. "I said, 'Oh my gosh, Tom, you're going to have to get another job,'" she recalled. Five weeks later, it was already too late. Judy was diagnosed with breast cancer. The treatment, her oncologist told her, would cost $75,000, assuming nothing went wrong that would drive the cost even higher. "Honestly, I thought I was going to die," Judy said. "I had cancer, and I couldn't pay for the treatment."[1]

Even the best medical care this country has to offer is no good unless you have health insurance to cover it. The rule of thumb is that for health insurance to be useful to most people, it has to be available, affordable, and adequate. For too many Americans, it fails one of those tests. That's why so many Americans have no health insurance at all. But that's only the beginning of the story. The other problem that health care reform had to take on was more subtle, but just as much of a moral outrage: the rapidly growing number of Americans who think they're covered and then find out differently, just when they need their insurance the most.

One of the ways the Obama administration and congressional Democrats tried to broaden the health care debate this time was by focusing not just on the uninsured, but also on the underinsured—the Americans who don't have adequate protection from sky-high medical bills that can send them straight into bankruptcy. By framing the debate in that way, the Democrats hoped to give health care reform a greater appeal than it has had in previous debates. Yes, health care reform was about the 46.3 million Americans who had no health insurance in 2008.[2] That figure has probably grown since the recession began; for every 1 percent rise in the unemployment rate, the number of uninsured Americans goes up by about 1.1 million.[3] But this time, the debate was also about the underinsured Americans—those who didn't have *enough* coverage. As of 2007, there were 25 million of them, a 60 percent increase in just four years.[4] That's a sign that the erosion of health coverage is a bigger and more complicated problem than many of us had realized, and a powerful argument for the urgency of reform.

For the 15 percent of Americans who have no health insurance, the lack of coverage comes at a high personal price. They're more likely to avoid getting medical care because of the cost, less likely to seek all the recommended follow-up treatments when they do get it, less likely to have a regular place to go for their medical care, and more likely to be hospitalized for preventable conditions than Americans who have health coverage. People who are uninsured tend to have low incomes, and more than eight out of ten are from working families. Many are young adults, and minorities are disproportionately likely to lack coverage. And as long as so many people are uninsured, those of us who are lucky enough to have coverage will pay the price, because health care providers shift much of the costs to us. In 2009, 8 percent of the cost of an average family premium—about $1,100 a year—went to cover the costs of treating the uninsured.

But the 14 percent of nonelderly adults who are underinsured have many of the same problems as the uninsured. More than half went without medical care they needed in 2007, passing up on doctors' visits, leaving prescriptions unfilled, or skipping tests and treatments that a doctor had recommended. That was true for two-thirds of Americans without health insurance. And in both cases, about half said they had trouble paying their medical bills, were holding off collection agencies, or had to take drastic measures to pay their bills, such as taking out loans or mortgages or going deeply into credit card debt. All together, about 75 million non-elderly adults—four out of ten—were either uninsured or underinsured in 2007.[5]

In a lot of cases, people are getting the skimpy health coverage because it's all they're being offered. When Tom Hodges was searching for a job, it's not as if he could make the workplace health insurance plan a factor in choosing which job to take. "If he had known up front, he wouldn't have taken the job in the first place," Judy Hodges said. "But when you go for a job interview, you can't say, 'Well, let me see your health insurance contract to see if it's adequate,' because they'll say, 'Bye-bye.'" Judy got her cancer treatment—the chemotherapy, the surgery, the radiation—largely because her persistence, and the help of an advocacy group called the Patient Advocate Foundation, persuaded the various providers to forgive most of her debts.

But Judy's inadequate health insurance was unfair to her at such a difficult time in her life, and it wasn't fair to the doctors who treated her, either. Every time she saw her medical oncologist, she said, "You know I can't pay you for this." Eventually, Judy recalls, the medical oncologist told her, "Don't ever say that again. You're putting me in a terrible ethical dilemma. I don't want to ever think that my decision to treat you is based on your ability to pay or not pay."[6]

All of this, clearly, relates to the cost of health care and the expensive health coverage that's out of reach for so many Americans. The fact that the ranks of the underinsured grew so quickly in just four years shows that workers are being hurt by health plans that pass on the costs in so many ways, such as putting limits on their benefits.[7] Nancy Davenport-Ennis, chief executive officer and president of the Patient Advocate Foundation, the group that helped Judy Hodges, says one of the biggest problems is that some companies have switched their workers to health plans that expose them to a lot of the costs through high deductibles.

But even more generous health plans, such as preferred provider organizations, may have limits built in that make them less generous in reality. "You can have a person in a PPO who looks pretty good, until you look at how many radiation treatments are allowed, and they're capped at twelve, and they need thirty," Davenport-Ennis said. Of all of the patients her group has helped who faced a financially devastating medical crisis, she said, more than nine out of ten were working and had health insurance.[8]

Certainly, a lot of large employers could do better for their workers. But when health insurance premiums are rising so fast, many businesses that are struggling to stay open may not have much of a choice. Between 2001 and 2008, health care premiums for small businesses rose 74 percent. In 1993, at the beginning of the debate over the Clinton health care reform plan, 61 percent of small businesses provided health coverage for their workers. As of 2008, only 38 percent did.[9]

But group coverage, the kind offered by employers, is only part of the story. The other part is the individual insurance market, which offers such limited coverage at such high prices that it just isn't an option for many people, even when they don't have any other way to get coverage. The failure to make the individual market work, despite many years of efforts by lawmakers at the federal and state levels, was a sobering reminder of how difficult it would be for reformers to tackle its problems this time around. But it was also a reminder of why it was so important to try.

Unlike people who get their health insurance through the workplace, anyone with an individual health insurance policy will have to pay the entire cost of the premium, because there's no employer to split the costs with them. That premium is likely to be expensive, because they won't belong to a "pool" of people whose health histories average out—the way they do in a group health plan. They're also likely to pay higher deductibles. And they can be turned down for coverage if they have a preexisting condition, or at the very least, the insurer can refuse to cover that condition. In a 2007 survey, the Commonwealth Fund found that nearly three-quarters of all people who had tried to get individual health coverage in the previous three years ended up not buying it—usually because it cost too much. More than a third were either turned down for coverage because of their health, were charged a higher premium, or could only get coverage that would have excluded a health condition.[10]

And yet, for many Americans, the individual market is the only place they can get health coverage. For people who have lost a job or left it voluntarily, they can continue their employer's health coverage for a while—a year and a half—through a program called COBRA. But COBRA is expensive, too, because people who use it have to pay the entire premium themselves, plus a 2 percent administrative fee. That kind of expense can create some real sticker shock, since most workers are used to getting some kind of premium subsidy from their employers. That's why only 9 percent of unemployed workers typically use COBRA to keep their health coverage.[11] The economic stimulus bill was supposed to help that situation a bit by paying 65 percent of the COBRA premiums for people who lost their jobs during the recession. That probably eased the pain for a lot of workers, but it's not a permanent solution.

Many of the worst health care stories we hear are the ones about people getting turned down for coverage of their preexisting conditions. Why should we accept an industry that denies people medical care for the very reasons that they need medical care? Unfortunately, this has been one of the most stubborn problems to solve in all of the years I've been involved in the health care debate. To keep their expenses as stable and predictable as possible, health insurance companies try to avoid attracting too many people who are in worse than average health. If they have too many unhealthy people whose care costs too much, everyone's premiums go up, and that chases away the healthy people, which in turn makes the remaining people's premiums go up even more. But some insurance companies have gone to extremes to keep their costs stable, and the way they have handled preexisting conditions is one of the most notorious extremes. One study found that insurance companies who offered individual coverage were charging people higher premiums or limiting their coverage for conditions as minor as hay fever, asthma, or old knee injuries.[12]

When I was in the Senate, we did try to take on the preexisting conditions issue. In 1996, Congress passed the Health Insurance Portability and Accountability Act, which was supposed to make it easier for people to change jobs without losing their health insurance. Unfortunately, the law came just two years after the failure of the Clinton health care reform effort, so most of my colleagues weren't in a mood to do anything too ambitious. And since the Republicans were in the majority at that point, only the lightest possible government regulation of private insurance could get through Congress. The main achievements of the law were to make sure people could move from one job to another without facing long waiting periods for coverage of preexisting conditions, and to make sure people who had insurance for a long time through the workplace could get individual insurance if they had exhausted all of their other options.

But the law didn't say how much the insurance companies could charge for that individual coverage, if it was for someone with a preexisting condition. To Karen Pollitz, a former research professor at Georgetown University's Health Policy Institute—and now a top official at the Department of Health and Human Services—that was "like locking the door but leaving the window open."[13] That's why, for individual coverage, companies came up with such a wide range of premiums for hypothetical cases—with various insurers quoting prices ranging from less than $1,700 a year to more than $15,000 a year to a family of four where one child had asthma.[14] And that's why the Hodges family's individual insurance premiums kept rising higher and higher until Tom finally had to find a less-than-ideal job just to get group coverage—which turned out not to be much help to them anyway.

There was another enormous problem in the individual insurance market that came to light during the health care reform debate. It was the practice of canceling people's coverage retroactively if the insurance company finds that the patient misstated anything, or left anything out, when they applied for the coverage. An investigation by the House Energy and Commerce Committee found that, among other things, WellPoint canceled a Virginia man's coverage because his insurance agent marked down his weight wrong. The company now called Assurant refused to cover a patient with lymphoma because of warning signs in a five-year-old CT scan, even though his doctor never told him about it. And UnitedHealth canceled the insurance coverage for an entire Michigan family, including two children, because the father didn't mention in their application that he had an abnormal blood count.[15]

There is more to the access problem, however, than just the difficulties with health insurance. If you have health insurance but you can't find a doctor, you are still out of luck. Anyone who has struggled to find a decent primary care practice in his or her area, for example, knows this is a problem that needs to be taken seriously. It has become increasingly hard to convince medical school students to practice primary care when they graduate, rather than become specialists, because primary care physicians are paid far less than specialists for their services even though both groups have to pay off the same amount of medical school debt. One recent study, for example, predicted there could be a shortage of anywhere from 35,000 to 44,000 generalist physicians for adult patients by 2025.[16]

Yet primary care, as we all know, is critical to the routine health needs of most Americans. Unless we want everyone with a sore throat to go to the emergency room for a strep test, we need to make sure that people have places to go to take care of those routine needs. And yet, contrary to the myth that other countries suffer longer waits than we do for medical care, we actually do poorly in making necessary care available to our citizens. In a recent survey of chronically ill patients in eight countries, only about a quarter of patients in the United States and Canada said they could go to a doctor the same day when they were sick, compared to nearly half in the United Kingdom and more than half in the Netherlands and New Zealand. American patients had shorter waits for specialists, but longer waits for medical care that they needed right away.[17]

Another persistent access problem we have is the shortage of doctors who are willing to treat Medicaid patients. The Medicaid program helps some low-income people who would be uninsured otherwise, but it only goes so far. Adults usually get it only if they have children, are pregnant, or have disabilities.[18] Even for that limited group of people, though, it can be a challenge to find doctors who will see them, because Medicaid pays such low rates to physicians. They vary from state to state, but they generally are far lower than Medicare rates. So physicians are less likely to take new Medicaid patients than people with any other kind of insurance.[19]

All of these problems bring their own set of political burdens if Congress tries to solve them. To make primary care more attractive, the most obvious solution is to change the payment structure so it pays more. But if that kind of change comes at the expense of the specialists, their lobbyists will fight back. Likewise, if you want to require the states to pay more for Medicaid services, you will make Medicaid that much more expensive for states that are already struggling with the program's costs.

The biggest political challenge, however, was how to deal with the very real problems of the health insurance companies without turning them into opponents of the plan—mobilizing all of their political power to block it in Congress or simply undermining it at every turn if it became law. This was a strategic problem that applied to the other health industry stakeholders as well, since virtually all of them have fought efforts to expand health coverage in the past. But it was particularly true of health insurers, given all of the ways they have denied Americans access to the coverage they need. For health care reform to be a success, the Democrats could not just turn the health insurance companies into the enemy. Like it or not, they had to give the industry a reason to cooperate with health care reform.

This was one of the hardest points to explain to the progressive groups who were fighting for reform, and even to many Democrats on the Hill. Clearly, the health insurance industry has a lot to answer for. It has been far too interested in the bottom line, and not nearly interested enough in the health of the people it is supposed to serve. It would be tempting for Democrats simply to beat up on the health insurance companies and force reform down their throats, and frankly, the insurance companies would not get a lot of sympathy if that happened. The political reality, however, is that such a feel-good strategy doesn't work. Like it or not, the health insurance companies would be part of the landscape after reform passed, and their support for the new law—or, at least, their willingess to tolerate it—would be crucial to its long-term success.

Instead, the smarter strategy was to bring the health insurance industry on board from the beginning, by giving them a powerful reason to go along with reform. That incentive, which was central to the entire effort this time, was to require all Americans to have health insurance. If the insurance companies knew that everyone would now participate in coverage—including all the healthy people who might pass up health insurance otherwise—they would not have to worry as much about large numbers of unhealthy patients driving up their costs, and they would not fight a crackdown on all of the outrageous practices they have used to exclude the people who need their help the most. That was the strategy the Obama administration pursued, and it held great promise. But it would be sorely tested along the way.

6 | OUR HEALTH CARE PYRAMID

To understand how all of these problems with our health care relate to each other—the rising costs, the uneven quality, and the unacceptable limits on access to care—try to picture a setup in which we spend so much money on the flashiest, most advanced technologies that we can't take care of many people's most basic needs. That is the state of our health care today. Our priorities are backwards, and it will take a monumental effort on everyone's part to turn that around.

Every nation's health care system is like a pyramid, starting with primary care at the base and working up to the most sophisticated technologies and procedures at the top. The top of the pyramid includes such things as advanced CT and MRI scanners, heart transplants, better anesthesia that can be used on more frail patients, and new developments such as laparoscopic surgery and "drug-eluting stents," which release medication over time to help keep formerly clogged arteries open. Most countries start spending money at the base of the pyramid, on primary care, and work their way up until the money runs out. We do it backwards. We start at the top of the pyramid, spending our money on all the latest medical marvels, and work our way down until the money runs out. And when it does, millions of Americans don't get the primary care they need, or the preventive care that might keep them from developing serious health problems later.

We pride ourselves on having the most advanced health care in the world, and the high-end technologies and new drug therapies are a large part of what we value about our medical care. The United States adopts new surgical techniques more quickly than most other countries, and new drugs usually come to our markets one to two years before they're available in other nations. Our CT and MRI scanners are available more widely than in most other developed countries. (Only Japan has more of both, compared to its overall population.) But we have become so devoted to our technology that other health care needs are getting shortchanged. We run more CT tests than any other country and more MRI scans than any country except Japan, and we pay far more for the tests than any of the other nations. And our hospitals have such a strong incentive to stay ahead of the technological curve that the basics are getting lost. They are putting more money into specialty services and technology than they're spending on expanding their bed capacity, because that is what they think they need to do to compete for market share.[1]

But what about the simple things that most people need—a regular doctor they know and trust, a place to go if someone is sick at night or on the weekend, or the ability to get the follow-up care the doctor says they should have? Unfortunately, that is where our money runs out. When we allow so many Americans to be uninsured or underinsured, and we allow the supply of primary care doctors to become so tight because we don't pay them enough for their critical services, we create serious problems for ourselves.

In an international survey in 2005, American patients with health problems reported more serious obstacles getting the care they needed than patients with similar health issues in five other countries. Americans were far less likely than patients in the United Kingdom, Canada, Germany, Australia, and New Zealand to have a regular doctor, far more likely to have skipped filling a prescription or having a follow-up test because it was too expensive, and more likely to have trouble finding anyplace to go for health care at night or on weekends—other than the emergency room. They were, however, less likely to have to wait to see specialists or have elective surgery. We do well in giving our citizens optional health care that pays the providers a lot of money. We just don't do as well in giving them necessary care.[2]

We also never seem to have the money to help people stay healthy. American adults receive only about half of the preventive services experts say they should get, such as cancer screenings and vaccines. In one study, fewer than half got information from their doctors on weight, exercise, and nutrition, compared to seven out of ten adults in the United Kingdom. That is a particular problem given that preventable illnesses, such as cardiovascular disease and cancer, are becoming a major cause of deaths and rising health costs.[3] There are different reasons for this, but the common theme is that we simply do not treat prevention with the importance it deserves. Patients don't seek preventive care because they may not be aware that they're at risk for illnesses. Our health care culture encourages doctors to treat illnesses, while prevention always gets a lower priority—especially since almost every minute of the doctor's day is spent seeing a large volume of sick patients. And employers don't see much reason to spend money on prevention when many of their employees probably will move on to other jobs.[4]

All of this shows the need for Americans, as a society, to take prevention much more seriously. Prevention and wellness have to become "cool." Take the increasingly serious problem of obesity. Two-thirds of Americans are either obese or overweight, and more than 25 percent of people are obese in thirty-one states. As recently as 1991, no state had an obesity rate higher than 20 percent.[5] Obesity is highly preventable, through nutrition counseling and better access to healthy foods, particularly in the schools. But if it's not prevented, it can lead to serious and chronic illnesses such as diabetes, which is also on the rise.[6] By 2006, treatment for obesity and its related conditions—such as diabetes and high blood pressure—accounted for 9 percent of all health care spending in the United States, a $40 billion increase from just eight years earlier.[7]

If we want to turn that around, we have to change people's attitudes toward high-calorie, large-portion meals so they are scorned, not celebrated. Part of the key is to raise people's awareness of how the food industry has manipulated the ingredients of certain high-calorie foods to make them irresistible, the trend David Kessler writes about in his insightful book, *The End of Overeating.* Our national leaders and the health care industry can only do so much about this—it's also up to individuals to take more responsibility for their nutrition and show enough discipline to eat healthier foods in smaller portions. But we do need to make healthy foods cheaper and easier to find, especially by making school lunches more nutritious and taking the junk food out of the schools. And, as part of health care reform, we had to give everyone better coverage for preventive care, such as nutrition counseling and screening for high blood pressure and diabetes.

Getting our health care spending right is a matter of setting the right priorities at every level. As long as we consider it more important to have all the latest medical technologies and drugs than to give everyone basic health care, we will continue to spend our money on the wrong things. We will keep spending more than any other country in the world, and those lucky enough to have health insurance will get to take advantage of all of the newest medical advances. And yet, we will still have millions of Americans who can't get even primary care or learn how to head off expensive conditions that could be prevented so easily. We will be spending our money the wrong way down the health care pyramid. To spend it the right way, we have to make the collective decision—in government, in the health care sector, and in our own lives—to make a different set of choices.

7 | KEEPING WHAT PEOPLE LIKE

Americans would love to find a way to fix our health care. They are aware of its problems, they have sympathy for the people who have struggled with it, and they're worried that they could be the ones going bankrupt because of a medical bill someday. But most people aren't sure what the right answer is. There are too many working parts and too many vested interests for most people to see an obvious solution. So they are vulnerable to the scare tactics that opponents always use when reformers try to tackle the industry's very real troubles.

This time around, the Obama team had to find a way to satisfy the two basic values most Americans have about their health care. They want a choice of health plans and doctors, and they want to be able to keep what they have. The easiest way to scare them away from supporting health care reform—even when they are fully aware that the problems will only get worse if nothing is done—is to convince them that reform will force them to accept health plans and doctors that are worse than what they have now. People are willing to support better health care for people in need, but not if it means sacrificing the quality of their own care. It happened with the Clinton health care plan, and if the Obama administration was not careful, it would have happened again.

In just one year—between spring 1993 and spring 1994—public support for the Clinton health care initiative fell from 71 percent to 43 percent. Several months after the effort collapsed in Congress, three experts on health care public opinion—Robert Blendon, Mollyann Brodie, and John Benson—analyzed the polls from that time and found that by April 1994, most Americans did not think they would be better off if the plan became law. They thought the government would have too big a role in their health care, that they would have to pay more money for their care, and that they would have less freedom to choose their doctors.

The analysts blamed the sudden drop in support on the complexity of the Clinton plan, which made it easier for Americans to believe the worst about it—and for opponents to make the harshest charges stick. By setting national limits on health care spending, building the new system on competing managed care plans, and requiring people to get their insurance through newly created health alliances, the plan convinced many people that they would be forced to join health plans they didn't want and to deal with government bureaucracies that might ration their care.[1] That, of course was exactly the message of the "Harry and Louise" ads, run by the Health Insurance Association of America. The most famous of the ads warned that "the government may force us to pick from a few health care plans designed by government bureaucrats," and featured the famous line from the middle-class couple: "They choose, we lose."[2]

The "Harry and Louise" ads are the most famous opposition campaign tactic from that time, but they were hardly the only ones that helped turn public opinion against the initiative. My Republican colleagues made effective use of a chart showing a tangled bureaucratic maze, implying that the Clinton plan would have turned health care for average Americans into a nightmare. (Ironically, the senator who created the chart was Arlen Specter of Pennsylvania, who switched to the Democratic Party and joined the reformers this time.)[3] There was even an article in *Reader's Digest,* which reached millions of homes in middle America at that time, that charged, "The Clintons must know this plan will result in rationing. . . . Quality will be a forgotten concept. They are taking away our choice of doctor."[4]

So it was no surprise when the opponents of health care reform once again tried to claim that the latest effort would have created a runaway bureaucracy standing between patients and their doctors. In my view, though, the complexity of the Clinton plan cannot explain the loss of support on its own. If you want to see true complexity, I always tell critics, try to write our current health care sector into legislative language. You simply cannot fix the problems with a five-page bill. What really doomed the reform effort in the 1990s was the relentless campaign of attacks, which fed into Americans' fears of los-ing what they had—even though they were aware of the problems with the current system.

Still, the fact that their opinions were so easily swayed was a lesson in itself. Even when conditions are at their best for big domestic-policy changes, Blendon, Brodie, and Benson concluded that "the tendency is for experts to overestimate the willingness of middle-class Americans to sacrifice and risk the uncertain consequences of major changes in their lives."[5]

The Obama team was determined to learn from that experience. During the height of the presidential campaign, they decided that Obama and his surro-gates should stress—at every possible opportunity—that his health care plan would *not* force Americans to give up what they have, if they are happy with it. The new mantra was a variation of the line Obama later used many times as president: "If you like what you have, you can keep it." The only thing that would change for most people, Obama would tell voters, was that their premi-ums would go down, because he would take steps to control those rising costs. For those who didn't have a good source of health insurance, there would be change—but once again, Obama and his advisers framed it in terms of ex-panding people's choices. They would be able to get insurance through a new federal pool, with a wide range of options of both plans and doctors. If they wanted to get their insurance through a new, government-run plan, that would be a choice, too.

That was the way Obama laid the groundwork for the next round of health care reform as he stumped around the country. "If you have health insurance, then you don't have to do anything," he said in his final debate with Senator John McCain in October 2008. "If you've got health insurance through your employer, you can keep your health insurance, keep your choice of doctor, keep your plan." For people who didn't have another source of insurance, Obama said, "What we're going to do is to provide you the option of buying into the same kind of federal pool that both Senator McCain and I enjoy as federal employees, which will give you high-quality care, choice of doctors, at lower costs, because so many people are part of this insured group."[6] The goal was to build on the strengths of the current setup while addressing the weaknesses.

Obama hoped to convince Americans he would preserve their choices, keep what they liked about their health care, and give new choices to people who currently have no choice at all.

There was a bit of a risk in promising that no one would see any changes at all to the health insurance they had. The legislation might not actually move people out of their health plans, but it could set off a chain of events that would lead some employers to stop offering health coverage. The Congressional Budget Office, for example, predicted that some businesses—mostly ones with low-wage workers—would drop coverage because it would be cheaper to pay a penalty and let their workers get coverage through the new federal pool.[7]

Still, since so many employers were dropping coverage already, leaving everything alone was no guarantee that people would keep what they had, either. And Obama's advisers were confident that the plan would leave the vast majority of insured Americans alone.[8] Eventually, he began wording his statements more carefully, arguing simply that "nothing in this plan will require you or your employer to change the coverage or the doctor you have."[9] Democratic leaders in Congress tried to stick to more general statements, such as pledging that the plan would "preserve access to the plan and doctor of your choice." The broader lesson still held, however: Obama and the Democrats had learned to reassure Americans with health coverage that their own health care would not be disrupted.[10]

And at least they were trying to find a message that would not stretch the truth. The Republicans, in reviving their antigovernment message to fight the plan, seemed to care only about what phrases would work the best. Many of their statements came straight out of a memo prepared by Republican pollster Frank Luntz, who specialized in poll-tested phrases that would make ideas sound better to the general public. (One of his better-known books was called *Words That Work.*) In his memo, Luntz recommended that Republicans call the reform plan a "government takeover" of health care and argue that it would lead to rationing and denied or delayed care.

"They don't want to hear that you're opposed to government healthcare because it's too expensive (any help from the government to lower costs will be embraced) or because it's anti-competitive," Luntz wrote. "But they are deathly afraid that a government takeover will lower their quality of care—so they are extremely receptive to the anti-Washington approach."[11] He wasn't looking for the best arguments that would not stretch the truth, just the ones that would stick.

Obama and the Democrats had found the right message: change health care without taking away people's choices or interfering with the health coverage they already had. Translating that goal into reality, however, would create political and legislative tensions that they would have to deal with every step of the way.

8 | LESSONS FROM OTHER COUNTRIES

Throughout the debate, a common refrain among members of Congress was that we had to find a "uniquely American" way to solve our health care problems. That's true, of course. We would never be able to win broad support throughout the country if people thought we were trying to replace everything they knew. But most of the nations that have covered all of their citizens have wrestled with the same kinds of issues we are trying to solve.

They have had to find the right balance between giving people the health care they need and keeping costs under control. They have had to prevent their doctors and hospitals from wasting money without cutting payments so deeply that the providers can't cover their costs. And they have had to find the right mix of public and private insurance—a subject that has prompted some bitter political fights, much as we have had throughout our own history.

So it is worth looking at how some of these other nations have struggled with the issues and found the answers. Not all of their solutions would work easily in the United States, and they generally have started with health care systems that have very different frameworks from ours. But when you look at the larger themes that all health care systems have to address, we have more in common with other nations than many might realize. The difference, though, is that other countries have found ways to cover all of their citizens—and protect them from being bankrupted by an illness—while still spending far less than we do.

We should also recognize another crucial distinction that sets us apart. Unlike all of the other industrialized nations, we don't actually have a health care system. We have a market. A system has certain basic elements that allow it to function smoothly: health coverage for all citizens, which everyone is required to join; a management infrastructure to administer the delivery of health care and the payment for all services; and a universal financing mechanism. Without any of those elements, we have a market that delivers generous care to the luckiest Americans and leaves millions of them to fend for themselves.

We also rely heavily on private insurers, who have to answer to their shareholders first and their customers second, as opposed to the way private insurance works in every other industrialized country, where they only have to answer to their customers. It is time to give up the idea that those countries have nothing to teach us, and to start learning how they have made their systems work.

Let's start with France, since the World Health Organization rated it the number one country in the world for overall health system performance.[1] Based on the popular image of the country, a lot of Americans probably would expect its system to be socialized medicine, which means that the government not only pays for health care, but provides it as well. That's not how their system works. It is based on private doctors who get paid for each service they perform, and people get their coverage through national health insurance funds, based on the kind of work they do.[2] (Unlike Americans, people in France don't lose their health coverage when they lose their jobs.)

The difference, though, is that France covers everyone, and at a far lower cost than we spend on our coverage. What people get for their money is comprehensive coverage of hospital, physician, and prescription drug expenses, and even services that we would consider luxuries—such as spa treatments, as long as a doctor has prescribed them.[3] The other thing that's unique about the French system is that the people with the most serious illnesses get the most coverage. The national health program picks up the full cost of treatment for cancer, diabetes, mental illness, and other expensive conditions. It even allows cancer patients to get any drug they want.[4]

The biggest issue France is wrestling with right now, like so many other countries, is how to control health care spending better. In general, the government keeps costs down by negotiating fees with doctors' unions and trying to keep annual budgets for the public hospitals under control. Still, France has already demonstrated that it can set up a far more efficient health care sector than we have. A big part of the reason is the smart cards French patients carry, which allow doctors to get reimbursed electronically and will eventually include their medical histories. Think of how much time and paperwork we would save in the United States if our own health care technology was this up-to-date.[5]

In Germany, Americans might find even more that we recognize from our own setup. Once again, people get their health insurance through their employers—though they don't lose it when they lose their jobs—and those insurance funds pay the doctors and hospitals. However, health insurance in Germany is provided through roughly 200 "sickness funds," which are privately run and compete with each other, but are not-for-profit. Germans can choose among different funds, which gives them more freedom of choice than we have in the United States, since American workers are limited to the health plans their employers offer.[6] So how do the German "sickness funds" compete if they can't make profits? By promising customers better service, such as offering extra coverage beyond the required benefits or being quicker to pay their claims.[7]

Like the French system, the German system suffers from chronic budget shortfalls and rising costs.[8] But it has attempted some innovative solutions that could hold lessons for the United States. Germany has an independent comparative-effectiveness institute, for example, that evaluates different medical services and makes recommendations to the German Federal Joint Committee, which determines what benefits will be covered.[9] It also uses "reference pricing," in which drugs that are close substitutes for one another are covered, but anyone who wants a substantially more expensive drug has to pay the extra cost.[10]

Clearly, the German system is still a work in progress. Even so, it has proven that a system of private providers and private, competing insurers can cover all of its citizens and still provide plenty of choices for everyone.

The lesson from Australia is different, but still relevant to our own reform debate. It is that other countries have fought their own ideological battles over the proper balance between the government and the private market, but have still found a way to cover all of their citizens.

Australia's national health care system has a tumultuous history, since it was passed once, torn down, and then rebuilt again. Its first universal health care program began in 1975, created by the Labor Party coalition government that was in power at the time. But after the conservative coalition, headed by the Liberal Party, came to power later that year, it gradually dismantled the new program (after promising to keep it) by scaling back the public system and promoting private insurance as an alternative. By the end of the conservative coalition's eight-year reign, the most important features of the national health care program had been lost. So when the Labor coalition returned to power in 1983, it relaunched and rebranded the program.[11]

The Australian health care system is basically a publicly funded one with private insurance wrapped around it. Australians get free public hospital care, with medical and drug coverage that requires some copayments by the patients. It is financed by a 1.5 percent income tax, and hospitals get their funds from federal and state revenues. Private insurance allows people to go to either private or public hospitals and have their choice of specialists there. Unlike our employment-based system of private insurance, however, Australians buy it individually—and only about 43 percent of the population has it.[12]

Since 1984, when the new program took effect, Australia has had ongoing debates about how much of a role private insurance should play and how much the government should encourage it. In 1999, after the conservative coalition had returned to power, the government began to offer rebates for everyone who bought private insurance.[13] The government said the subsidies were necessary because people had been dropping private health insurance, calling that trend "the single most serious threat to the viability of our entire health care system."[14] But critics have argued that the rebates are an unnecessarily expensive way of promoting private health insurance, so now the Labor government, under Prime Minister Kevin Rudd, has been trying to cut back the subsidies for wealthier people.

Taiwan is an example of a more recent development in health care reform: studying many different countries and taking the best ideas from all of them. Until the 1990s, Taiwan had more than ten different public health insurance programs, but 41 percent of the population was still uninsured. After a period of rapid economic growth created demands for a better system, the Taiwanese government began studying other countries' health care systems to find the best ideas for a national health insurance program that would extend coverage to all of its citizens[15]—in part to preempt a challenge from the opposition party. They were doing this right around the time we in Congress were trying, and failing, to pass the Clinton health care reform plan. The difference was, the Taiwan health care reform effort succeeded.

The result, which went into effect in 1995, was a single-payer health care program much like Canada's (or our own Medicare program), in which the government pays for medical care delivered by a mix of public and private providers—with the private providers playing the main role in the delivery of medical services. But the designers of Taiwan's system tried to improve on other countries' models—by not letting the rich opt out, as Germany does, and by having one insurance system rather than the 3,500 different health insurance plans that operate in Japan.[16] The one thing the designers did not want to do, though, is borrow ideas from the United States. As Hongjen Chang, a former chief executive officer of Taiwan's Bureau of National Health Insurance, told *Washington Post* reporter T. R. Reid, "In the end we said, 'No, this is not the way we want to go.'"[17]

The new program went into effect quickly, and a bit chaotically, when it began just two months after the creation of the Bureau of National Health Insurance, which runs the system. Still, Taiwan rapidly brought most of its population into the system, and 99 percent of the country is now covered. Like France and Germany, Taiwan gives people smart cards with their medical records and billing information, which helps keep its administrative costs down to 2 percent—the lowest in the world.[18]

The providers get paid for every service they perform, but the providers consider the fees too low, so they try to make up for it by doing as many services as they can. Unfortunately, this trend has led to rushed visits with patients and wasted health care spending. Taiwan's health officials think as much as a third of the nation's health spending may go to overuse and misuse of health care—a figure eerily close to the estimates in our own country.[19]

All of these nations' health care systems have substantial differences with our own, and some of their solutions wouldn't go over so easily in the United States. Still, there are general lessons we can learn from each of these countries. France shows us that it is possible to have a public-private mix that protects everybody, especially the sickest, and preserves people's choice of doctors—if we accept that everyone has to be in the system and everyone looks out for each other. Germany demonstrates that it is possible to have a healthy competition between health plans that isn't based on profits, and certainly isn't based on denying care for the people who need it the most.

Australia shows us that other nations that have fought the same ideological battles we have, with the same kinds of tensions between government and the private sector, have not let those battles get in the way of extending health care to all of their citizens. And Taiwan illustrates how we now have enough examples of international health care reforms that a pretty good hybrid system can be built, using the best examples from other countries and learning from their mistakes. There are problems with these countries' approaches, of course, and we should learn from them, too. A constant theme is that it is possible to go too far in containing costs, or simply to use too blunt an instrument, as the doctors and hospitals in Germany, Australia, and Taiwan would tell us.

Still, the positive lessons are the most important ones for our own reform efforts. These countries consider health care such a basic right that they accept an important trade-off: everyone has to participate, but in return, everyone has health coverage, doctors have to treat them, and their insurance has to pay the claims. It costs money to cover everyone, but as Taiwan found out, those costs can bring health care inflation under control, which more than covers the price.[20] It is also possible to expand health coverage in several steps, as long as they are big ones. France gave national health coverage to all industrial and commercial workers right after World War II, then added farmers and agricultural workers in 1961 and the self-employed in 1966, and finally brought in all of the rest of the uninsured in 2000.[21]

Most of all, these countries have gotten the moral element right: they do not let their people lose their health coverage, and they do not let them go bankrupt because of health care bills. These are fundamental tests of a nation's character, and it is shameful that we have failed the tests for so long. There were important economic reasons to fix our health care problems, but the moral reasons were the ones that led so many of us to see the reform effort as a calling, not just another issue. For those of us who were fortunate enough to be involved, these were the reasons we were eager to give health care reform another try. We knew full well that there would be plenty of obstacles ahead, and many of them were exactly the ones we predicted.

And then there were the obstacles we never saw coming.

Part Two

THE PLAN

1 | THE PHONE CALL

It was a rainy Saturday afternoon, four days after the election, when the newly elected president called me with a proposal. I was at the Regency Hotel in New York with my wife, Linda, Senator Byron Dorgan of North Dakota and his wife, Kim, and our friends Chip and Betsy Barclay. Somewhere around 3:00, President-elect Obama called me on my BlackBerry. I ducked into a quiet area behind the elevators, knowing that the call might be about a possible assignment in the new administration.

Instead, he had two jobs for me. He proposed that I become a senior counselor to the president, overseeing his health care reform effort from the West Wing. At the same time, he also wanted me to become the new secretary of the Department of Health and Human Services. I would have two substantial challenges: developing the policies and the strategy to steer his health care reform plan to passage in Congress, and running a massive federal department with nearly 65,000 employees and an annual budget of more than $700 billion.

I wasn't actually sure this was a good idea. It certainly would strengthen my ability to lead the health care reform effort if I had a presence at the White House, and not just at Health and Human Services. But both jobs carried enormous responsibilities, and each would have been competing for my full attention. More importantly, though, it was not clear to me that health care reform was as important to the new administration as I felt it should be. Obama had talked about health care constantly on the campaign trail, even more than Bill Clinton had in 1992, and his rhetoric had suggested it was at the top of his list of priorities. But I had been hearing talk—thirdhand, admittedly, but still worrisome—that some of his top advisers were questioning whether it would be prudent to tackle health care reform at the beginning of the administration. The full scale of the economic crisis was just becoming apparent to all of us, and it seemed that rescuing the economy might take so much of the new president's time and attention that health care would move to the back burner.

My initial conversation with the president-elect didn't resolve my concerns. But Obama did suggest that I think about what my conditions might be for taking the jobs, and talk to Pete Rouse—my old Senate chief of staff, who later became Obama's Senate chief of staff—to see if they could be met. Pete would be joining the White House as a senior adviser, and it was nice that I could bring my concerns to a friend on the new president's team. Still, I felt that it was an uncomfortable exchange because of my reservations. But these were important questions to resolve, because they would help determine the success or failure of an issue I cared deeply about.

The details of my own role, and the resources I would need to be successful, were negotiable. But what was not negotiable was the need for health care reform to be a true priority for the new administration—a top-tier issue worthy of an early start and the complete commitment of the White House, from the president on down. To make our long-term economic future more secure, and to give our country a true health care "system" worthy of the name, the reform effort deserved at least that much. And given how quickly a new president can lose his early popular support—and, therefore, lose his leverage with Congress—I believed Obama's best possible window of opportunity was to take on health care reform as early as possible.

I would later find that my unease was justified. Some of the new president's top economic advisers were, indeed, convinced that health care reform should wait. Larry Summers, the director of the National Economic Council and former secretary of the treasury, was concerned that the president would have his hands full with the biggest economic crisis since the Great Depression. He asked whether this was really the best time to take on health care, too. Gene Sperling, a veteran of Bill Clinton's economic team and now counselor to Treasury Secretary Tim Geithner, suggested that the administration should first seek an agreement with Congress to extend the life of Social Security before moving on to health care. Peter Orszag, the Office of Management and Budget director, tried to mediate the health care reform argument, but seemed more sympathetic to putting it off.

This debate within the president's inner circle would become a running concern of mine throughout my association with the Obama administration, from those early conversations about my new role to the end of that role three months later. There were times when it was not clear that the president himself was fully committed to taking on the problem early on, given that he did not shut down the talk of a delay. To be successful at health care reform, with all of its complexity and all of the political forces standing in the way, a president has to be completely committed to the fight. But every time I grew frustrated and asked him whether this was truly a priority for him, his answers were so convincing that they easily put my doubts to rest. And as I learned more about the president's operating style, I realized that his approach is to continually challenge assumptions and encourage the full airing of different views.

Not all of Obama's advisers were sure this was the right time to take on the battle. But I believe the president himself was sure—and that meant health care reform just might succeed after so many years.

I first met Barack Obama in 2003, when I was the Senate minority leader and he was a state senator jumping into a crowded race for the Democratic nomination for the U.S. Senate in Illinois. One of my leadership duties was to meet Senate candidates, get a sense of who was strong and who was not, and help decide how much support the party should give them. Senator Peter Fitzgerald, a somewhat iconoclastic Republican who had rubbed some of his GOP colleagues the wrong way, was retiring from his Illinois seat in 2004, so we had a good chance to pick up that seat for the Democrats if we had a solid candidate. I remember being impressed with one of the leading candidates at the time, Dan Hynes, the state comptroller. I also met with another of the likely front-runners, Blair Hull, who had become a multimillionaire trading securities on Wall Street.

But I got a particularly good impression of Barack, which was reinforced later when I returned to Illinois to attend a press conference with Dick Durbin, the senior senator from the state. Durbin was always one of the best communicators in our caucus, but I noticed that Barack was an eloquent speaker as well and carried himself with a healthy sense of confidence. I told Dick I thought Barack had a bright future ahead of him. At the time, Dick was worried about whether Barack would be able to get a fair hearing from the state's voters: "But he's got such a funny name!" Later, Dick and Barack would build a close working relationship and friendship when they served in the Senate together, and Dick was one of his most enthusiastic champions during the presidential campaign.

Barack had an incredible streak of luck during his Senate race, as all of the other top-tier contenders fell away. Hull self-destructed when his divorce records revealed bitter allegations of abuse from his ex-wife, Hynes got dragged down in a nasty battle with Hull, and Barack coasted through the political carnage to win the nomination. Then his likely Republican opponent, Jack Ryan, a former investment banker, dropped out after reports surfaced that his ex-wife had accused him of pressuring her to go to sex clubs. The new Republican candidate, Alan Keyes, was no threat at all; a hard-line conservative activist and former presidential candidate, he had to move from Maryland to Illinois to run. And, of course, Barack's electrifying keynote address at the 2004 Democratic convention in Boston made him a national figure overnight. So he was suddenly able to raise a lot of money, and he offered to help raise funds for other candidates—including me, as I fought to keep my own seat. And as his election looked more and more like a sure thing, he sought me out for conversations to learn about how the Senate works.

On election night, Barack became the new Illinois senator—but I was suddenly out of a job, having narrowly lost my seat to a strong challenger, Republican congressman John Thune. Barack quickly contacted me to express an interest in some of my staff members. He was particularly impressed with Pete Rouse, my chief of staff, and wanted to hire him for the same job in his office. Pete initially turned him down, saying he was tired of the Senate and wanted to look for something else. But eventually, Obama convinced Pete to take the job for just six months, to get him started. Pete, of course, ended up sticking around for far more than six months.

Barack and I kept in touch, both directly and through Pete, over the next two years. So when Obama began to think seriously about running for the presidency in the fall of 2006, Pete asked if I would talk to him about it. I was happy to do that, naturally, but the conversation was also a clear signal that a request for an endorsement would be next. That would present a real dilemma, since I had other friends in the race who had served in the Senate with me as well—notably Hillary Rodham Clinton, another star senator whom I had known for years and worked with during my last four years in office. There was also John Edwards, the former North Carolina senator and the 2004 Democratic vice-presidential nominee, as well as Joe Biden and Chris Dodd, with whom I had worked closely during my years as Senate Democratic leader. But when I pondered who to endorse in the race, I tried to take a realistic look at who would be in the best position to win the White House.

During her time as New York's junior senator, Hillary had been a tireless worker with a serious mind for policy, particularly on health care and education. But I concluded that Barack had the best chance to offer what the voters seemed to want for 2008, which was a fresh face with no political baggage who could offer the country a truly different set of policies. He would represent a break with the past—and not just the eight years of George W. Bush's presidency, but the eight years of Bill Clinton before that. Besides, Barack had already reached out to several members of my old team—not just Pete, but also close advisers such as Steve Hildebrand, who became Barack's deputy campaign manager, and Denis McDonough, my former foreign policy adviser who took on the same role for the campaign. So I had already built up such an interest in Barack's future, through our personal friendship and through the growing number of my former aides in his circle, that it seemed natural to throw my support behind him.

That decision led to some strain in my relationship with both of the Clintons for quite a while, particularly because I was unable to reach Hillary to give her an advance warning before I announced my endorsement in February 2007. Barack's campaign did not want me to call the other candidates until 48 hours before the announcement, to keep the news from leaking. So when it was time to make the calls, I traded voice mails with Hillary, but we never connected. In hindsight, I probably should have called Bill Clinton, but that idea did not occur to me until it was too late. Fortunately, we were able to patch up our relationship after the election, when Hillary moved on to her new role as secretary of state, a job she has approached with all of the same energy and seriousness of purpose she showed in the Senate.

———

When the election was over, it was not a foregone conclusion that health care would be my issue with the new administration. In fact, the first time the president-elect and I had talked about a possible role for me—in a phone call on the Thursday after the election—I half-jokingly suggested that if I could do anything I wanted, I would want to be secretary of state.

It was not a totally random suggestion. Over the years, I have had a strong interest in foreign policy, dating back to my first job in Washington as the foreign policy aide to Jim Abourezk, my senator from South Dakota at the time. I have continued that interest over the years through my friendship with Madeleine Albright, the former secretary of state, and through my work as a cochair of the National Democratic Institute, which runs programs to promote democratic institutions and practices throughout the world. But it was not a serious wish, since the wheels already seemed to be in motion to give the job to Hillary—and since John Kerry, another friend from my Senate days and the 2004 Democratic presidential nominee, also coveted the job. I had no desire to get in the middle of that conflict.

There had also been talk that I might become the new president's White House chief of staff, but that job quickly went to Rahm Emanuel, the Illinois congressman who had one of the sharpest political and policy minds in Washington and had helped engineer the House Democrats' victory in the 2006 elections. Instead, I suggested to the president-elect that he use me as a kind of all-purpose consultant to work on special projects. The president-elect, however, made it clear he had me in mind for a health care role. "I'd like to make it more definitive than that," he said. "What about secretary of Health and Human Services?"

That would have been a natural progression from the role I was given on the transition team: heading up the team of about a dozen people who would work out the first steps on health care reform. In addition, the president-elect and I did have a bit of history on health care. When he was a senator, we had talked a few times about the issue, and as a presidential candidate, he was kind enough to write a supportive quote for the jacket of my previous book, *Critical: What We Can Do About the Health-Care Crisis*. I had e-mailed Pete a draft of the book, and he shared it with Barack, who largely agreed with the ideas in the book. The one disagreement we had was over the need to require everyone to buy health insurance, which I supported and Barack did not. That issue would become the one defining difference between him and Hillary Clinton as they debated health care during the primaries. But it was not a big enough difference to keep him from thinking about me for the Health and Human Services job.

Unfortunately, the job did not sound too appealing to me. For one thing, I had never run a bureaucracy of that size before. More importantly, though, I did not believe I could have a real impact in the health care reform debate if I was not based at the White House. I had seen how it worked in the Clinton administration, when Donna Shalala was the Health and Human Services secretary and Ira Magaziner headed up the reform effort at the White House, and while they did the best they could in their separate roles, I am certain that everything would have gone more smoothly if Donna had had both jobs. In any administration, power and proximity go hand in hand—meaning that to be able to negotiate the congressional initiatives that matter most in a presidency, you must have regular access to the president and his top advisers. I suggested that I could be a more effective health care reform advocate if I was based at the White House, perhaps on a temporary basis.

The president-elect said he would think about that and call me back. So I believe that when we talked again that Saturday, he was truly trying to respond to my concerns from the first conversation. By heading up the new White House Office of Health Reform, in addition to being the Health and Human Services secretary, I had a better chance of having the proximity I would need to lead the reform effort successfully. But I still needed to discuss the idea some more, both to make sure I would have the resources I needed and to satisfy myself that health care reform would have the proper priority in the new administration. The president-elect suggested I talk to Pete about what conditions I would need to take the jobs.

That led to a meeting the following Thursday at the transition office with Rahm, Pete, and John Podesta, the founder and president of the Center for American Progress. John was cochairing the transition team along with Pete and Valerie Jarrett, a close friend of the Obamas' who would later become a White House senior adviser. At that meeting, they satisfied me that all of my conditions could be met. I wanted to make sure I would have the same access to the president and his senior staff that I would have had as part of the White

House team. I wanted to bring along my trusted staff—Timothy Hogan, Jody Bennett, and Lindsey Wagner—and ensure that they had the same status as other White House staff. Finally, I needed to know that, in whatever way the new administration signaled its top priorities, health care would have the same status as energy. That way, I could make sure it would not lose its rightful place in the top tier of the agenda.

They assured me that there would be no problem meeting any of those conditions. I would also get to pick my team at Health and Human Services, which was crucial, since a strong team would make it easier for me to handle the workloads of both jobs. I was already counting on the help of Jeanne Lambrew, my collaborator on *Critical* and a veteran of Bill Clinton's health care policy team, who would have been the deputy director of the new White House Office of Health Reform, and Mark Childress, my former chief counsel in the Senate, who would have become my chief of staff at Health and Human Services. Another key to being able to juggle my own duties, I decided, was to divide health care reform into two phases and shift my emphasis accordingly. During the congressional debate, I planned to spend about three-quarters of my time at the White House, to give the negotiations with Capitol Hill as much attention as they needed. After the reform bill had become law, if we were that lucky, I would reverse my work pattern and spend three-quarters of my time at Health and Human Services, since I would have to shift my focus to the implementation of the new law.

With my concerns addressed, I told Rahm, Pete, and John that I would take the jobs. In the meantime, I would be in charge of the health policy team for the transition. We all exchanged hugs as I left the meeting, and I looked ahead to the challenge of helping the president-elect turn his campaign promises into law. It was a task that would be critical to the future of our economy— and determine whether Barack Obama, who had made health care reform more central to his campaign than any recent president, could truly deliver the change he had promised.

2 | THE MAKING OF THE OBAMA PLAN

When he entered the presidential race in February 2007, Barack had a lot to prove to the voters. They knew he could deliver an eloquent speech with confidence and purpose, and they knew he had a special ability to inspire people to transcend their differences. But they did not know whether he could master the intricate details of policy. He had only been in the Senate two years, not long enough to make a big mark through his legislative work.

He was certainly capable of it; anyone who spent two minutes with him knew he was one of the most intellectual members of the Senate, full of curiosity and creative thinking. But most voters would not get the chance to spend two minutes with him, and much of the early media coverage was skeptical about whether he could do anything more than give a good speech. Over the course of a two-year campaign, the voters would have to be able to answer that question from a distance.

Health care seemed to be as good an issue as any to prove he had substance, and not just rhetorical flash. Besides, his campaign advisers believed he didn't have much of a choice. His top rivals for the Democratic nomination would force an early, and detailed, debate over health care whether he wanted it or not. John Edwards, the former senator from North Carolina and John Kerry's running mate in 2004, put out a health care reform plan in February, just a few days after Barack entered the race. The approach of the Edwards campaign, the Obama team felt, was to be first with a proposal on every issue even if they had to sacrifice some specifics to do it. And even though Hillary would not outline her own plan until months later, the Obama campaign knew she would make it as detailed and well researched as possible, because she, too, had something to prove. Because the entire country knew her role in the unsuccessful reform effort of the 1990s, she had to turn a weakness into a strength.[1]

Barack had been studying and thinking about health care for the past two years in the Senate, so it wasn't as if he was new to the subject. He had a series of discussions with various health care experts—arranged by his Senate policy director, Karen Kornbluh—and he had the advantage of having a physician, Dora Hughes, on his staff as his health care adviser. And although he was not on either of the two Senate committees that focus on health care issues, he recognized the importance of the issue, and he put together a health care reform bill that focused largely on improving quality. (He became a member of one of the committees, the Health, Education, Labor, and Pensions Committee, in 2007 just before he launched his presidential campaign.) When his advisers found that quality alone was not enough to get the public interested in health care reform, he began to shift his emphasis to costs and coverage. But in his bestselling 2006 book, *The Audacity of Hope*, he offered a rough glimpse of what that early Senate bill would have looked like.

In his "example of what a serious health-care reform plan might look like"—based on the Senate bill—Barack proposed having the Institute of Medicine design a model of a basic, high-quality health care plan that would include primary care, preventive care, catastrophic coverage, and management of chronic illnesses. People would be able to buy the model health care plan through either the Federal Employees Health Benefits Plan, the health program that covers federal workers and members of Congress, or through a new set of state-run purchasing pools. The new plans, as well as Medicare and Medicaid, would have to switch to electronic claims and electronic health records. And with the money saved through those lower administrative costs and other reforms, the federal government would subsidize low-income families so they could join the new health plans, a step that might also make it possible to require all parents to sign their kids up for health coverage. Barack even toyed with the idea of chipping away at the tax break for employer-sponsored health coverage, bringing in extra funds for the new system by taxing the "fancy, gold-plated executive health-care plans that fail to provide any additional health benefits."[2]

His advisers kept working to expand the plan, though, and that work provided a good foundation for a campaign proposal when the right time came. In May 2007, Barack unveiled his plan in a speech at the University of Iowa Hospital in Iowa City, Iowa. In his speech, he told the story of a family from Decorah, Iowa, that was on the verge of bankruptcy from rising health care premiums because the husband had survived a battle with cancer. "We're not a country that rewards hard work and perseverance with bankruptcies and foreclosures. We're not a country that allows major challenges to go unsolved and unaddressed while our people suffer needlessly," Barack told the crowd. "This is not who we are. And this is not who we have to be."[3]

The campaign plan proposed a series of steps to control rising health care costs. To make work-based coverage less expensive, Barack said the federal government should reimburse employers for some of their catastrophic health care expenses, as long as the employers channeled that money into reducing their workers' premiums. He called for encouraging disease-management programs and innovative ways to coordinate care better, and he promised to invest in electronic health records. He promised to make the insurance market more competitive by preventing insurers from "abusing their monopoly power through unjustified price increases." And he vowed to bring down drug costs by allowing Americans to buy drugs from other countries, making generic drugs more widely available, and using the purchasing power of the federal government to negotiate lower drug prices for Medicare.[4]

All together, the campaign's advisers predicted that the various cost savings in the plan could save the average family as much as $2,500 in premiums per year. That estimate came from a memo prepared by David Blumenthal, David Cutler, and Jeffrey Liebman, all respected health care economists and policy analysts. They based their estimate on the savings they thought would come from the "reinsurance" proposal (helping employers cover the catastrophic costs), the improvements in health information technology, the increased use of disease-management programs, lower overhead spending, and less uncompensated care.[5] This was the thinking behind the $2,500-per-family savings figure that Barack would use throughout the campaign—and would later set as a target for the transition team, telling us he expected "hard numbers" on how we would actually produce those savings.

On the quality side, Barack made an important contribution to the campaign debate by endorsing comparative effectiveness research. He promised to set up an independent institute to "start measuring what's effective and what's not when it comes to different drugs and procedures, so that patients can finally start making informed choices about the care that's best for them."[6] He said he would require providers to start reporting preventable medical errors, as an incentive to take them more seriously and make sure they happen less often. That was also part of Barack's broader commitment to greater openness in health care; he said he would make the industry more transparent about costs and quality by requiring hospitals and providers to report more information about both areas.[7]

But it was the access side of Barack's plan that would get the most attention—his plan for making health coverage available to every American. He said he would make all parents get health coverage for their children, and require all employers to either cover their workers or pay a fee to help the federal government do it. He called for an expansion of Medicaid and the State Children's Health Insurance Program to provide more public coverage to low-income families. And since individuals, small businesses, and the self-employed have the most trouble getting coverage, he proposed creating a new National Health Insurance Exchange to make a variety of approved health plans available to them. If they couldn't afford any of the plans, there would be federal subsidies. All of the plans would operate under new rules: no one could be rejected for being sick or having preexisting conditions.

The plans could be offered by private insurers, but there would be a new option, too. One of the plans would be "a new national health plan which will give individuals the choice to buy affordable health coverage that is similar to the plan available to federal employees."[8] The term *public option* appeared nowhere in Barack's speech that day, nor was it anywhere in the details of the fifteen-page plan the campaign released. But that was what he was proposing. The idea didn't create even a ripple in the news coverage of his speech. But that simple idea—give people a health plan roughly similar to the Federal Employees Health Benefits Plan if they had no other source of coverage—would later become both the rallying cry of progressives who were tired of private-market failures and the excuse for conservative opponents to warn, once again, of the dangers of "government-run health care." It triggered an ideological fight that nearly destroyed the entire effort, and with it, all of the other reforms that Americans badly needed.

Not everyone thought it was a good idea for Barack to put out a health care plan with so many details. Several experts advised sticking to general principles. If you get into any level of detail, they told the campaign, health care stakeholders will pick apart anything that could be remotely controversial—such as benefit levels for coverage—and your opponents will kill you with attack ads. But health care reform had now become a test of the seriousness of any candidate in the Democratic primaries. If Barack wanted to have any shot at the nomination, his advisers told the experts, he needed a serious health care plan.[9]

Barack's plan had the benefit of recent experience in health care reforms at the state level, as well as elements of how the thinking had evolved about national health care reform since the 1990s. The most important lessons from state experience came from the Massachusetts health care reform law of 2006, which set a goal of health coverage for all residents of the state. It came close; as of 2008, only 2.6 percent of state residents were still uninsured, the lowest rate in the country. And this was under a Republican governor, Mitt Romney, who was now running for the Republican presidential nomination. Massachusetts did it by requiring everyone in the state to get health insurance, requiring most employers to contribute to their workers' coverage or pay a fee, expanding the Medicaid program, and creating a new Commonwealth Care program to subsidize health insurance for people with incomes up to three times the federal poverty level.[10]

Barack did not embrace all of the Massachusetts plan. He refused to require everyone to get health insurance, which was the main source of leverage the state used to get everybody to participate. From the beginning, he thought the idea had uncomfortable Big Brother overtones.[11] And when advisers debated a softer version of the mandate—such as requiring everyone to get coverage only after insurance costs had been brought down to a certain level—he replied that if affordability was the problem, that's what they ought to focus on.[12] The closest he was willing to come was to require all parents to cover their children, on the theory that kids were the one group whose health care fate was not in their own hands.

Still, one of the centerpieces of Barack's plan, the health insurance exchange, was inspired directly by the Massachusetts model.[13] As part of the 2006 reform, the state created a Health Connector, an independent, quasi-governmental agency that runs an exchange to provide health insurance to individuals and small businesses. It sets standards for that coverage and has certified six private insurers to offer it, as part of a program called Commonwealth Choice.[14] So far, Connector officials think it has been a great success in getting uninsured people into the system. However, they're the first to admit that it has not gotten health care costs under control, and they're worried that if they don't take the next step and control costs soon, they will lose some of the coverage gains they have made.[15] They do allow Massachusetts residents to get out of the requirement for everyone to buy health coverage if they truly can't afford it, by applying for a certificate of exemption if they suffered financial hardships—such as eviction notices or having their utilities cut off—or if buying health insurance would make them suffer "serious deprivation of food, shelter, clothing or other necessities."[16]

The public option, meanwhile, was the product of the evolution of thinking in Democratic circles since the 1990s. In 2003, political scientist Jacob Hacker published a paper called "Medicare Plus," in which he proposed letting people buy into an expanded Medicare program if they didn't already have coverage through the workplace or traditional Medicare.[17] Over the next few years, the idea took hold with progressives, who knew the country wasn't ready for a Canadian-style single-payer system, but saw the Hacker idea as the next-best thing: a new Medicare-style program for a limited group of people. Some even thought it might be a first step toward a single-payer system, an idea John Edwards acknowledged when he included a public option in his own health care plan. "Over time, the system may evolve toward a single-payer approach if individuals and businesses prefer the public plan," the Edwards plan stated.[18]

That wasn't what Barack had in mind when he included the public option in his own plan. He wasn't looking for a back-door way to slide into a completely new health care system. But he did agree with the other argument in favor of the public plan: that it would create a healthy competition with private insurers, forcing them not only to do a better job of covering people, but also to do it at more reasonable rates. Later, this would become a critical argument for including it in health care reform despite all the controversy. If Congress really wanted to keep health care costs at a reasonable level for individuals and small businesses, this was an effective way to do it.

So now Barack had his campaign health care plan. He also had the basis for another, more secretive project. While he traveled across the country in pursuit of the presidency, his Senate staff quietly worked with the staff of Gordon Smith, an affable moderate Republican senator from Oregon, to develop a bipartisan health care bill they could introduce together. The Obama-Smith bill, if it had ever been introduced, would have looked a lot like Obama's campaign plan, since a lot of the work on the bill was reflected in the campaign plan. Only a handful of aides in both offices knew about it. But the thinking was that Obama could work on it from his position on the Health, Education, Labor, and Pensions Committee, while Smith could advance it from his seat on the Finance Committee, the other Senate panel that handles health care.

Smith ended up losing his seat to Democrat Jeff Merkley in the 2008 election, but at the time that Barack was starting out on the presidential campaign trail, Smith looked like a fairly safe bet for reelection. Barack's Senate staff never would have let on publicly that they had a backup plan in case he didn't make it to the White House. But that's what the Obama-Smith health care bill was. Whenever Barack returned to the Senate, he would have a worthwhile legislative project waiting for him.

Except that he never returned.

3 | THE PRIMARIES

The health care debate in the Democratic primaries began unusually early. On March 24, 2007, the Center for American Progress Action Fund and the Service Employees International Union hosted a forum at the University of Nevada–Las Vegas that was entirely about health care reform. Unfortunately, it happened a bit too early for Barack to give his best performance. He had not yet released his health care plan, so for the most part he had to stick to general principles.

He had been a presidential candidate for less than two months at that point. And he went on after John Edwards, who at that point had a health care plan that he could talk about at length. Hillary had not released one of her own either, but because of her history with the subject, she could talk about it with authority and discuss how the politics of the issue had changed since the 1990s. A depressed Barack later told his campaign manager, David Plouffe, that he had "whiffed" at the forum.[1]

Still, Barack clearly had a broad sense of where he was headed as he spoke to the audience that Saturday morning. He committed himself to seeking universal coverage—health care for all Americans. He said the plan would have to bring down health costs and get more for the money we do spend, and that "employers, government, and individuals are all going to have to put up something." He vowed to seek more money for preventive care and for better management of chronic illnesses. He said he would propose a better system of letting individuals join a health care "pool" so they could spread their costs with others more easily. And he endorsed the idea of "pay or play," which calls for employers either to cover their workers or to pay into a fund to help their workers get coverage elsewhere. Significantly, he said nothing about requiring all individuals to get health insurance.[2]

Most of all, though, Obama accurately predicted the importance that health care reform, whether it succeeded or failed, would have for his presidency. "Every four years, we hear somebody has got a health care plan," he said. "Every four years somebody trots out a white paper, and they post it on the Web. But the question we have to challenge ourselves is, do we have the political will and the sense of urgency to actually get it done? I want to be held accountable for getting it done. I will judge my first term as president based . . . on whether we have delivered the kind of health care that every American deserves and that our system can afford."[3]

If you listened to Hillary and John that day, putting their remarks together with Barack's, you would have gotten a good sense of the consensus that was already emerging in Democratic circles about what should be done. Even given what we now know about his personal behavior, we should acknowledge that John Edwards made important contributions, at the time, to the health care debate. At the forum, he advanced the issue by talking about the need for "shared responsibilities," and spelling out exactly what those would be. Employers would have the "pay or play" requirement, the government would have to set up "health care markets" similar to the exchange Barack would eventually propose, and individuals would have to get health insurance.[4]

And Hillary made a lot of thoughtful points about the insurance practices that would have to change, particularly the refusal to cover preexisting conditions—"none of us are going to be insurable if we don't change this system"—and the reluctance to cover preventive care that could save money in the long run, especially with the growing frequency of chronic conditions such as diabetes. She talked about the need to move to electronic medical records to cut down on wasted administrative spending. And she noted the importance of adding a "backup government-sponsored approach to complement the employer system" for individuals and small businesses who can't get insurance, echoing the public option that John had already discussed.

There was another important political reality that Hillary acknowledged at the forum, and would talk about many more times on the campaign trail. Everyone was waiting to find out what lessons she had learned from her role in the failed 1990s health care reform effort. The big lesson, she said, was that the Clintons did not explain well enough to the American public that they would not be forced to give up coverage that they liked. "We don't want to have people feeling like, oh, my goodness, the government is going to come in and they're going to tell me what I have to do and what doctors I have to go to," she said. "That was never, ever part of the plan, but some people got worried about that."[5] She got the message, and throughout her campaign, she tried to assure voters that they could keep what they liked—in language remarkably similar to the assurances Barack would use. "If you like what you have now," she told a questioner at an online news conference in September 2007, "you don't have to change anything."[6]

Hillary announced her health care plan in three stages over the course of the year. She put out her plan to control costs in May, her proposals for improving the quality of care in August, and, finally, her plan for covering all Americans in September. The general framework was not too different from what Barack had proposed, or from what John had outlined. She, too, proposed giving individuals and small businesses a new menu of health plans that would fit their needs, though she would have done it by opening up the Federal Employees Health Benefits Program that members of Congress and federal workers use. She would have included a public option that would "compete on a level playing field" with private plans. She would have banned insurers from rejecting people for preexisting conditions and limited how much they could vary the premiums. And she would have controlled costs by reducing payments to Medicare managed-care plans, allowing the government to negotiate drug prices for Medicare, and improving the quality of health care in a variety of ways, such as covering preventive services and funding comparative effectiveness research.[7]

The big difference between her and Barack, however, was that she would have required all Americans to get health insurance. Where Barack saw a harsh, and possibly cruel, new requirement that would force people to buy health coverage they can't afford, Hillary saw the one mechanism that was crucial to getting everyone covered and eliminating the instability caused by people who don't pay for health insurance until they're already sick. And she believed there were ways to make the mandate as painless as possible for people who truly faced financial hardship. Her plan would have created a tax credit to subsidize coverage for people who don't earn a lot of money, making sure that the premiums they had to pay never would have risen beyond a certain percentage of their income.[8] Still, this one disagreement would become the defining health care battle of the Democratic primaries, creating bitter fights that masked the fact that Barack and Hillary agreed on nearly everything else.

When Barack unveiled his health care plan on May 29, Hillary had to figure out how to respond. Just say it's not universal coverage, her advisers said, because if it doesn't require every American to buy health coverage, it will never come close to getting all Americans to participate. But if that was the line the campaign took, her advisers warned, it would also commit Hillary to including such a requirement in her own plan, a commitment she had not yet made. "Well, I'm going to have to have one anyway, right?" Hillary replied.[9] So that day, the campaign's policy director, Neera Tanden, issued a statement making the challenge official: "Senator Clinton believes that in addition to making healthcare more accessible, we have to achieve true universal healthcare so that every American has health coverage."[10]

Barack didn't reject the idea of requiring everyone to have coverage because of some politically calculated scheme. If anything, his stand was a disadvantage to him in the Democratic primaries, because nearly everyone, including me, was telling him the only practical way to achieve universal coverage was to require everyone to participate. Without that requirement, there's too much incentive for people to delay getting health coverage as long as they can, refusing to pay the premiums that support other people when they're sick, and then trying to get coverage when they need it. The insurance companies have gone way overboard in trying to prevent this from happening, but it is still a valid concern, because it is a rational way for people to react when insurance is voluntary. Barack, however, thought most people go without health coverage for a more basic reason—because they can't afford it—and didn't think it was reasonable to try to force them into the system. "He thought it was pushing people too hard—'I'm going to make you buy something, but I can't show it to you, and I can't tell you how much it's going to cost you,'" recalled David Cutler, the Harvard health care economist who advised the campaign. Barack's view, he said, was that "I can't start out that way."[11]

Both Hillary and John had the requirement in their plans, however, and they both attacked Barack for not including it in his. Without it, they said, Barack's proposal was not really universal coverage. In a June 2007 debate in New Hampshire, John cited a back-of-the-envelope estimate by the *New Republic*'s Jonathan Cohn that Obama would leave 15 million Americans uninsured.[12] "We have a threshold question about whether we're going to have truly universal care," Edwards said. "I believe that unless we have a law requiring that every man, woman, and child in America be covered, we're going to have millions of people who aren't covered."[13]

Later in the year, as the first primaries approached, Hillary picked up on the 15 million estimate—which had now been verified by MIT economics professor Jonathan Gruber—and used it to hammer away at the credibility of Barack's health care plan. "When it came time to step up and decide whether or not he would support universal health care coverage, he chose not to do that," Hillary said at a November 2007 debate in Las Vegas. "His plan would leave fourteen million Americans out. That's about the population of Nevada, Iowa, South Carolina, and New Hampshire."[14]

Barack fought back by insisting that if we bring the cost of health insurance down, more people would get it. "She thinks the problem for people without health care is that nobody has mandated, forced them to get health care. That's not what I'm seeing around Nevada," he said at the Las Vegas debate. "What I see are people who would love to have health care. They desperately want it. But the problem is they can't afford it."[15] Later in the campaign, after John Edwards dropped out and the race started to turn into a drawn-out primary battle between Barack and Hillary, Barack's questions about the coverage requirement took on a harder edge. He seized on the fact that Hillary's plan did not specify what she would do about people who failed to get the required coverage. "If they cannot afford it, then the question is, what are you going to do about it? Are you going to fine them? Are you going to garnish their wages?" Barack asked in a January 2008 debate. "You know, those are questions that Senator Clinton has not answered with respect to her plan, but I think we can anticipate that there would also be people potentially who are not covered and are actually hurt if they have a mandate imposed on them."[16]

The Obama campaign also started hitting Hillary with ads and mailers that tried to make her sound insensitive to people's financial problems. One mailer in February 2008, which drew complaints from the Clinton campaign, warned,

"The way Hillary Clinton's health care plan covers everyone is to have the government force uninsured people to buy insurance, even if they can't afford it. . . . Punishing families who can't afford health care to begin with just *doesn't make sense*."[17] The mailer said nothing, though, about Hillary's proposal to limit how much income people would have to spend on health insurance premiums, which was her mechanism for making the coverage affordable. Likewise, an Obama campaign television ad that aired in April 2008, shortly before the Pennsylvania primary, charged, "What's she not telling you about her health care plan? It forces everyone to buy insurance, even if you can't afford it. And you pay a penalty if you don't."[18]

The Clinton campaign responded with a Pennsylvania television ad that accused Barack of making "false charges" about her plan: "She has a plan everyone can afford. Obama's will cost taxpayers seventeen hundred dollars more to cover each new person. Hillary's plan covers everyone. Obama's leaves fifteen million people out." The $1,700 estimate, however, came from another Jonathan Gruber paper that compared Hillary's plan to one with no mandates at all—unlike Barack's plan, which at least had the mandate to cover children.[19] And a robocall from the Clinton campaign to Pennsylvania voters charged that Barack's plan "imposes a nine-hundred-dollar hidden tax on families," which was a huge stretch based on an estimate of what we all pay to cover uninsured people—and the assumption that there still would be a large number of uninsured people under Barack's plan.[20] Truth, of course, is the quickest casualty of the toughest political campaigns. The longer the Democratic primaries dragged on, the greater the danger that each campaign would make it harder for the eventual winner to do what needed to be done to fix the health care problems.

It seemed at times that the nomination battle would never end. But when it did, the two did their best to patch up their differences, on health care as well as everything else. Barack did not change his stand on requiring all Americans to have health insurance—yet. He would not begin to reconsider his position until after the election was over. Still, one of his most important hires from Hillary's old campaign staff was Neera Tanden, who had been one of the most vocal advocates of the mandate. She became his domestic policy director, and later a senior adviser at the Department of Health and Human Services Office of Health Reform. (Tanden is now the chief operating officer of the Center for

American Progress.) And when Hillary gave her speech at the Democratic convention in Denver, she put aside whatever doubts she had spread about the effectiveness of Barack's health care plan. "I cannot wait to watch Barack Obama sign into law a health care plan that covers every single American," she told the cheering delegates.[21]

As for Barack, on the night he accepted the nomination at a massive public celebration at Denver's Invesco Field, he gave the crowd just a hint of the personal stake he had in the health care debate. During the primaries, he had talked frequently about how his mother, Stanley Ann Dunham—who had died of ovarian cancer in 1995 at age fifty-three—had to fight with her insurance company to make sure her cancer wasn't considered a preexisting condition. "As someone who watched my mother argue with insurance companies while she lay in bed dying of cancer," he said, "I will make certain those companies stop discriminating against those who are sick and need care the most."[22]

As he prepared to turn his attention to the general election, Barack had at least one good reason to think he could succeed where past presidents had failed. This time, some of the most powerful special interest groups, including organizations that had fought furiously against reform in the past, were sending signals that they would not stand in the way again.

4 | THE STAKEHOLDERS

In the summer of 2008, shortly after Obama had locked down the Democratic presidential nomination, his campaign headquarters in Chicago got a visit from a surprising guest. Karen Ignagni, the president and chief executive officer of America's Health Insurance Plans, the trade group that represents about 1,300 health insurance companies, flew in to deliver a message in person to the nominee's health advisers.

The group wanted all Americans to have health coverage, she said, and it was willing to accept a health care reform package that included a "guaranteed issue" requirement—meaning, all health insurance companies would have to accept anyone who applied, regardless of whether they had any health problems. No longer would health insurance companies be able to turn down people with preexisting conditions. There was one condition, though. If Obama won the election, she wanted him to accept a reform package that would require all Americans to sign up for health coverage. To the health insurers, it was the only way to make sure people wouldn't take advantage of the new rules by waiting to buy insurance until they were already sick.

It was a conflict that needed to be worked out, but Ignagni's visit represented a larger shift in the political environment that went beyond any single person or interest group. The stakeholders were looking for ways to be involved in the next reform effort, and even help it along this time. Labor and consumer groups had always supported reform, but now some of the biggest players in the health industry—health insurers, pharmaceutical manufacturers, doctors, hospitals, and medical device makers—and prominent business voices were sending signals that they would cooperate with health care reform rather than mobilizing to kill it.

This was partly because of self-interest. If millions of uninsured Americans gained health insurance, the health industry groups stood to gain millions of new customers, and a successful effort to constrain health care spending could save businesses from the out-of-control rise in premiums. But there was also a broader recognition among all of the players that the health care sector couldn't keep going the way it was going. And as an Obama victory began to look more likely, the business and health care stakeholders recognized what the rest of us were seeing. The stars were lining up for health care reform for the first time since the defeat of the Clinton plan, and the smartest interest-group leaders wanted to make sure they had seats at the table.

The repositioning of America's Health Insurance Plans was a perfect example. The group had been created in 2003 by the merger of two insurance industry organizations that had caused us problems in the past—the American Association of Health Plans, a thorn in our side during the congressional debates over the Patients' Bill of Rights, and the Health Insurance Association of America, which created the "Harry and Louise" ads that helped defeat the Clinton plan.

So their track record was not the kind that would ever make you think they would support a new reform effort. Indeed, I gave a speech to the group in February 2007, shortly after the Democrats gained control of Congress, in which I warned them that they were perceived as the National Rifle Association of health care. They had voted with Republicans on virtually every issue, I told them, and it wasn't always clear whether they cared about their customers or just their shareholders. To have a better relationship with the new majority, everyone would have to work a lot harder to find common ground.

By that point, though, they were trying to play a more constructive role in the health care debate. In November 2006, just after the election, the group had proposed its own plan for giving every American access to health insurance. The plan did not ask a lot from the health insurance industry itself. Its main suggestions were to expand the two main low-income programs, Medicaid and the State Children's Health Insurance Program, and create a new account to allow people to buy any kind of health coverage with pretax dollars.[1] Still, the fact that the group was willing to put out any kind of coverage proposal for all Americans sent a strong signal that it wanted to have a place in the next reform debate.

And shortly after Obama was elected, the group put out a new plan that added the crucial trade-off. It proposed accepting everyone who applies for health coverage—with no exclusions for preexisting conditions—as long as all individuals were required to get health insurance.[2] This became their negotiating position once the Obama administration and Congress began working on the reform plan.

Another organization that signaled, early on, that it was interested in supporting the next health care reform effort was the Pharmaceutical Research and Manufacturers of America. The powerful lobbying group, which nearly everyone in Washington calls PhRMA for short, could have done a lot of damage if it had run an ad campaign against the plan. Instead, top executives of the group contacted Obama campaign advisers to deliver a clear message: they wanted to be part of the solution.

The communication between PhRMA and the Obama campaign was not one-sided. The campaign made a deliberate effort to reach out to PhRMA and other key stakeholders as well, believing that, as health care adviser David Cutler put it, "You weren't going to do this by having enemies. You were going to do this by having friends."[3] Still, PhRMA's offer to cooperate may have been partly due to the influence of the group's president and CEO, Billy Tauzin, a former Republican chairman of the House Energy and Commerce Committee—and before that, a conservative Democrat—who had always been interested in the art of making legislative deals.

Another intriguing development was the advertising campaign run by the American Medical Association, the same organization that had fought "socialized medicine" so many times in the past. For the 2008 presidential election, the physicians' group reinvented itself as a "Voice for the Uninsured," the name of its ad campaign that spent millions of dollars to urge the presidential candidates to put health care reform high on their agendas. "Louise's problem is so critical that she has the best doctors in the country working on it. Louise's problem is her insurance plan has eliminated her choices," read one ad that ran in *Time* magazine right before the election. It was one more important signal that the issue was returning to the top of the national agenda.

———

Perhaps the best examples of stakeholders recognizing their long-term interests, however, were the business leaders who issued general—but important—statements about the urgency of health care reform. In 2005, Howard Schultz, the CEO of Starbucks, told the story of how the rising cost of health care made it increasingly difficult to offer health insurance to his employees—because his company was now spending more on health insurance than it was on coffee.[4] In September 2008, at the height of the presidential campaign, the Business Roundtable, which represents the CEOs of Fortune 500 companies, put out its own health care reform plan. It was built, not surprisingly, on business-friendly priorities—such as requiring all Americans to have coverage and allowing health insurers to offer coverage across state lines—but it also endorsed subsidies for low-income people.[5]

Even Wal-Mart, the retail giant notorious for skimping on health care coverage, tried to change its image by becoming a vocal supporter of reform. In February 2007, Wal-Mart joined with the Service Employees International Union, one of the nation's leading labor groups, and several other partners, including the Center for American Progress, to call for health insurance for all Americans by 2012. The coalition, called Better Health Care Together, did not suggest a detailed reform plan. But getting Wal-Mart to join such a coalition was a huge symbolic step, and it led to continued involvement by the retail chain in the search for a bipartisan solution to the health care crisis.

The Better Health Care Together campaign was one example of an intriguing development in early 2007: the rise of the so-called strange bedfellows coalitions. Stakeholders that normally would be at odds were joining together to insist that reform could wait no longer—that whatever their political differences, it was time to work on whatever common ground they could find.

A month before Wal-Mart and the Service Employees International Union joined forces, a surprising variety of health care industry and consumer groups announced their support for a plan to expand coverage, first by bringing the remaining uninsured children into the system and then by helping adults through tax credits and broader eligibility for Medicaid.[6] The Health Coverage Coalition for the Uninsured teamed up the advocacy groups Families USA and AARP with industry powerhouses such as America's Health Insurance Plans and the American Medical Association, as well as important players such as the

American Hospital Association, the Blue Cross Blue Shield Association, Pfizer Inc., Kaiser Permanente, and UnitedHealth Group.

Around the same time, another strange bedfellows coalition combined the forces of two other business groups—the Business Roundtable and the National Federation of Independent Business, the lobbying organization for small businesses—with the Service Employees International Union and AARP. The new coalition, Divided We Fail, would establish a strong presence during the presidential campaign. Its signs were a common sight in New Hampshire during the primaries, and its television ads, which featured a memorable combination of elephant and donkey noises, were in frequent circulation. Their slogan was, "Divided we fail, but together we can do anything."[7]

It certainly seemed that a critical mass of stakeholders was willing to support the next health care reform effort. But some of the early "happy talk" can be deceptive. There were a lot of supportive statements from business groups in the 1990s, too, and yet their support quickly evaporated once the Clinton health care plan began moving through Congress. The Chamber of Commerce, for example, had officials who concluded the organization should support health coverage for everyone with mandatory contributions from businesses—once again, because rising health care costs were becoming a huge burden for businesses that provided health insurance. But in February 1994, when a Chamber official prepared to testify that the organization could accept a requirement that all employers cover their workers, an up-and-coming House Republican named John Boehner and his allies pressured the Chamber to change its stand. It did, and the testimony was rewritten to say that the organization "cannot support any of the mandate proposals that have been advanced in legislation by President Clinton or members of Congress."[8]

Likewise, the National Federation of Independent Business (NFIB), one of the members of Divided We Fail, was sending signals throughout the presidential election campaign that it wanted to get past the old political stalemates and find a solution to the health care crisis. During the 1990s, the group took a hardline position against the Clinton health care plan and even lured away some of the Chamber's members.[9] This time, however, the group's president and CEO, Todd Stottlemyer, insisted that small businesses had a strong interest in finding a solution.

Of the nation's 47 million uninsured Americans, he said, 28 million were small business owners, their workers, and their families. And in the time since the defeat of the Clinton plan, NFIB's members had grown more insistent that something had to be done to make health coverage less of a burden for them. In just eight years, he often pointed out, the average small business premium had shot up 129 percent.[10] "It was my belief that some form of health care reform was going to pass," recalls Stottlemyer, now an executive vice president at Inova Health System. "So then you've got to decide—do you want to be at the table, or do you want to be on the menu?"[11]

Stottlemyer brought NFIB into the Divided We Fail coalition, teaming up with Bill Novelli, then the chief executive officer of AARP. "If Reagan can shake Gorbachev's hand," Stottlemyer said, "I can go over and shake Bill Novelli's hand." Stottlemyer got an earful from some NFIB members who couldn't understand the point of talking to groups such as AARP and the Service Employees International Union. But his view was that it's easier to find common ground if you talk to your opponents than if you don't. I remember being impressed with Stottlemyer when I met with him in late 2008, thinking that his reasoned approach to health care might mean that the politics of the issue truly had changed.

But in January 2009, Stottlemyer stepped down—not because of the political pushback he was getting, he says, but because he was tired of traveling all the time and not seeing his children. By the time health care reform got underway in Congress, NFIB had become one of its most vocal critics again.

5 | OBAMA vs. McCAIN

I have always considered John McCain a friend. He thinks for himself and has shown great courage in his Senate career in doing what he believes is right, whether his party agrees with him or not. Unfortunately, I don't think he took the health care reform issue too seriously when he ran for president. He put together a health care plan because he needed one, but you could tell his heart was not in it.

John's idea was mostly based on standard Republican thinking on health care, which holds that many of the problems would be solved if people simply had more freedom to shop around for the best health care deal for themselves. Americans do want to have as many choices in health care as possible, as we have seen, but personal choice alone cannot solve the biggest problems that need our attention. It cannot bring down costs or improve quality by itself, because our health care is not transparent enough to allow people to make well-informed decisions. And it cannot solve the insurance practices that deny coverage to so many people, because individuals and small businesses don't have the bargaining power to change these things.

John seemed to understand this before he won the Republican nomination. Shortly after I became the Senate majority leader in 2001, he worked with Ted Kennedy and John Edwards on our biggest health care priority at the time, passing the Patients' Bill of Rights through the Senate, because he understood that many of the managed care companies were going overboard with their denials of coverage. And he supported the idea of reimporting cheaper drugs from other countries, a position that, to his credit, he continued to hold as the Republican nominee even though most of his party opposed it. But for the most part, as a presidential candidate, John bought into the idea that rather than trying to create a true health care system, we should turn it into even more of a market. And he served up the predictable scare tactics against Barack's plan—that it would be a big-government nightmare that would eventually lead to a Canadian-style single-payer system.

Throughout the Republican primaries, it was clear that this was the only approach that would gain traction with the party's voters. Virtually all of John's opponents insisted that free-market principles and individual choice were the best solutions to our many health care problems. "If we go in the direction of socialized medicine," former New York mayor Rudy Giuliani said during a January 2008 debate, "where will Canadians come for health care?" If more Americans bought health coverage on their own, Giuliani said, health care costs would come down and quality would improve because "the only thing that reduces cost and increases quality is a significant, dramatic, large consumer market, not government control."[1] Even former Arkansas governor Mike Huckabee, who spoke thoughtfully and eloquently about the need to take preventive care more seriously, insisted that the way to provide the best health care was to "turn it over to each individual consumer and let him or her make that choice."[2]

The one notable exception to the pattern was Mitt Romney, the former governor of Massachusetts, who had presided over the passage of the innovative health care reform law that inspired key parts of Barack's plan. He was every bit as ideological as the other Republican candidates, but he, at least, had a solid accomplishment to back up his claim that "we don't have to have government take over health care to get everybody insured. That's what the Democrats keep on hanging out there. The truth is, we can get everybody insured in a free market way." Romney, however, had to play down the biggest "big government" aspect of the Massachusetts law—the requirement that everybody get coverage—because his opponents were putting him on the defensive about it. So ultimately, he had to back away from much of his own accomplishment. "I would not mandate at the federal level that every state do what we do," he said.[3]

John McCain's health care plan, which he announced in Des Moines, Iowa, in October 2007, was designed to put as much control and responsibility in the hands of consumers as possible. In a major change, he would have ended the tax break for employer-sponsored health insurance, in which the health coverage is not counted as taxable income to the employees. This is a tax break many of us enjoy without realizing it. Instead, he would have traded it in for tax credits to help Americans buy health insurance on their own. With an annual tax credit of $2,500 for individuals, or $5,000 for families, people would have been able to shop around for whatever health plan fit their needs the best, John argued.

That approach, in his view, would have led to the creation of more low-cost and creative insurance options. "The 'solution,' my friends, isn't a one-size-fits-all big government takeover of health care," John told his Des Moines audience. "It resides where every important social advance has always resided—with the American people themselves, with well-informed American families, making practical decisions to address their imperatives for better health and more secure prosperity."[4]

He also included an idea that was sure to backfire. To increase competition in the health insurance market, he proposed letting insurance companies sell coverage across state lines.[5] Since different states have different laws about what benefits must be covered, and some states are stricter than others, it's not hard to predict what would happen. Insurance companies would base themselves in the states that allow the skimpiest benefits, and there would be a "race to the bottom" that would make it harder and harder for Americans to find adequate coverage. It might be possible to make the idea work if all plans had to include a minimum level of benefits, but nothing in John's plan suggested that he would have provided that kind of protection.

Some of the other aspects of John's plan made valuable points that need to be heard more widely in the health care debate. As a counterpoint to individual freedom, he said Americans also need to show more personal responsibility and take steps to prevent the spread of chronic conditions such as obesity and diabetes. And he took an admirable risk by suggesting that we rethink our approach to paying providers by paying them a single sum for high-quality care, rather than a series of payments for each service.[6] But the overall plan suggested that John had something to prove. It seemed deliberately designed to convince Republican voters that he shared their conservative ideological views—at a time when many were not sure he did—rather than to challenge them to examine why a market-based approach doesn't always work with health care. "Conservatives believe in the pursuit of personal, political, and economic freedom for everyone," John said. "In health care, we believe in enhancing the freedom of individuals to receive necessary and desired care. We do not believe in coercion and the use of state power to mandate care, coverage, or costs."[7]

But by taking steps that would move away from the employer-based health care system Americans have had since World War II, McCain lost his ability to convince voters that Obama had the most radical plan for health care. As Jeanne Lambrew, my collaborator on *Critical* and now the director of the Department of Health and Human Services Office of Health Reform, pointed out at the time, millions of Americans who get their health insurance through employers are shielded from the worst practices of the individual insurance market—being denied coverage or charged extra premiums because of chronic conditions—and they would have become vulnerable to all of those practices if they left their employer health coverage.[8] John's plan was a red flag to Americans who want to keep what they have. And it was a generous gift to the Obama campaign.

Barack was not always dead set against taxing any health care benefits. In the early health care proposal described in *The Audacity of Hope*, he suggested that "if necessary, we could also help pay for these subsidies by restructuring the tax break that employers use to provide health care to their employees." He would not have targeted everyone who gets the tax exclusion, but he would have reconsidered the tax break for "fancy, gold-plated executive health-care plans."[9] And his advisers looked at the idea when they were trying to come up with revenue sources for his campaign health care plan, because it's a standard suggestion for raising enough funds to expand coverage.[10] But they quickly rejected it, figuring some employers would cut back on health coverage if they lost the tax exclusion. So when McCain took the whole idea a giant step farther, by taxing all employer-sponsored health care benefits, the Obama campaign's line of attack was pretty much set.

On the day after John accepted the Republican nomination in St. Paul, Barack was already predicting dire consequences if John's health care plan became law. In a speech at the Schott glass company in Duryea, Pennsylvania, Barack warned that the company's executives would "say to themselves, 'Can we really afford to keep on giving health care if we're not getting [a] tax break?'" The workers might get a $5,000 tax credit, Barack said, but "your health care may cost twelve thousand dollars or fourteen thousand dollars. And good luck trying to get health care if you've got a preexisting condition, or if you're fifty-five or sixty, close to retirement. Good luck trying to go out on the open market without an employer-sponsored health care plan." From then on, through the end of the campaign, the Obama campaign made sure that the end of the tax break was all that most voters heard about McCain's health care plan.

An Obama campaign television ad in October 2008 called John's proposal "the largest middle-class tax increase in history" and warned that it "could cost your family thousands. Can you afford it?"[11] Another pointed out that the tax credit would have gone directly to the health insurance companies, "leaving you on your own to pay McCain's health insurance tax."[12] I obviously disagreed with John's health care plan, but the ads exaggerated the impact it would have had. For one thing, it would not have cost all families "thousands." That would be true in cases where the employer did stop offering coverage, and it would have been disastrous for Americans in that situation. For those whose employers maintained coverage, however, the tax credit probably would have been big enough to cover the increase in people's income taxes in most cases.[13] And the tax credit would have gone directly to the insurance companies to make sure people didn't spend it on other things.[14]

Barack was on more solid ground when he warned, during the third presidential debate, that younger workers might take the tax credit and buy health insurance on their own, leaving only the older and less healthy workers in their employer health care plans. If that happened, premiums would have risen for everyone who was left.[15] Still, Barack's constant refrain—"for the first time in history, you will be taxing people's health care benefits"—was so sweeping that it was sure to make it harder for him to consider even a limited tax once he won the presidency. Such considerations were not high on the minds of his campaign advisers, though. Everyone was focused on winning the election, and not allowing themselves to think much about the realities of governing if Barack actually won.

It's too bad that the taxation of health care benefits became such a flashpoint in the presidential campaign. I certainly don't agree with the idea of ending the tax exclusion completely, but over the long run, we may need to consider a more limited exception—perhaps a way of taxing health care benefits progressively as they get more generous, the way we tax income at higher rates as people's earnings rise. We do need some mechanism to make people more conscious of the costs of health care, and the richer people's coverage is, the less incentive they have to make sure they don't overuse medical care. John did make an important contribution to the health care debate by looking for a way to lessen the impact of the tax exclusion. He just took the idea too far.

When McCain talked about Barack's health care plan, he mostly stuck to the standard ideological script of warning about "big government" taking over. "His plan will force small businesses to cut jobs, reduce wages, and force families into a government-run health care system where a bureaucrat stands between you and your doctor," he said in his convention speech.[16] During the presidential debates, he spent a lot of time painting Barack's plan as a threat to small businesses. "If you're a small-business person and you don't insure your employees, Senator Obama will fine you. Will fine you. That's remarkable," John said during the second debate.[17] That wasn't true, of course. Barack's plan did have the "pay or play" requirement for large employers, but it specifically said that "small businesses will be exempt from this requirement." In fact, it would have offered small businesses a tax credit to pay for half of the premiums if they insured their workers.[18]

John even warned that Barack would have fined parents for not insuring their children—but he was actually taking aim at the only mandate Barack was willing to include after resisting all of the pressure from Hillary and John Edwards to require everyone to get coverage.[19] The one thing McCain never did, much to the surprise of the Obama campaign, was to single out the public option as the big threat to private health care. Obama's advisers were sure the McCain campaign would use that issue to stir up the big-government fears—much as the congressional opponents of the reform effort later did.[20] And yet, somehow, John never got around to it.

This time, the typical attacks on "big government" health care did not have enough power to stop the Democratic tide on election night, from Barack on down to the newly expanded congressional majorities. Shortly after the networks declared him the winner, Barack—now the president-elect—asked the nation for patience in taking on all of the challenges that had just landed on his plate. It was not just health care reform, after all. It was also two wars, long-delayed energy and education needs, and now the most frightening economic calamity since the Great Depression. "The road ahead will be long. Our climb will be steep. We may not get there in one year or even in one term," he said. But "I promise you, we as a people will get there."[21]

Over the next several weeks, it would our job on the transition team to help him figure out the most realistic way to get there—and how to keep health care reform from getting shoved to the back of the line.

6 | PREPARING THE ROAD MAP

As the head of the transition team's health care task force, I had six different duties to fill up my time. Our group needed to plan the policies and strategy for moving ahead on health care reform. We also wanted to keep the issue visible in the public eye and find ways to keep people engaged in the effort. We had meetings with the major health care stakeholders to make sure they felt involved, meetings with the president-elect's economic team to make sure the health care team had a voice in their discussions of the crisis, and interviews with candidates for the top jobs at the Department of Health and Human Services. And, of course, I had to prepare for my own Senate hearings and the vote to confirm me as the new health secretary.

All of those duties were important, and all would prove crucial to the success of health care reform. But the most immediate challenge, and the one that would make the best use of my knowledge of the Senate, was to advise the president-elect on the best strategy for getting health care reform through Congress. The political environment for reform was better than it had been in decades. It may have been even better than it was in the 1990s—because now that the Democrats in Congress had seen the consequences of failing on health reform, they were much more motivated to succeed this time. And many of the stakeholders seemed more motivated, too.

But that didn't mean all of the obstacles were gone. There is always a certain amount of tension between the White House and Congress, even when they're controlled by the same party, over who is really in charge of the biggest legislative initiatives. There were differences to work out between fiscally conservative Democrats and the rest of the party, differences between the Senate and the House, differences among committee chairmen, and the unique rules of the Senate that make it so hard to pass anything unless it has overwhelming support. We also had a delicate, perhaps impossible, balance to find: the legislative strategy would have to allow just enough time for the members of Congress and the public to consider the details, but not so much time that the usual opponents could pick them apart.

In our advice to the president-elect, the health care task force tried to address each of these challenges, learning as much as we could from the Democrats' failure in the 1990s. The biggest lesson, we thought, was to stay as hands-off as possible and let Congress write the initial bill. The president-elect had made it clear throughout the campaign what he wanted, and his election was a clear vote of confidence in his plan from most of the public. But there is a difference between putting out a campaign plan as a framework for legislation and trying to write a complete bill, which is the job of the legislative branch. "Despite apparent demands for leadership, members of Congress want to be authors, not scribes," the health care team told the president-elect in our first official transition memo. "If we offer to do more than offer guidance in the early phase, members of Congress will have less incentive to work through the policies and politics and wait for the plan to arrive. They will also feel less ownership of the process and product."[1]

Not all of the key players in Congress wanted us to stay away. Aides to Max Baucus, the chairman of the Senate Finance Committee, asked us for feedback on the eighty-nine-page "white paper" he produced outlining the possible components of a health care bill. It was strikingly similar to the president-elect's campaign plan, except that it would have required everyone to get coverage.[2] Likewise, Ted Kennedy's aides wanted us to endorse his idea for the best legislative strategy, which was to negotiate an advance agreement on a single health care bill—possibly the same one in the House and the Senate—and then try to pass it through both chambers. We encouraged both of them to keep working at their ideas, but did not try to shape them.

The problem with the Clintons' health care strategy, and that of the congressional leadership, was not just that they wrote a complete bill at the White House. Bill Clinton has always insisted that was what Dan Rostenkowski, then the chairman of the House Ways and Means Committee, asked him to do. The problem was also the way they did it, in a secretive process, and the way they then let the bill languish after Clinton's September 1993 speech to Congress, giving the opponents time to mobilize and turn large segments of the public against it. All of us on the health policy team made the collective decision that, the more we tried to control the process, the more danger there would be for the health care bill. It was time to let members of Congress work through the issues for themselves, cheering them on but letting them do their work.

Still, we would have to stay involved enough to try to persuade fiscally conservative Democrats to support health care reform. Otherwise, we would never get it off the ground. Our advice to the president-elect was to reach out to the House "Blue Dog" Democrats, the fifty-two-member coalition that focuses on reducing the deficit and reining in entitlement spending, to convince them that a short-term increase in federal spending on health care reform would pay off in savings down the road. "No plan—no matter how elegantly designed or executed—can succeed unless we convince Blue Dogs and other moderate Democrats and Republicans to adopt an open mind about the need to spend now to save money across the entire health system," we wrote.[3]

The key to our success, we believed, was to draw a direct connection between health care reform and the revival of the economy. The first and most urgent task at hand, once the president-elect took office, was to convince Congress to pass a massive stimulus bill to keep the economy from sliding into another depression. It would have been natural for the Blue Dogs to worry about how much we had just spent on the stimulus and decide that we could not afford health care reform—rather than seeing health reform as the key to relieving cost pressures on businesses, which would make the economic recovery efforts more likely to succeed. "There is a real risk of your agenda being swamped by the need to address the financial market meltdown and growing budget deficit," we wrote. "If the economic recovery plan becomes mired in debates over its size or content, the ability to follow on with health reform will be diminished. Underscoring the linkage between the health and economic problems will become more important as critics and opponents gear up to label a push for health reform and other priorities as opportunistic."[4]

Even though we tried to avoid taking sides publicly on Kennedy's legislative strategy—the one-bill approach—and thought there would be real advantages if the issue could be advanced in that way, we didn't think it would work. There were simply too many disagreements to work out between liberal and centrist Democrats, and different strategies required in the Senate and the House. Rather than using the traditional approach—develop the policy first and then try to get the funding—we suggested reversing the order, winning the funding first and then developing the policy. We proposed using the budget resolution—a non-binding spending blueprint Congress approves every year—to create a reserve fund for health care reform big enough to make the passage of reform more likely. This way, the first vote would only have to be a test of the general commitment to reform, not an endorsement of any specific approach.

This also had, in our view, one other advantage. It would give lawmakers more time to develop the health care reform bill, but also allow Congress to debate it and pass it more quickly once it was ready, giving less time for special interests to mobilize and create the dreaded "death by a thousand cuts."[5] Ultimately, this was the strategy Congress adopted in April 2009. It put a deficit-neutral reserve fund in the spending blueprint, meaning the funds would be there as long as the bill paid for itself.[6]

Finally, we had to decide what role, if any, we would find for the centerpiece idea I had promoted in *Critical*. It was the idea of creating a Federal Health Board to set the rules and fill in the framework of a new health care system, much the way the Federal Reserve System sets monetary policy. Just as the Federal Reserve puts those decisions in the hands of economic experts, the Federal Health Board would allow health care experts—nominated by the president and confirmed by the Senate—to make the detailed decisions that are often too difficult to be handled by our political system. It would set policies to keep health insurers from avoiding patients with high-cost health problems, promote coverage of the procedures and drugs that are proven to work the best, pay doctors for healing patients rather than just for performing the most services, and make health care more transparent. The president-elect had praised the idea in his quote for the book jacket, saying it "holds great promise for bridging this intellectual chasm and, at long last, giving this nation the health care it deserves."

I believe he did recognize the value of the idea, and understood why it might help promote policies that are necessary but require more political courage than Congress usually has. But ultimately, the idea never got very far in the transition discussions. My sense was that the president-elect thought it would become too much of a political fight in itself—from members of Congress who would not want to delegate those decisions to independent experts, and from Republicans who would use it as yet another piece of evidence that the Democrats wanted a "government takeover" of health care. Conservative columnist Tony Blankley, for example, said it would lead to "the end of independent private-sector health care in America."[7] Other members of the transition team thought that this was not the issue we wanted to spend our time debating.

I still believe that the idea is an important one, and that the policies that would do the most to make our health care more rational will not be realized until Congress becomes one step removed from the process. But that fight would have to wait until another day. We had more than enough on our hands for this round.

About a week before Thanksgiving, word leaked out that I would take on the dual health care jobs at Health and Human Services and at the White House. Immediately, my in-box flooded with about 500 e-mails, and I took about fifty calls congratulating me on the new roles. One of them was from former vice president Al Gore. Everyone associates him with the issue of climate change now, but he and I had talked many times about health care reform when we served in the Senate together. He was fascinated by health care and could talk about it in incredible detail. Just about all of the reaction to my nomination was positive, including from some Republicans, such as Senator Orrin Hatch of Utah, who told reporters that I was a "great choice" who could work with both parties.[8] And, of course, one of my biggest supporters was Ted Kennedy, who had called the president-elect to encourage my nomination when he heard I was in contention for the job.

I spent much of the next several days talking to key members of Congress and meeting with stakeholders, including representatives of the American Medical Association, the American Hospital Association, the AFL-CIO, and the Divided We Fail coalition, including Todd Stottlemyer of the NFIB. You would expect a certain amount of predictable statements from them about their eagerness to work with the new administration. But I came away from those meetings with an incredible sense of optimism, just like the feeling so many voters had during the campaign, that health care reform might actually happen this time. Nobody was warning of any serious problems ahead. This just might be the transformational time that so many of us had hoped it would be.

On December 5, I traveled to Denver to speak at a health summit hosted by Ken Salazar, then a senator from Colorado. Ken, a close friend who got along well with senators from both parties, would later become the interior secretary in the new administration. But at the time, he was intending to stay in the Senate and play a role in the health care debate from his seat on the Finance Committee, where he would have been great at helping the different factions find common ground. I was struggling with a cold that day, but I was able to get my main points across. The goal of health care reform, I told the audience, would be to create a health care system that performs better and gives every American more access to care, higher quality, and lower costs. It would shift from a focus on sickness, treating people after they already have health problems, to keeping them healthy and preventing them from getting sick in the first place. We would have to do a better job managing chronic illnesses, change the way we pay doctors and hospitals to reward quality rather than the number of services they provide, and address the shortages of primary care providers and nurses that make it harder for people to get the health care they need.

I also used the speech to announce a new strategy for keeping the public engaged in the reform debate: a series of community discussions around the country, including many in people's homes, that would allow Americans to discuss and submit their ideas for what we should be doing. It was part of a broader strategy to make the health care reform process as open and inclusive as possible so people did not get the sense that we were cooking up policies behind closed doors, as they did during the Clinton effort. The Associated Press picked up on this theme in its coverage of the event: "President-elect Barack Obama and his aides are determined not to repeat the mistakes the Clinton administration made 15 years ago in trying to revamp the nation's health care sector. That means applying some of the lessons learned—moving fast, seizing momentum and not letting it go."[9] So far, all of the reaction was better than I could have hoped. But then, we were still only talking about reform at the 30,000-foot level.

Soon, however, we got some encouraging signs from the president-elect as we began to focus on the details of the health care strategy. On December 11, I joined him at a press conference in Chicago, where he formally announced my nomination as health secretary and my appointment as the director of the new White House Office of Health Reform. I was thrilled that Jeanne Lambrew, my collaborator and trusted adviser, was there, too, as the president-elect announced that she would join me as the deputy director of the health reform office. "Year after year, our leaders offer up detailed health care plans with great fanfare and promise only to see them fail, derailed by Washington politics and influence peddling. This simply cannot continue," Obama said. "The runaway cost of health care is punishing families and businesses across our country. We're on an unsustainable course, and it has to change."[10]

I was prepared for some tough questions about my role at the lobbying firm Alston & Bird. I was not a lobbyist there, but I did provide my analysis on health care issues and Congress to some of the firm's clients. It would have been natural for reporters at the press conference to bring that up, as some already had in previous articles, given that the president-elect had campaigned on reducing the influence of lobbyists and special interests. But this was Obama's first press conference since Illinois governor Rod Blagojevich had been arrested on charges of trying to sell his Senate seat. All but one of the questions that day were about Blagojevich. I didn't get a single question about my work for Alston & Bird.

That afternoon, we headed to Obama's Senate office in Chicago for a two-hour meeting about how to move ahead on health care reform. To my pleasant surprise, the president-elect told us, for the first time, that he might be willing to reconsider his thinking on two of the strongest stands he had taken during the campaign: his opposition to requiring everyone to get health insurance, and his refusal to consider any taxation of health care benefits. These were no small concessions. These were the defining health care battles he had fought against Hillary Clinton in the primaries and against John McCain in the general election. But the president-elect's message to us that day was that he would not close his mind to new arguments or evidence that either of these policies would make a better health care bill. He was not prepared to change his positions that day, he told us. But if our collective judgment was that these provisions would improve the bill or make it more likely to pass, he would listen.

The president-elect even suggested he might be willing to consider an idea I have favored as a possible way to reduce doctors' malpractice premiums and cut down on defensive medicine. The idea is to give doctors a "safe harbor" against malpractice lawsuits as long as they follow the established best practices in medical care—ordering tests or procedures when we know they're useful, or not ordering them when we know they have little to no benefit—and as long as there's a compensation fund to help people who were truly the victims of medical mistakes. This came up because we were trying to figure out how to convince the various stakeholders that we weren't going to be locked into the usual debate lines. If we considered taxing the benefits of the most generous, "Cadillac" health plans, we would anger labor unions, who often have negotiated for those kinds of benefits at times when management has been reluctant to increase their wages. And if we considered the safe harbor idea, we would be sure to provoke the wrath of lawyers' groups, who would consider it an unnecessary concession to those who want to limit medical malpractice lawsuits. But if we were willing to do things that might cause tension with our allies, we would prove that we were serious about reform, and that might give us more leverage to win concessions from our opponents.

At that time, I thought there was about a 30 to 40 percent chance that we could produce a truly bipartisan bill. Having bipartisan support not only would have made it easier to pass the bill, it also would have made it harder for talk show hosts and the usual special-interest opponents to scare the country about the changes. It was not that we were getting any special, back-channel overtures from Republicans about wanting to work together. I simply believed that, given all of the momentum that seemed to be building to fix the system's problems after so many years, Republicans would not just walk away and refuse to participate. They would offer their own ideas, I thought—serious, fully formed ideas based on free-market principles and individual choice—and it would become a contest of ideas. And then we would have worked out the most broadly acceptable health care reform bill that we could. I did not expect that Republicans would decide it was in their better interest simply to oppose us at every turn, as if it were 1994 all over again.

In fact, we hoped to arrange some joint events with prominent Republicans on select issues as a way of highlighting health care reform's importance to the economy and potential areas of agreement. Our plan was to host a series of events in March and April 2009. One might have featured Mike Huckabee, the former Republican presidential candidate, speaking about the need to reduce obesity. Another might have had California governor Arnold Schwarzenegger, who had promoted health care reform in his state, talking about the need for shared responsibility between individuals, employers, providers, and the government for expanding coverage and controlling costs. There could have been an event with former Senate majority leader Bob Dole, my former Senate colleague and partner at Alston & Bird, on the need to cover everyone to stabilize the health care market, and another with former House Speaker Newt Gingrich on the importance of improving health information technology.[11] We did not have any commitments that they would join us, but given the work they had done on these issues, we thought there was some chance that these events would come together.

So far, everything was going so well that it was easy to believe we might achieve the long-awaited health care breakthrough. But it is also easy to get carried away. Despite all of the positive press coverage and encouraging reactions—to my nomination and to the overall health care effort—I had seen enough of these kinds of cycles to know that they don't last.

All too often, I thought at the time, what goes up, comes down.

7 | OPENING THE DOORS

As we worked on the early strategies for health care, we were determined to learn from the failures of our health reform effort in the 1990s, and one of the most important lessons was to be more inclusive of Congress and stakeholders from the start. Government is always better when its leaders hear as many different points of view as possible, and gather ideas from the widest possible spectrum of people who will be affected by their decisions. That is not just the lesson of the health care reform effort of the 1990s. It is also the essence of what Obama's campaign for the White House was all about. By promising to open up the workings of government to the public as much as possible, and by using a sophisticated Internet presence during the campaign to keep up an active dialogue with his supporters, he gave the nation an idea of what might be possible if government could mobilize more people to become involved in its work.

So it made sense for our health care working group to take the next step—using an active Internet outreach strategy to ask for people's ideas and conduct a running conversation about how to reform health care. It would be a way for us to be as different from the Clinton health care task force as possible, seeking out views from people throughout the country rather than relying just on Washington experts. It would also distinguish us from the eight years of the George W. Bush presidency, which became known for hiding more and more information from the public rather than opening up its work for scrutiny. And finally, it would allow our health care working group—as well as the rest of the transition team—to keep up the incredible energy that the campaign had built up throughout the country, harnessing the public's desire for involvement by asking them to help us govern.

Just a few weeks after the campaign had ended, our health care team posted the first video for a feature on the transition Web site that asked people for their comments on the country's biggest challenges. The feature, called "Join the Discussion," was supposed to round up people's views to help guide the transition team's discussions of the agenda. Two of the health care team members, Dora Hughes and Lauren Aronson, made a video asking people to post comments about what worries them the most about health care. By the time the comment period closed, more than 3,700 people from around the country had posted their thoughts.[1] It was a point of pride for the health care group to draw so many comments, since there was a bit of a friendly competition between the different issue groups to be first on the Web site with some new feature. But, more importantly, it also showed the potential for technology to open the process of government in a way that had not been possible before.

Some of the comments were pretty much along the lines of what we were already thinking: contain costs for people who already have health coverage, encourage preventive care, shift the focus from treating illnesses to keeping people well. But we also heard concerns about insurance companies being too concerned about maximizing their profits, doctors charging too much for routine services, nurses being spread too thin to care properly for hospital patients, and pharmaceutical companies having too much influence over which drugs are approved and what prices they can charge. We got a lot of comments from people who wanted to change to a single-payer health care system, like Canada's. But we also heard from people who wanted to delink health coverage from the workplace, which was the goal of John McCain's health care plan. And at least one person wanted to encourage greater use of health savings accounts, which come with high deductibles, meaning that you save your own money to cover your first few thousand dollars of medical expenses. In Washington, the accounts are mostly favored by Republicans, as a way to make people more conscious of the cost of their health care. But the fact that we were getting such a wide variety of views was a good sign. It meant that people were interested and engaged in the discussion. In a follow-up Web video, I urged them to keep the comments coming so we could hear all of their ideas and make the process as open as we possibly could.

It is the personal stories of troubles with the health care system, however, that pack the biggest emotional punch and are the most likely to make members of Congress recognize the urgency of health care reform. So for our next step, we wanted to do more than just gather written comments. We wanted to hold a series of forums throughout the country so people could tell their stories in person and discuss with each other what might be done to fix the problems. But instead of organizing the forums on our end, we reached out to the public and asked them to organize the discussions themselves. It was a perfect way to build on the grassroots-driven style of the Obama campaign, which used social networking to give supporters the tools to mobilize on their own—extending the campaign's reach far beyond anything it would have had otherwise.

We gave people advice on how to moderate their own forums, using a "host and moderator guide" they could download from the transition Web site. The guide suggested a sample agenda for the meetings, told hosts how to explain the purpose of the meetings, and advised them to "conduct the meeting like President-elect Obama would: respecting everyone, listening to everyone's opinion, and engaging in spirited discussion without being disagreeable."[2] We especially encouraged them to take note of audience members who had compelling personal stories that might boost the case for reform. At the end of the meetings, we asked the hosts to submit summaries of what they had discussed and ideas for reforms that the transition team should consider—or at least principles, if the audience members couldn't agree what the solutions should be. The project was an amazing success. By the end of December, people had held more than 9,000 community forums around the country to discuss how we could create a better health care sector.[3]

I chose two forums to attend myself: one at a fire station in Dublin, Indiana, and the other at a senior wellness center in the southeastern section of Washington, D.C. The Indiana forum had been organized by an emergency medical technician named Travis Ulerick, who saw the problems of the uninsured through his job—sick or injured patients who couldn't afford the ambulance rides—and concluded that the current market works far better for the well-off than it does for people with lower incomes. The other was put together by Angela Diggs, the administrator of the Congress Heights Senior Wellness Center. They were very different experiences. The Dublin forum had a wide variety of audience members, from doctors who thought insurance decisions were affecting their ability to practice good medicine to patients who were frustrated at how much it cost them to have routine physical exams. The seniors' forum in Washington, D.C., was focused more narrowly on senior citizens and their concerns, such as Medicare's often mysterious coverage rules. But both were incredibly valuable as a way to hear people's concerns firsthand, which is how policymakers make the emotional connections they need to solve problems.

One of the stories that affected me the most came from Dolly Sweet, a survivor of breast cancer who was now battling lung cancer. The medication she was supposed to take cost $35,000 a year—more than she received in Social Security benefits. So she made the only choice she thought she could make: "I canceled the medicine." It was a stunning moment. I felt deep sympathy for her, and then my sympathy turned to anger. It defies all sense that the treatment of cancer should become an economic choice. And yet, that was the kind of story we were hearing from around the country—people having to choose between their health and buying groceries, or paying their mortgage or rent. Dolly Sweet showed incredible courage that day. When I asked her what happened after she canceled the medicine, she just smiled and said, "I'm still here." But the awful dilemma she faced was a vivid reminder of what health care reform was all about.

When all of the meetings were over, we had a good idea of what the audiences cared about the most, thanks to the summary reports the moderators turned in and the surveys all of the audience members were asked to fill out at the end. The final report on the community forums, which was released in March 2009, covered the results of 3,276 summary reports from the moderators and more than 30,000 surveys filled out by the audiences. By far, the biggest concern was rising health care costs; more than half of all audience members put that down as the issue they were most worried about. People were also concerned about not having enough coverage of preventive care, not being able to get insurance because of preexisting conditions, and the overall quality of the health care they get. There was a rough consensus on the general principles, if not the exact methods, for solving the problems. People thought that a reformed health care sector would serve Americans better if it treated everyone fairly, gave patients plenty of choices in their care, was simpler and more efficient, and offered broader coverage—such as including mental health coverage as a standard benefit.[4]

There would be one more event to continue the theme of openness, this time with members of Congress and various health care stakeholders offering their input. In a December memo to the president-elect, our health care group proposed holding a White House summit on health care to allow all of the major players to offer their ideas. Americans would participate by submitting video questions, by watching the live broadcast on C-SPAN, and by holding town hall meetings and viewing sessions throughout the country. Rahm Emanuel had proposed the idea, based partly on a bipartisan summit on welfare that Bill Clinton had held in 1995, and we had refined it to include as much of the new technology and mass-mobilizing techniques as possible.[5]

It was too much to hope that a single summit at the White House would guarantee that Democrats and Republicans would stay on the same page throughout the health care debate. But we would have a much better chance of success if we at least started on the same page.

8 | HEALTH CARE vs. THE ECONOMY

When the president-elect announced my nomination at the December 11 press conference in Chicago, the nation was reeling from an economic disaster that was throwing millions of Americans out of work and threatening the survival of businesses across the country. Yet he challenged the nation to see health care reform not as a distraction from the crisis, but as part of the way to solve it. "Some may ask how at this moment of economic challenge we can afford to invest in reforming our health care system. And I ask a different question. I ask, how can we afford not to?" he said. "Instead of investing in research and development, instead of expanding and creating new jobs, our companies are pouring more and more money into a health care system that is failing too many families. . . . If we want to overcome our economic challenges, we must also finally address our health care challenge."[1]

It was as powerful a statement as I could have hoped for, and it suggested that we all saw a direct linkage between health care reform and the rescue of the economy. Behind the scenes, though, this was far from a settled question. In fact, one of the most important debates we would hold over the next two months was whether we could still afford to take on health care reform, as key members of the president-elect's economic team argued that it should be put on hold because of the crisis. This was a natural question to ask. It was their responsibility to figure out how to get the economy back on track, and they were rightly concerned about any initiatives that might work against an economic recovery. The question we had to resolve, then, was whether health care reform would be a threat to the economic recovery efforts, or whether it was part of the solution.

The discussions started in December, as part of the regular meetings I attended with the economic team. Peter Orszag, who had been the director of the Congressional Budget Office and was about to become the new director of the Office of Management and Budget, was at most of these meetings. So was Larry Summers, the former treasury secretary and Harvard University president who was in line to be the new director of the National Economic Council. Tim Geithner, the president-elect's nominee to be the new treasury secretary, was there, as was Gene Sperling, an old friend and respected economist who would be Geithner's counselor. Carol Browner, the former Environmental Protection Agency administrator who would be the new White House coordinator of climate and energy policy, often attended as well, since the president-elect's economic advisers saw his plan for reducing carbon emissions—a "cap and trade" system that would limit the amount of greenhouse gases companies can release into the air—as a likely way to raise revenues that could be used to fund other projects. The president-elect joined us at some of these meetings when his schedule permitted.

There was a lot on the line for health care reform, as the argument for delaying it seemed to be gaining traction. Larry Summers, in particular, raised hard questions about the wisdom of moving ahead now and asked whether an ambitious health care effort in the middle of an economic crisis might be more than the nation could handle. The general argument—made most passionately by Larry, but shared by others on the economic team—was that the economy was on the verge of collapse. Everything we were learning about the crisis made it appear worse than before, and the forecasts were becoming increasingly dire, especially for job losses. The size of the stimulus package we were about to propose to Congress was growing all the time; by the time of the president's inauguration, it would reach $825 billion. (The final price tag of the package, as passed by Congress, would be slightly lower: $787 billion.) How could we afford to invest in health care reform now, when we would have to spend yet more federal funds to expand coverage? And how full could we make the president-elect's plate when everyone agreed his most urgent task would be to rescue the economy?

I didn't consider any of them hostile to health care reform. They were simply giving the president-elect the mix of views that he needed to decide his agenda priorities. And none of them was suggesting we should outright cancel our plans for health care reform. In fact, Larry came up to me after one meeting and said, "Please don't misunderstand me." It wasn't about whether to take on health care reform, he said—it was about where it should come in the order of the president-elect's priorities. Gene Sperling told me the same thing, and he had a unique take on what the proper sequence should be. He thought we should attempt to reform Social Security and extend its life first, and then move on to health care. That might surprise readers who recall all of the bitter political fights over Social Security, but Gene's argument was that there was actually more collective support for strengthening the program's long-term finances than there was for changing the health care sector. And by taking on Social Security first, he thought, the new administration would show that it was committed to fiscal responsibility and reducing the deficit.

I was not sold on the Social Security idea. The program does face long-term financing challenges, but they are still years away. In the environment we faced in December 2008, there was no question that the economy had to be the top priority. When the house is on fire, you put the fire out. Nothing else comes before that. My concern, however, was that the economic team didn't seem to recognize how health care reform could contribute to the recovery. As long as businesses continued to struggle with out-of-control health care costs, they would not be able to expand or rehire laid-off workers, and the economy would take that much longer to recover from the knockout punch it had suffered. Yes, health care reform would increase federal spending in the short term. But if it were done in the right way, it would bring down total health care spending—and that would relieve pressure on businesses and help them recover faster.

This was the exact argument the president-elect made on the day he announced my nomination. And yet, when some of the economic advisers made their case for delaying the health care effort, he did not really push back. He mostly sat and listened. At that point, I began to wonder if he was changing his mind as he surveyed the damage from the economic disaster. That would be an understandable reaction, but from my point of view, a delay could have dealt the health care effort a blow that it might not have survived. If the tide turned against keeping health care in the top tier of the agenda, we might have lost the best window a new president has to attempt something as politically difficult as health care reform.

At one point, Joe Biden, my longtime Senate colleague and now the vice-president-elect, began to think it would be wiser to delay the health care effort. At an economic team meeting in early January, he spoke at length about why it would be too much to attempt health care reform in the middle of the crisis, just as some of the other advisers had argued. Later, I sensed that Joe felt a bit bad about arguing so strongly against my position, and after the inauguration he invited me to breakfast at the vice president's mansion to make sure the debate didn't come between us. Joe was focused on getting the stimulus package to succeed, and he would later become the president's point man on monitoring its progress to make sure the money wasn't wasted. But when health care came up at future meetings, he said, he would take his cues from me.

As the stimulus package came together, we did win an important short-term victory. The package would include three important "down payments" on health care reform: federal funding for health information technology, preventive care, and comparative effectiveness research. The final stimulus bill included $20 billion to help hospitals and physicians convert to electronic medical records; $1.1 billion for comparative effectiveness research, spread across three agencies; and $1 billion to create a "prevention and wellness fund" to pay for programs to help reduce chronic diseases. There would also be a new federal council to coordinate the research.[2] Our health care team pushed for those funds, in part because there was wide acceptance of the need in those areas, and—more importantly—because we could legitimately say they would create jobs. But it would also help us establish a link between health care and the economy that might help us build the case for tackling the two together.

On January 8, I had my first confirmation hearing, before the Senate Health, Education, Labor, and Pensions Committee. It couldn't have gone better. My family was with me for moral support. I got a generous introduction from Bob Dole. Ted Kennedy was there to chair the hearing; he looked a bit frail, but surprisingly good under the circumstances. He sounded as sharp and as eloquent as ever, clearly determined to make health care reform succeed this time. The Democrats on the committee welcomed me back as an old friend, and the Republicans were incredibly gracious as well. But they were clearly concerned that the majority Democrats would roll right over them if they tried to oppose a health care bill they didn't like.

Senator Mike Enzi of Wyoming, the top Republican on the committee, laid it on the line in a pointed question. Would I discourage my former Democratic colleagues in the Senate from using the budget reconciliation process, a special procedure for spending and tax policy changes that would allow them to pass health care reform with fifty-one votes—and bypass any Republican filibusters?

I gave him a direct answer: Yes, I would. The goal of the new administration, I said, would be to use "regular order"—where the committees write the legislation, it comes to the Senate floor, and if the Republicans mounted a filibuster, the Democrats would need sixty votes to break it. "You have a physician," I said—referring to Senator Tom Coburn of Oklahoma, one of the Republicans on the committee—and "you have people that have worked these issues, as many of you have, for many, many years. We need that input. We need that involvement and that engagement."[3]

It was true that this was our goal, but it was not as if the transition team had never considered using budget reconciliation as a last resort. At the time, Senate Democrats only controlled fifty-eight votes in the Senate; they would not reach sixty until later that year, when Republican senator Arlen Specter of Pennsylvania switched to the Democratic Party and Al Franken won his drawn-out battle with Norm Coleman over the Minnesota Senate seat. In the health care team's December memo to the president-elect, we suggested that we should decide whether to use budget reconciliation if Republicans tried to block the bill—and that if we did, we should look to the example of the creation of the State Children's Health Insurance Program in 1997, which was done through budget reconciliation.

It would bring its own set of problems, we pointed out. Republicans were already insisting that we take the option off the table, and even if we used it, the process has specific rules that would give us trouble continuing any spending that lasted for more than ten years.[4] Still, in the spirit of bipartisanship and openness that we were trying to maintain, we really did prefer to get Republicans' input and pass health care reform with the broadest support we could get.

Five days later, I got the devastating news that made all of those strategic decisions seem a lot less important. My brother Greg had a brain tumor, and it was one of the most aggressive kinds. He needed the best care we could find. Suddenly, all of those policy discussions about health care took a backseat to my brother's real, and urgent, health care needs. I spent much of that day looking into our options, and prepared to join him as soon as he could fly back from Japan. Health care reform would have to wait.

Because Greg's brain tumor sounded so similar to Ted Kennedy's, I reached out to Vicki Kennedy to see what advice she had. She put me in touch with Larry Horowitz, who had coordinated Ted's care. Larry, in turn, recommended that we turn to Dr. Allan Friedman and Dr. Henry Friedman of Duke University to do the surgery and the vital postoperation therapy that Greg would need. It would be a "debulking" operation, in which the surgeons would try to get as much of the tumor out as possible. They had virtually no chance of removing all of it, so radiation and chemotherapy would have to do the rest. Allan had performed Ted's surgery, so Duke University did seem to be the best option. Since Greg wouldn't be able to fly alone, my brother Steve, who lives in Seattle, flew to Sapporo to accompany Greg on the flight to North Carolina. Dave, my other brother, agreed to meet us there.

That Saturday, I drove to North Carolina with Linda, my mother, and Dr. Lorraine Hale, a close family friend who had accompanied my mother to Washington for the inauguration. On Monday, the day before the president-elect was to be sworn in, Dr. Friedman and his team of doctors performed the surgery. It went as well as we could possibly have expected; the doctors thought they had removed about 98 percent of the tumor. Greg came out of the surgery incredibly well, under the circumstances. But he would face many months of difficult radiation and chemotherapy treatments. The only silver lining in any of this was that, unlike many Americans, Greg had insurance that covered most of his expenses. He had a high deductible and coinsurance to pay, but he would not be driven into bankruptcy by his medical bills. It would been devastating if he had to worry about financial ruin on top of everything else. But this was one more reminder, on a personal level, that millions of Americans do not have this kind of protection.

We stayed with Greg through Inauguration Day. It must have been a strange sight to see us all gathered in Greg's hospital room, with our champagne and plastic glasses, watching the new president on television as he set the tone for all of us who were preparing for roles in his administration. But the president's words that day spoke eloquently to the challenges ahead, and to the very question that consumed all of us: deciding how many major projects we could take on at one time. "There are some who question the scale of our ambitions, who suggest that our system cannot tolerate too many big plans," the president told the freezing crowd that seemed to fill every inch of the National Mall. "Their memories are short, for they have forgotten what this country has already done, what free men and women can achieve when imagination is joined to common purpose, and necessity to courage. What the cynics fail to understand is that the ground has shifted beneath them, that the stale political arguments that have consumed us for so long no longer apply."[5]

But when I returned to Washington, I found that the scale of our ambitions was exactly what the president's advisers were still debating. Indeed, in my absence, it became harder for my own advisers to push back against those who thought that a health care reform effort now would work against the goal of economic recovery, rather than helping it. It seemed that the momentum was shifting, and that despite all of the time the president had spent laying the groundwork, a full-blown health care reform effort might have to wait—possibly until after the best window of opportunity for it had closed.

It was not even clear that all of the president's advisers thought an early health care reform effort made sense as a matter of political strategy. David Axelrod's concerns about health care reform were a perfect example. He had been the strategist who guided the president to victory in the election, and now he had the difficult job of helping the president decide how to make the best use of his limited time. With all of the crises competing for the president's attention—an economic calamity, two wars, and years of deferred work on great national needs—finding the right sequence was quite a challenge. But when we met shortly after the inauguration, Axelrod was not at all enthusiastic about putting health care reform at the top of the list. The 85 percent of the public that already had health insurance had never really shown that much concern about the plight of the uninsured or health care quality, he thought. If they care about anything, Axelrod argued, they care about rising premiums, which have the most direct impact on everybody.

On the surface, he was right. That is what most of the polls showed. My reading of the political history of health care, however, was that people's level of concern depends on how much exposure they have had to it. If they don't use it much, they're not concerned. As soon as they need it, however, they see the problems firsthand, and they become more frustrated and less confident. Axelrod, however, had to worry about the impact that health care reform might have on the success of the new administration's other priorities. So his view was that he should advise the president to spend his first days in office on the issues that the public cared the most about: ending the Iraq war, doing a better job in Afghanistan, improving our ability to meet our own energy needs, strengthening our schools, and, most of all, pulling the economy out of its tailspin.

It was time to find out, once and for all, whether the president still thought health care reform was as important a priority as it used to be. I asked Rahm Emanuel, the new White House chief of staff, for a meeting to clarify the president's position. We decided to meet on the Sunday after the inauguration. When I got to Rahm's West Wing office, I could tell the White House was in a complete state of upheaval. Boxes were everywhere, carpets were rolled up, and walls were being patched and painted. After Rahm greeted me, the president himself walked in unexpectedly. He gave me a warm hug and asked about Greg, and I gave him the full update. Then, I asked him directly: Was health care reform still as important to him as it was in the days when he first offered me the job?

His answer offered a revealing insight into one of the best aspects of his character. Yes, he told me, health care was more important than ever. He and Rahm both assured me that health care would be included in his first budget proposal to Congress. But when the economic advisers argued their case for delaying it, he said, he listened without arguing back because he wanted to hear all sides of the debate. We share a common trait, the president told me: We're both good listeners. That is the mark of good, open-minded leadership. But that didn't mean he agreed with the economic advisers. It just meant he wanted to give them a fair hearing.

"Tom, health care is the most important thing we will ever do," the president said. "It will be my legacy. And it is more important to me now than ever before. Don't ever doubt that."

9 | MELTDOWN

Being a caregiver is one of the most difficult, and exhausting, challenges anyone can face. You have to devote whatever time and energy it takes to take care of your family member's needs, while somehow making the time to give your work the attention it deserves. I was lucky enough to be surrounded by a family who could step in and take responsibility for Greg's care. Sidney Jackson was not as lucky. In March 2003, his wife died, and he was left alone to look after an adult daughter with special needs. For Sidney, then in his sixties, it proved all but impossible to maintain a full work schedule and care for his daughter at the same time.

Sidney was a driver for the Carey limousine service in Washington, D.C. One of the people he drove regularly was a close friend of mine, Leo Hindery, a Democratic donor and founder of InterMedia Partners, a private equity firm that invests in a wide variety of media outlets. Leo lives in New York, and he often asked for Sidney's driving services when he visited Washington. Sidney had helped him out during a 1997 visit, when a broken arm made Leo's travels more difficult, and he had considered Sidney a friend ever since.

So after watching Sidney struggle for two years to take care of his daughter while keeping up a full work schedule, Leo made him an offer. In 2005, he hired Sidney away from the limousine service to become his personal driver—part-time, but at a full-time salary. Leo came up with this arrangement because he wanted Sidney to be able to stay home more often and take care of his daughter, driving only on those occasions when Leo needed his services. It was an act of compassion that few people can provide, and of those who can, most wouldn't even consider it. Leo used his wealth to help a friend get through one of the most difficult periods of his life.

Around the same time, I was adjusting to life in the private sector, for the first time after twenty-six years in Congress, after my loss to John Thune in the 2004 election. I had spent ten years of my time as the Senate Democratic leader, including a year and a half as the majority leader, and now I was settling in to a busy but lower-profile life in Washington. I was patching together several new roles, serving as a special policy adviser at Alston & Bird, working on health care issues at the Center for American Progress, and teaching at George-town. I also served on various advisory boards, including InterMedia's board.

One day in May 2005, Leo was kidding me about my new life. Does it bother you, he asked, having to hunt around for parking spaces now? No, it's okay, I said, laughing off the question. No one likes hunting for parking spaces, of course, but it didn't bother me any more than it would anyone else. Still, Leo of-fered to save me the trouble. He didn't need Sidney's services most of the time, he said—so why not let Sidney drive me to some of my appointments, when Leo wasn't in town and it was convenient for Sidney to do so?

It was hard to argue with the logic. I was keeping up a full and active sched-ule, including a lot of travel, so having a driver at least some of the time would be a big time-saver. And if Leo didn't need Sidney most of the time anyway, and Sidney could fit in my trips around his daughter's needs, the arrangement would work out well for everyone. It was a completely casual arrangement be-tween friends, I thought, and that was all that mattered.

It was also the arrangement that would bring my role with the Obama ad-ministration to an end.

The issue came up in early January, as the Senate Finance Committee examined my finances as part of its vetting process for my confirmation hearing. Since the Finance Committee and the Health, Education, Labor, and Pensions Commit-tee both handle health care issues, both would hold hearings before the full Senate voted on my nomination to be the new Health and Human Services secretary. Just as I was preparing to appear for my first hearing—before the Health, Education, Labor, and Pensions Committee—the Finance Committee staff started asking questions about Sidney's services. They wanted to know why I had not reported his driving services as income for three years and paid taxes on it.

Actually, I had discovered my error and paid the back taxes, and this is what caught the committee's attention. On January 2, I had filed an amended return reporting Sidney's services as income, a move I thought was an extra cautious way of clearing up any possible questions about the issue. For most of the time Sidney drove for me, it had never crossed my mind that there might be tax implications. My accountant never raised the driver arrangement as an issue either—because I never told him about it. I always considered it a favor from a friend, not a form of income to myself. Now that I was being vetted for the Health and Human Services nomination, however, we had to look at every possible tax issue from every possible angle. We concluded that it was a close call, and different people might come to different conclusions, but the safest thing to do would be to amend my returns to count Sidney's services as income for all three years.

There were other issues we had to resolve, too. For example, Linda and I had charitable contributions that we could no longer count as deductions, because we had mistakenly made the payments to the two directors of a South Dakota charity, rather than the charity itself. Altogether, we had to pay an additional $140,000 in taxes to cover those three years. It was an enormous hit to our finances, but one that we hoped would clear up any remaining doubts and allow my nomination to move forward. The Finance Committee continued to ask questions, however, and it became clear that the issue wasn't going away. At one point, Linda and I combed through the house looking for receipts for some of the charitable donations.

As a former senator, I understand the importance of what the Finance Committee was doing. They were providing congressional oversight of the new administration—through detailed scrutiny of the president's nominees—and that is how Congress, at its best, can hold the executive branch to high ethical standards. What most people don't realize, though, is the toll the process can take on the nominees. You have to spend weeks walking through your finances in far more detail than most of us can easily handle. Even those of us who have dealt with the tax code in our policymaking roles can miss something in our personal finances. And mistakes can turn into raging scandals.

About a week after the inauguration, I met with the Finance Committee staff and answered questions for three hours. It went well, but they informed me that, fairly soon, they would have to announce to the public that I had not paid the car-and-driver taxes until the beginning of the year. Later, I met with Max Baucus of Montana, the chairman of the committee, and Charles Grassley of Iowa, the ranking Republican. Both said they were not sure they could support my nomination. In fact, Max asked if I was sure I still wanted to go through this.

I did, at that moment. But I was becoming less sure every day.

My life was being consumed by twin crises: one professional, the other personal. My tax issue and Greg's illness competed for my attention throughout much of the month of January. Greg had successfully completed his surgery, but now he faced two and a half months of proton beam radiation, an unusually precise method of treatment that fires protons into the tumor and spares healthy cells close by. We were extremely fortunate, once again, to have the generous help of Ted and Vicki Kennedy, who knew the rigors of the therapy all too well. They let Greg and my brother Dave, who would take care of him during the therapy, live in their Boston apartment for the entire course of the treatment. This would make Greg's next few months much easier for him, to my great relief. But just as Greg was preparing for this new phase of his treatment, my professional crisis was about to escalate into a full-scale firestorm.

I was with Greg and Dave at the Kennedys' Boston apartment on the night of Friday, January 30, when the Finance Committee released the report detailing my tax problems. Immediately, the story dominated all of the cable news channels, and news outlets started speculating that my nomination could be in serious trouble. Reporters started e-mailing me for reaction, but I was in no position to deal with all of the inquiries; we were supposed to meet with Greg's doctors that night. Jenny Backus, who had been in the transition health care working group and would join the Health and Human Services staff, fielded most of the calls and patiently walked reporters through the details.

That weekend, it immediately became clear to me how badly my political standing had deteriorated in just a few days. On Sunday night, I called Orrin Hatch at home to get his reading of how serious the tax issue was. Orrin was the second-ranking Republican on the committee, and he would be able to give me a candid and well-informed assessment of what would come next.

Unfortunately, Orrin told me, this looked serious. It was no longer clear how many Republicans on the committee would vote in favor of my nomination—if any would support me at all.

That one phone call captured how completely my circumstances had changed. I was no stranger to partisan combat, having lived with it for ten years as the Senate Democratic leader, but any of the old tensions with my Republican colleagues seemed to have faded away in the years since I had left the Senate. A few weeks before, I had been warmly greeted in the Health, Education, Labor, and Pensions committee by senators from both parties. And I had looked forward to helping both sides find the path, as elusive as it might be, to a broad, bipartisan agreement on health care reform. Now, I had become a polarizing figure, with one side of the aisle for me and one side against me. It was the last way I wanted to start the new job.

On Monday, I met with the members of the Finance Committee in a closed session to walk through the issues with all of the senators. The way it ended showed that the partisan divide over my nomination was now wide and seemingly permanent. All of the Democrats told reporters they had full confidence in me, while the Republicans either suggested they would oppose me or said the matter needed more investigation. Baucus did issue a statement declaring his support for me, saying he was still convinced I would be "an invaluable and expert partner" in health care reform.[1] I went out and told the reporters that the Obama administration was right to hold its nominees to a high standard, and that the American people were right to expect public servants to pay their taxes. I apologized for my mistakes, and said I still looked forward to working with both parties to give America a better health care sector.

As I thought about it overnight, however, it became clear that the reality was no longer that simple. It might have been possible to move forward with my nomination, but it was no longer desirable. I might have been able to prevail after a lengthy political battle, but the last thing the administration needed was to spend time and political capital on a troubled nomination. People only had one message for all of us in Washington—"pay your taxes"—and they had every right to feel that way. I might have survived, and the personal pressure of my twin crises would have subsided eventually. But I would have started off as a wounded nominee, with none of the bipartisan goodwill I had built up at the beginning of the process.

The health care reform effort deserved better. After one hundred years of failure, it was time to break through the old ideological barriers and make our health care more rational and more humane. To break through those barriers, we needed someone who had the trust of lawmakers from both parties—someone who could help the new administration listen to all sides, find the combination of changes that could pass Congress, and keep everyone focused on the ultimate goal. When people can't get health insurance, can't trust the quality of their medical care, or risk being bankrupted by the costs, it would be a tragedy if their problems remained unsolved because of the distractions that consume Washington's attention every day. If you become a distraction yourself, you cannot achieve the goal that so many Americans are counting on the new administration to achieve. All you can do is make it easier for others to achieve that goal.

The next day, I told the president I had reached the end of the road.

There are very few crises that are truly as dire as they seem at the time. In the days after I withdrew, there was a lot of breathless speculation that the job of passing health care reform had gotten tougher. I'm happy to report that that was not the case. Kathleen Sebelius, the former governor of Kansas, is now in place at Health and Human Services. She not only knows the issues firsthand— from the eight years she spent as the Kansas insurance commissioner—but has formidable political skills as well, having worked closely with both parties as the Democratic governor of a Republican-leaning state. And Nancy-Ann DeParle, who oversaw the Medicare and Medicaid programs during the Clinton administration, stepped in to run the Office of Health Reform. She has been a constant presence on Capitol Hill and worked tirelessly to find solutions to the series of legislative stalemates, both large and small. Both are valued friends, and I have kept in touch and tried to be helpful as they have put in countless hours to keep the health care effort on track.

No one is indispensable to the success of an issue as big as health care reform, but everyone can help to overcome the many powerful forces that have always stood in its way. That is the spirit I have adopted as I have settled back into the private sector. When my advice could be helpful to the administration, and to the leadership in Congress, I tried to provide it. When the parties seemed hopelessly deadlocked in their health care priorities—which they were, unfortunately, throughout almost the entire effort this time—I tried to do my part to suggest ways out of the deadlock.

Being on the outside gave me enough distance to be able to judge the events from a long-term perspective, no longer tied down by the day-to-day fights. Still, I wasn't exactly a neutral observer, because I wanted the president to succeed. And I wanted my friends to succeed. Besides Kathleen and Nancy, I valued my friendships with Senate Majority Leader Harry Reid of Nevada— who had been one of my strongest defenders from political attacks during my Senate majority leader days—and with Speaker Nancy Pelosi of California, my House counterpart in the Democratic leadership during my last few years in the Senate. It would be their responsibility, as the health care bill moved closer to the finish line, to hold on to every vote they could find without sacrificing the complex and interrelated changes needed to fix the system.

Along the way, these leaders, together with the committee chairmen and the administration's health care team, would have to keep the reform effort on track in a Congress that is usually reluctant to take on big challenges. They would have to deal with personality clashes, conflicting political needs, and the return of the big ideological battles that had always held America back from the goal of achieving the health care reform it deserves.

Now, the fate of that goal was in their hands.

Part Three

NO MARGIN FOR ERROR

1 | THE WHITE HOUSE STRATEGY

On Tuesday, February 24, President Obama walked into the House chamber, made his way through the crowd of cheering senators and House members, and stepped to the podium to deliver his first address to a joint session of Congress. It wasn't considered an official State of the Union address—since he had just been sworn in five weeks before—but for all practical purposes, that is what it was. Obama congratulated Congress on passing the massive stimulus bill fewer than two weeks earlier, an act that surely saved our economy from an even more disastrous collapse. Although the Republicans in the chamber listened politely that night and even applauded from time to time, everyone was aware of the unfortunate backstory. Only three Senate Republicans, defying enormous pressure from their party colleagues, had joined the Democrats to pass the stimulus package that the nation desperately needed.

Now, Obama asked lawmakers from both parties to join him in an even more difficult task. The time had come, he said, to end decades of struggle and finally give the nation comprehensive health care reform. It was an economic necessity, he told the lawmakers and a national audience, because health care costs were rising out of control. Health care caused a bankruptcy every thirty seconds. In the previous eight years, premiums had grown four times faster than wages. Small businesses were shutting down under the costs, and the national budget was being swallowed up by the expense of the federal health care programs. This did not mean the two parties could bridge their differences easily, Obama said, or that all of the stakeholders would like the changes that would be needed. But he would invite members of Congress and industry leaders to the White House the following week to start trying to find common ground.

"I suffer no illusions that this will be an easy process. Once again, it will be hard," Obama told Congress. "But I also know that nearly a century after Teddy Roosevelt first called for reform, the cost of our health care has weighed down our economy and our conscience long enough. So let there be no doubt: health care reform cannot wait, it must not wait, and it will not wait another year."[1]

On that night, it seemed that Obama just might succeed where other presidents had failed. The political environment for health care reform wasn't perfect. Members of Congress were already exhausted from their frantic push to finish the stimulus, and Ted Kennedy, whose political and legislative skills could have added tremendous power to the effort, was sidelined again by his battle with brain cancer. But in so many other ways, the conditions were as good as they ever get. We had a young, energetic, and popular president calling for reform. The Democrats had the largest House and Senate majorities in years. Many of the health care stakeholders were looking for ways to help the cause of reform, not block it. And the Democrats had a wealth of experience from the 1990s to help them design a better strategy for this round.

Henry Waxman listened that night with especially keen interest. One of the most skilled legislators and investigators in Congress, Waxman was starting his eighteenth term as a House member from California—he was first elected in 1974, right after the Watergate scandal—and had just become the chairman of the powerful Energy and Commerce Committee. From that post, Waxman would be in a position to help steer two of Obama's top domestic priorities to passage: health care and climate change legislation. He and I had been friends for many years, and during my last two years as Senate minority leader, he graciously allowed me to hire his top adviser, Phil Schiliro, for my policy staff. Phil became indispensable to me, just as he became indispensable throughout the health care debate in his latest role, as Obama's top liaison to Capitol Hill.

Waxman had been especially interested in health care policy since his days in the California State Assembly, and had been at the forefront of the issue for decades as the top Democrat on the Energy and Commerce health subcommittee. He also remembered the failure of the 1990s all too well, in which most Americans didn't think health care reform offered anything to them. One hopeful sign this time, as Waxman listened to the speech, was that Obama pointed out clearly what was in it for Americans who already had health insurance: lower premiums.[2]

For Chip Kahn, one of the health industry leaders whose support Obama would need, this was all familiar territory. In the 1990s, he had been the executive vice president of the Health Insurance Association of America, the organization behind the "Harry and Louise" ads that did so much damage to the Clinton health care effort. Now, Kahn was the president of the Federation of American Hospitals, an organization that represented a different segment of the health care industry—one that had a strong economic stake in health care reform. So for this round, Kahn was supporting reform, not fighting it. His group wasn't always the most vocal advocate, but the fact that Kahn would get involved at all, given his history, was a powerful symbol of how the political momentum had shifted. This time, key industry stakeholders became allies rather than opponents.

In the case of the Federation of American Hospitals, the motive was clear. Hospitals struggle with the costs of providing care to the uninsured, Kahn said, so expanding health coverage is a matter of survival for them. "We do have national health insurance in this country, and that's the hospitals," Kahn said. "By law, they have to provide services to people who need them." This time, Kahn said, the new administration showed every indication that it would listen to industry groups. And the way Obama was framing the argument seemed to get the effort off to a strong start. "It looked brilliant at the time, and it had the sense of inevitability," Kahn said.[3] Of course, it had the sense of inevitability in 1993, too.

The White House strategy was full of lessons learned from that experience. This time, the president would push Congress to start on health care right away and pass it quickly—not let a bill hang out there in the public spotlight, losing momentum and public support. Rahm Emanuel was especially vocal about this point. He worked in Bill Clinton's White House during the last health care effort, when the plan wasn't unveiled until September and then stalled as Clinton got distracted by a series of foreign policy crises, giving opponents plenty of time to mobilize against it. The administration was also determined to push for an open process this time, with the White House health care summit being the most visible example. This would prove that the Obama team had learned from the criticisms of the Clintons' secretive process. And there would be strong efforts to get as many health care industry players on Obama's side as possible, to keep them from flooding the airwaves with attack ads.

There were also two related, and crucial, decisions that were driven largely by the president's economic team. This reform plan would have to slow the growth of health care spending, and it would have to be fully paid for. These would be relatively new challenges for the Obama team, since the campaign plan was able to rely mostly on nonthreatening ways to reduce health care costs, such as expanding health information technology and managing chronic diseases better. The most effective ways to cut back on spending and pay for expanded health coverage would require sacrifice from one health care stakeholder group or another. This was a reality the White House now had to face. But if the administration and Congress could find plausible ways to reduce costs and pay for the reform package—and explain them to the public—they had a chance at keeping the support of centrists and independent voters, who were likely to worry greatly that health care reform would add to the deficit.

Finally, this would not be another case of the White House sending a complete bill to Capitol Hill. The Obama administration was determined to hand over the writing of the actual health care bill to Congress, which is the way the process should work. But the framework had been set by the president during his campaign, and the Democratic committee chairmen were unlikely to make radical changes to that framework. The administration would encourage lawmakers to follow the general principles it had set for itself: fix the problems without jeopardizing what people like about their coverage, give people new choices without forcing them to change their doctors or their health plans, and write the reform bill using as open and inclusive a process as possible. A bipartisan reform bill would be the preferred option, if it was even remotely achievable, to make it harder for opponents to scare half the country. If it was not achievable, however, that could not stand in the way of saving people from facing financial ruin simply because they need medical care.

Two days after his speech to Congress, Obama set out to prove his commitment to pay for health care reform. He submitted his first budget proposal, which made room for a $634 billion, deficit-neutral reserve fund as a "down payment" on the health care bill Congress would write later. This was based on the strategy we had proposed in the transition, arguing that this would allow Congress to take a test vote on its general commitment to reform before working out the details. It also allowed Obama to prove he would take on health reform in a responsible way, with specific suggestions on how to pay for the broader coverage. In the budget, he laid out several general principles for what Congress should try to achieve with reform: it should protect people from rising premiums, reduce health care spending, and put the nation on "a clear path to cover all Americans." And it should give people a choice of health plans and physicians, encourage preventive care, and make medical care better and safer.[4]

But one of Obama's main suggestions for funding health care reform didn't get very far. He wanted to limit how much people who earned more than $250,000 a year could deduct for charitable contributions, a change that could have raised $318 billion over ten years. The following week, Max Baucus, the chairman of the Senate Finance Committee made it clear he didn't think much of that idea. This was no small matter, since the committee not only would have a large share of the health care workload, but also handles all tax legislation in the Senate. "I'm curious, to say the least, about that, because those proposed savings are generally outside of health care reform," Baucus told Treasury Secretary Tim Geithner at a hearing on the budget proposal. He questioned the "viability" of the charitable deduction change, and said the administration should try harder to find savings within the health care system, since one of the goals of health care reform was supposed to be the reduction of unnecessary costs.[5]

Charitable groups protested the proposed change as well. Independent Sector, an organization that represents charities and foundations, said it would reduce charitable contributions that were "needed more than ever in these difficult economic times."[6] But for all practical purposes, any prospect that the change would move forward ended on that day. When the chairman of the Senate's tax-writing committee doesn't like a proposed change in the tax code, it isn't going anywhere. So about half of the administration's funding package was already off the table. Both the House and the Senate would have to search harder for politically acceptable ways to pay for reform.

The White House summit, on the other hand, was a big success. On March 5, more than fifty members of Congress and more than eighty representatives of health care interest groups gathered in the East Room for an afternoon of talks about how to fix the problems with our health care. There would be other open discussions with stakeholders, but this was the most visible example to date of the administration's commitment to an open, collaborative process. One of the featured guests was Travis Ulerick, the emergency medical technician who had hosted the Dublin, Indiana, health care forum I had visited in December. This time, he was the speaker who introduced Obama, and he told a national audience his story about meeting people who couldn't afford to visit the doctor or ride in an ambulance.

When Obama opened the summit, he acknowledged that "there are those who say we should defer health care reform once again, that at a time of economic crisis, we simply can't afford to fix our health care system as well." But if health care reform didn't happen now, he said, families, small businesses, and government health care programs would be crushed by the burden of rising costs. To meet this economic challenge as well as the moral challenge, Obama said, Congress should send him "comprehensive health care reform by the end of this year."[7]

The administration officials, members of Congress, and interest group representatives broke up into five breakout sessions to discuss what they considered the biggest problems. At the end, everyone sounded ready to make concessions and rise to the challenge. Obama warned his progressive supporters—whom he jokingly called "you liberal bleeding hearts out there"—that any health care reform bill would have to cut costs, because "if people think that we can simply take everybody who's not insured and load them up in a system where costs are out of control, it's not going to happen. We will run out of money."

Henry Waxman sounded a practical note: "We all need to recognize there are going to be trade-offs, but if we don't get the trade-off exactly the way we want it, we've got to recognize there's a broader public goal and purpose."[8] This was the view he thought everyone at the summit shared. He remembered how different it was in the 1990s, when all of the health care stakeholders claimed they wanted reform, but then insisted it had to be exactly the way they wanted it. That day, however, Waxman thought the other stakeholders saw the next round exactly the way he saw it. This time, it would be not about narrow interests, but the pursuit of a broader goal.[9]

And Chuck Grassley, the top Republican on the Senate Finance Committee, noted that "Max Baucus and I have a pretty good record of working out bipartisan things" and predicted the committee would take up a health care bill in June.

"If you aren't ambitious on a major problem like this that the country decides needs to be done," Grassley said, "it'll never get done."[10] Chuck is a conservative Republican, but he also has a close working relationship with Max—closer than almost any other senators from opposite parties. If Chuck was truly ready to work with Max on health care reform, it just might have a chance. Or so I hoped.

In April, Congress signed off on the health care reserve fund idea when it adopted its annual budget resolution, a nonbinding blueprint for the spending it expects to approve during the rest of the year. This reserve fund wasn't as fully developed as the president's version, though. It didn't set aside any specific amount of money, and it didn't endorse any particular ways to health care reform. It just said that whatever Congress passed on health care would have to be paid for, so it wouldn't increase the deficit, and the budget committees could adjust the amounts that other committees could spend on it.[11] Still, the approval of the resolution helped set the stage for the reform effort to proceed.

It also set an important marker about how far the Democrats might have to go to pass reform. From the beginning, Democrats had discussed whether they should use a valuable, but little understood, process called budget reconciliation to make it easier to get a reform bill through the Senate. Normally, any health care bill would probably need sixty votes to pass the Senate, since that's what it takes to break a filibuster. But under budget reconciliation—which makes a series of policy changes that affect spending or taxes—the rules are different. The legislation can't be filibustered, and you only need fifty-one votes to pass it. There are a lot of disadvantages to the procedure, because you can't use it for every kind of legislation. Every piece of the bill has to be directly relevant to the budget, and it has to help reduce the deficit for two decades. If it doesn't, your opponents can strip it out. But we used budget reconciliation to create the State Children's Health Insurance Program, the most significant expansion of coverage of the 1990s. The Republicans used it in 2001 to pass Bush's tax cuts, too.

This time, however, Republicans were up in arms about the possibility that the Democrats might use budget reconciliation to pass health care reform. It would be a great blow to the power of the minority party to fight bad legislation, they said, and it would destroy any chances of the two parties working together. That's why Mike Enzi had asked me about it during my hearing in the Health, Education, Labor, and Pensions Committee. I had told him that reconciliation was not the way the administration wanted to go, and even now, both the White House and Senate Democratic leaders wanted to avoid that route if possible. But the leadership also knew it would be unwise to rule out reconciliation completely, in case Republicans fought reform every step of the way and a bipartisan agreement became impossible. So the budget resolution said that if the Democrats decided to use budget reconciliation, all of the committees would have to approve their bills by October 15.[12] For all practical purposes, that would be the deadline for the Democrats to decide if they could bring any Republicans on board.

Soon, the White House was able to show some results from its efforts to win cooperation from potential critics in the health care industry. On May 11, Obama announced that six leading industry groups had agreed to take a series of voluntary steps to save enough money to bring down the annual rate of health care spending growth by 1.5 percentage points. If this actually happened, it could save as much as $2 trillion over ten years. The groups that signed on to the agreement included the American Medical Association, the organization that had fought so many past health care reform efforts, and America's Health Insurance Plans, the voice of the health insurers that would face so many new regulations under reform but would also gain millions of new customers.[13] Later, some of the groups suggested that Obama had overstated how specific their commitment was, which itself suggested that the commitment was less than solid.[14] But it was a step that probably removed at least a few well-funded groups from the ranks of the opposition.

And one of the groups that signed the agreement, the Pharmaceutical Research and Manufacturers of America, also negotiated a separate deal for itself. It agreed to contribute $80 billion in savings over ten years to the health care reform effort, an amount that would later make it possible for the reform bills to include discounts on brand-name drugs for seniors with Medicare prescription drug coverage.[15] But in return, PhRMA wanted assurances that the White House would resist any effort to use the government's purchasing power to negotiate lower Medicare prescription drug prices—a popular proposal that was sure to resurface in Congress, and that Obama himself had endorsed in his campaign.[16] Unfortunately, the deal became a political embarrassment for the White House in August, when PhRMA disclosed it—and the White House had to acknowledge it—to head off an effort by the House to put the provision in its bill.[17] Once the deal became public, it was a lightning rod for attacks by congressional Democrats and outside progressives, and Democratic leaders insisted they weren't bound by it.[18]

All of the White House strategies for health care reform were smart ones, with plenty of good reasoning to back them up. But nothing about health care reform ever goes smoothly, and in the long run, these plans also created their own problems. Going fast was the right legislative strategy, in theory, but it also conflicted with the goal of winning at least some Republican support for the effort. In the Senate, this was not just a nice goal, but a necessity, since the Democrats did not have the sixty votes needed to break a filibuster until Al Franken won a lengthy court battle over the Minnesota Senate seat in June. And despite Grassley's optimistic words, the Senate Finance Committee would spend so long trying to get a bipartisan deal, with so little to show for it, that the health care effort still lost valuable time and momentum.

The open process was a good idea as well, but it had practical limits, since there was always going to be a point where members of Congress—particularly those in the leadership—would have to negotiate the toughest items behind closed doors. They were not about to give up their right to do that, and when they didn't, Obama faced tough questions from critics and the media about why he didn't live up to his promises of greater transparency. And the efforts to win over stakeholders probably spared the White House some of the political attacks health care reform might have faced otherwise, but they also raised new questions about how these "deals" affected the integrity of the health care bill. At the same time, they undermined the White House goal of letting Congress write the bill, since members of Congress were bound to react badly when they were supposed to honor deals they didn't negotiate.

The biggest irony, though, may have been the way that the hands-off strategy toward Congress turned from a strength into a liability. It was an article of faith among all of us, myself included, that the White House had to let Congress write the bill this time and give it only the most general guidance about what Obama wanted. I still believe it was the right decision, in the beginning. Lawmakers would have reacted badly—particularly the committee chairmen—if the administration had started out by handing a detailed bill to Congress and telling members to pass it, since the conventional wisdom was that the Clintons had made a mistake by doing so in the 1990s.

By the summer, though, the Senate Finance Committee got bogged down in its search for a bipartisan agreement. Although it was a worthy goal that had a brief chance of success, it went on too long and allowed opponents to mobilize, just as they did with the Clinton health care plan. At that point, the health care effort needed more aggressive intervention.

Obama was not sitting on the sidelines during all of this. Behind the scenes, he was talking to Baucus every day and having constant conversations with Democratic leaders about the need to get moving. But Baucus wanted more time, and Harry Reid thought it was important to give it to him. As the Senate majority leader, Reid wanted to give the committee chairmen more autonomy than I did when I held the job. And Obama thought it was important to let the Senate leaders and committee chairmen do their jobs. He did not want to embarrass them by putting public pressure on them or letting the world know about their private talks.

Both of these strategies might have seemed perfectly reasonable at the time. The end result, however, was that the "go fast" strategy was derailed—with disastrous consequences. A more public push from either Obama or Reid, or both, might have prevented some of the problems that were far more damaging than anything they could have said to Baucus. It is easy to say this with the benefit of hindsight, of course, and they did not have that luxury. But the truth is that a timely change of strategy might have headed off some of the later events that nearly killed health care reform.

2 | THE SENATE

In May 2009, Chris Dodd of Connecticut met with the other Democrats on the Health, Education, Labor, and Pensions Committee to plot their strategy. Chris was filling in for Ted Kennedy, the chairman of the committee, who had become weakened by his battle with brain cancer and could not return to full-time work. On this day, it was especially clear that the Democrats could not let Kennedy's illness stop them. There was growing concern that the Finance Committee—the other Senate panel that would take the lead on health care—might produce a bill first, and that it would be full of compromises from the very beginning.

Everyone knew there would have to be compromises later in the process, as Congress moved toward a final bill. But most Democrats wanted to start out with the strongest, most progressive position possible. They did not want to give up their highest priorities before the real negotiations even started. So Dodd and the other Democrats made their decision. They would move fast, and do all they could to lay out the clearest Democratic position.[1] That way, progressives would be satisfied that the Democrats were trying to produce the best possible reform.

This was not the only reason Dodd's committee wanted to move so quickly. Everyone shared the White House view that they had to move fast so opponents wouldn't have time to tear the bill apart. Dodd also had plenty of other responsibilities competing for his time, notably on the Banking, Housing, and Urban Affairs Committee, where he served as chairman. And no one wanted to lose momentum while so many health care stakeholders were lining up in support of reform. But the meeting captured a broader concern that was in play at the time: the growing nervousness about what the Finance Committee might do to the reforms most Democrats wanted.

As it turned out, there was no danger of the Finance Committee releasing its bill first. But the episode proves how much competition there was between the two committees, as they tried to find the best strategy for getting a strong health care bill through the difficult terrain of the Senate. In a place where you need not just a majority, but a "supermajority" of sixty votes, was it best for the Democrats to try to work out deals with the Republicans early, or was it better to hold out for their best vision of how to solve the problems? Max Baucus wanted to try to find common ground with the Republicans early. Chris Dodd wanted to start with the best vision of how to solve the problems and see how close we could get in the end.

As I talked to administration officials and members of Congress throughout the spring, I could see that the nervousness over the direction of the Finance Committee bill had spread far beyond Chris Dodd's committee. At this point, it was the biggest private concern of just about everyone involved, from the White House and the Department of Health and Human Services to the House and Senate leaderships, progressive Senate Democrats, and virtually all of the outside groups that supported reform. They did not want the Finance Committee to give away so much, in the pursuit of a centrist deal, that the final bill would not be worth the effort. This was the strategic tension the Senate Democrats would wrestle with from the beginning of the process through the final days of the debate.

No one can say for sure what would have happened if Ted Kennedy had been able to participate more actively. Kennedy had been the driving force on health care for Senate Democrats for many years. His primary challenge to President Jimmy Carter in 1980 was fueled in part by their disagreements over the issue, and he had been a legislative powerhouse during the health care battles of the 1990s. Republicans often say that he knew how to work with them, and that's certainly true. But Kennedy also knew when to push the envelope, especially on health care, to end up with the best possible deal. I believe that is what he was trying to do this time, as he participated as much as he could by long distance.

I believe Chris Dodd was trying to push the envelope, too. An energetic, experienced legislator who could talk knowledgeably about everything from health care to education to banking, Chris was probably Kennedy's closest friend in the Senate. The two shared so many political views that their bill almost certainly captured the direction Ted would have wanted. And in many ways, Dodd's was the better of the two Senate bills. The Finance Committee was in charge of a broader set of issues, so its bill took on a bigger scope. But the Health, Education, Labor, and Pensions bill did a better job of setting the new rules at the national level, rather than deferring to the states in a way that makes it hard to guarantee success. It also had more generous subsidies to make sure people could afford health coverage. It included a public plan to compete with private insurers, which would have been the key to so many improvements in the private market. And it was done quickly, in keeping with the need to keep the entire health care effort on the fast track.

Max Baucus did play a large role in setting the course of the health care debate—with decidedly mixed results. It's no secret that Max and I had disagreements on issues and legislative strategy during my years as the Senate majority and minority leader. And, of course, he is the chairman of the committee that launched the grueling tax investigation that ended my nomination. There has been a lot of speculation that his role in it was a form of retribution for his disagreements with my management approach as Senate Democratic leader. One television news special even said I was "taken down in a political knife fight."[2] It certainly was a painful episode in my life, but calling a tax investigation a "knife fight" is a bit over the top. I was much more dismayed by my rapid loss of support among Republicans than by anything Max did.

And the fact is that he did make a strong contribution to reform by showing complete commitment and immersing himself in the details so thoroughly. He took ownership of the health care effort in a way that Daniel Patrick Moynihan, the Finance Committee chairman in 1993, did not. Moynihan showed little interest in health care reform, and while his lack of commitment was not the primary reason for the effort's failure back then, it certainly didn't help. Baucus was determined to give reform his total support, and he kept charging ahead even during the toughest days of the effort. And his proposals, particularly on ways to deliver health care differently and pay providers more efficiently, had a big impact on the final shape of the law.

Unfortunately, Max was also persistent at times when he should have changed course. He was so determined to win an agreement with Chuck Grassley and his other Republican colleagues that he dragged out the negotiations long after it was clear that they no longer had any value. There was a short period of time when I believe a bipartisan agreement might have been achievable. But the talks should have ended, one way or another, before the August recess. Once the town halls erupted with anger from the right, and the Republicans came under so much more pressure not to agree to anything, the talks weren't real negotiations anymore. They were just a stalling game.

In fact, some Democrats believe the window for bipartisanship ended long before that. Ron Wyden, a Democratic senator from Oregon, had already proven that a bipartisan agreement on comprehensive health reform was possible. In 2007, he and Robert Bennett, a Republican senator from Utah, had collaborated on a proposal that would have joined the two parties' health care priorities in a unique way. It would have covered all Americans, satisfying the Democratic goal of universal coverage, but it also would have allowed anyone to stop getting health insurance through the workplace. Any employee could have taken the amount their employer paid for health coverage, as a tax-free payment, and used it to buy coverage in a private plan offered through new state agencies. In Wyden's view, this would have satisfied the Republican goal of creating more competition and giving people more choices in their health coverage.

Wyden and Bennett's solution might have gone too far for a lot of people's tastes, since it would have been a major move away from the employer-based health care system. But it was attractive enough to win the support of ten Senate Republicans, including Grassley and Lamar Alexander of Tennessee, the same senator who would later say the reform effort should be scrapped because "we don't do comprehensive well."[3] To get such a bipartisan agreement through Congress, however, Wyden believes the Obama administration would have had to lay the groundwork at the beginning of the year. "There was an opportunity for the administration to go to the country and say, 'We've been trying this for seventy-five years, and both sides have valid points,'" Wyden said. If the administration had done that early in the year, he said, Congress might have ended up with a bipartisan bill.[4]

Obama would not have embraced Wyden and Bennett's proposal, since he had campaigned on the need to keep the employer-based health care that everyone knows and likes. But even if he had agreed with the general strategy of urging the country to accept major trade-offs for both parties, the reality is that Obama had his hands full with the economic crisis at the beginning of the year. The passage of the stimulus package had to be the top priority. And unfortunately, by the time it was finished, any goodwill between the two parties had vanished. "Once the window for bipartisanship closes, it closes really quickly," said Wyden.[5] And after it closed, Bennett paid the ultimate price. In May 2010, conservative Tea Party activists blocked him from winning the Republican nomination for another Senate term—in part because he had worked with Wyden on health care.[6]

Max Baucus began planning for the next round of health care reform long before Obama won the presidency. He wanted to allow plenty of time for the members of the Finance Committee to learn about health care policy, because there is a steep learning curve, and most senators can't be expected to have the expertise on the deeply complicated problems reform had to solve. So in June 2008, he and Chuck Grassley cohosted a daylong health care summit at the Library of Congress, where senators from both parties heard presentations and panel discussions on all aspects of health reform. They learned about other countries' health care systems, the strengths and weaknesses of the employer-based health care system, the problems with the private health insurance market, ideas on how to slow the growth of health care spending, proposals on how to change the way we get our health care, and the reform ideas that have been tried in the states.[7]

And on November 12, 2008, just a week after Obama was elected, Max Baucus put out an eighty-nine-page "white paper" outlining his plans for expanding coverage and improving the quality of our health care. It was an impressive, thoroughly researched, and thoughtful guide to his own views on what a health care bill might look like. It was similar to the framework of Obama's campaign plan, but there were some striking differences. Baucus embraced the idea that all Americans should be required to have health insurance, for example, and he suggested that people between the ages of fifty-five and sixty-four should be able to buy Medicare coverage. And he had specific suggestions on how to solve the full range of issues, from uneven quality to the need for more primary care physicians.[8] This was his way of announcing to Washington that he had done his homework and intended to be a central player in the Senate debate.

As 2009 began, the Finance Committee held a series of hearings to continue to educate its members, including three roundtable discussions with representatives of insurance companies, physicians, hospitals, business groups, consumer groups, and academic experts. The roundtable sessions exposed the committee members to a wide range of views on how to expand coverage, how to improve the way health care is delivered, and how to pay for it.[9] And as the committee began to assemble its first draft of a health care bill, Baucus scheduled three private "walkthroughs" in April and May, so committee members from both parties could get an advance look at what might be in the bill and learn how the pieces were supposed to work.

Baucus and Kennedy shared an important goal on health care: They wanted to start the process as early in the year as possible and finish the bill in 2009, a goal they reaffirmed in a letter to Obama in February.[10] This way, they could avoid the trouble Bill Clinton faced by not launching the health care effort until late 1993, allowing it to get bogged down the following year, during election season. However, Baucus also wanted the bill to have bipartisan support from the very beginning. He saw bipartisanship not just as a nice goal, but as a practical need.

Unlike Kennedy's committee, the Finance Committee had several centrist Democrats who would have been more comfortable supporting a bill if it had at least some Republican support. Blanche Lincoln of Arkansas, for example, came from a state that had voted for John McCain over Obama by 20 percentage points.[11] And there was the reality that, at that point, the Democrats did not control 60 seats in the Senate. They would not be able to break a Republican filibuster without some help from the other side of the aisle. Finally, Baucus believed social reforms are always more durable if they had at least some support from both parties—as Medicare did in 1965—because that gives both parties a vested interest in making the program work.

Kennedy's committee, meanwhile, divided up the work so the burden of his absence didn't fall too heavily on any one senator. Chris Dodd presided over the day-to-day work on the bill, but he also had his hands more than full as the chairman of the Banking Committee. He also wanted to give other Democrats on the Health, Education, Labor, and Pensions Committee a chance to take ownership of major pieces of the bill—partly because they were anxious to be involved, but also to make sure they would be more vested in the success of the effort. So other top Democrats took over the work on different pieces of the bill. Tom Harkin of Iowa, who later became the chairman of the committee after Kennedy's death, worked on the bill's measures to encourage preventive care and boost public health programs. A strong progressive with deep moral convictions about helping the powerless, Tom was thoroughly grounded in these issues from his years of experience as the top Democrat on the appropriations subcommittee that funds health care programs.

Barbara Mikulski of Maryland focused on the bill's measures to improve health care quality, while Jeff Bingaman of New Mexico, who also sat on the Finance Committee, specialized in the central issue of expanding health coverage. And Patty Murray of Washington, who was also a member of the Democratic leadership, worked on measures to address critical needs in the health care workforce, such as incentives for medical professionals to work in underserved areas.

Chris Dodd never got the credit he deserved for his work on the reform bill. He held the committee's work together at a time when Ted Kennedy, while able to participate from Massachusetts, was unable to return to full-time work. And this was while Chris had to juggle a workload that included a lead role on bills to regulate tobacco and tighten the rules on the credit card industry, oversight of the financial bailout program, and legislation to rewrite the rules for Wall Street. Given all that he had on his plate, it was amazing that Chris was able to put together such a strong reform bill and get it through his committee so early.

His view of bipartisanship, however, was different from the way Baucus approached it. Chris worked as hard as he thought he could to win Republican support for the bill, even leaving out major sections of the bill—such as the public option—to allow more time for negotiations between the two sides. Still, he argued that bipartisanship was not an end in itself. The most important goal, he said, was a bill that would truly solve the problems people had with health care—not a bill that had broad support but was too weak to be effective.[12]

In the Senate, the ideological divide is not usually as great as it is in the House. There is still a divide, of course, and it has been growing worse in recent years

as some of the newly elected senators have tried to import the more confronta-
tional tactics of the House. But most senators represent broader and more diverse constituencies than their House colleagues, and there are more senators
who are used to working in a collegial way with the other side.

Still, the Senate Finance Committee's closed-door walk-throughs of its bill
during the spring made it clear that conservative Republicans were ready to fight
the health care bill all the way. Grassley, at that point, was still working closely
with Baucus, and there was still reason to think he might be open to a health
care agreement. But it was getting harder to find any other Republicans who
might be willing to join him.

By the beginning of the summer, Obama decided it was time to give Congress a deadline. Even under the best conditions, it is hard to get Congress to
pass major legislation on a fast track. There are too many different opinions
and too many competing interests that have to be addressed. Parts of the year
have to be devoted to the routine business of Congress, which is to pass the
yearly spending bills that fund the government. And there are several breaks
built into the year that members of Congress expect the leadership to honor,
including a recess that lasts the entire month of August.

So on June 2, Obama called Senate Democrats to the White House and
gave them a new timetable. He wanted the House and the Senate to pass a
health care bill before the August recess, and he wanted a final bill on his desk
in October so he could sign it into law.[13] This would give Congress the deadline
pressure it often needs, and it would fulfill a central goal of the White House
strategy: keep the bill moving forward before opponents could start tearing it
apart. But the deadline did not leave much time for the leadership or the committees to round up the votes they needed, even among Democrats. And without the votes, there would be no bill to send to Obama's desk.

It was Kennedy's committee that went first, with Dodd in charge. On June 17,
the Health, Education, Labor, and Pensions Committee began the first official
work session on its bill. The markup, as it is called, is the first chance for members of a House or Senate committee to propose and vote on changes to a bill.
If their changes are voted down, they may have another chance when the bill
goes before the full House or Senate.

The first day of the markup got off to a shaky start, however, as the committee Republicans tore into Dodd over an unfortunate prediction of the cost of the bill. The Congressional Budget Office, which analyzes bills and tries to estimate what they will cost, took a rough look at an early draft of the bill that was missing important sections. Based on what the budget office saw, it concluded that the bill might increase the deficit by $1 trillion over ten years, while extending coverage to about 16 million people—only about a third of the uninsured.[14] Mike Enzi of Wyoming, the top Republican on the committee, complained that the bill would cost too much and would not cover enough people.[15] John McCain grumbled that the bill was "a joke." And Lamar Alexander proposed that they start over with a new bill—an idea he would keep repeating through the end of the process.[16]

It was a bit silly to get so worked up about the early estimate, because it could not possibly give an accurate picture of the legislation. As Chris rightly pointed out, it was based on a draft bill that left out key questions, such as whether there would be a public plan to compete with private insurance and whether employers would be required to cover their workers. Those were issues that he intended to keep negotiating with the Republicans while the committee worked through the other parts of the bill. Later, the committee also trimmed back the subsidies to help people pay for health insurance. By the end, the cost estimate dropped to around $600 billion.[17] Unfortunately, all the public heard was that the bill cost a lot of money without covering most of the uninsured. It was not the way the Democrats needed to start the debate.

The Finance Committee was supposed to begin its own markup in June as well. But on the same day that Dodd was trying to start work in his committee, the Finance Committee postponed its markup until July.[18] It was struggling to keep down the costs of its own proposal, and Baucus was still trying to find a way to bring more Republicans on board. In his view, it was time to narrow the negotiators down to a core group that might be able to make more progress.

Soon, Baucus pared down his group to seven senators. Besides himself and Grassley, there were three Republicans: Olympia Snowe, the Maine moderate whom most Democrats saw as one of their best hopes for GOP support; Orrin Hatch of Utah, who had worked so closely with Ted Kennedy on the 1997 law that created the State Children's Health Insurance Program; and Mike Enzi, who was also the top Republican on Kennedy's committee and had been so critical of its efforts. And there were two other Democrats. One was Kent Conrad of North

Dakota, a centrist who chaired the Budget Committee and worried about health care's impact on the deficit. He and I had come to the Senate together, and over the years we became good friends and worked together on many issues. And there was Jeff Bingaman of New Mexico, the low-key, widely respected progressive who had also worked closely on the Kennedy committee bill.

This was the group that became the focus of the Finance Committee's effort to find a bipartisan agreement on health care reform. After about a month of talks, Hatch left the group in July, claiming that Baucus "has not been given the flexibility necessary to construct a realistic healthcare reform bill that can achieve true bipartisan support."[19] With Hatch's departure, the group gained a new name: the Gang of Six. Over a period of nearly three months, the senators would meet thirty-one times, spending more than sixty hours talking over such issues as how to make private health insurance affordable for struggling families and what kinds of reforms the insurance market needed.

They kept talking, as it became clear they were the administration's best hope for a bipartisan deal. But as the weeks dragged on, it would become increasingly evident that there was no deal to be had.

One other important element of the health care strategy seemed to be working, though. On July 8, three hospital groups—the American Hospital Association, the Catholic Health Association of the United States, and the Federation of American Hospitals—reached an agreement with the Finance Committee and the White House to accept $155 billion in payment reductions over ten years.[20] This was the result of negotiations that had been going on since the spring. Baucus had reached out to the hospital groups, reasoning that there was money to be saved with the hospitals and that they wouldn't have as many uninsured patients to take care of anyway. But he also believed that the hospitals needed to be on board, since they were major employers in every congressional district and could make a lot of trouble if they opposed the bill.

For Chip Kahn, the president of the Federation of American Hospitals, there were a few conditions that made it acceptable for the hospitals to give up so much money. The legislation would be written in a way that guaranteed the payment cuts wouldn't take place unless the number of uninsured people actually dropped. The Senate bill would contain a formula that adjusted the hospitals' payments if there was evidence of expanded health coverage.

And while there were no specific guarantees, he said, there were two "working assumptions" in the negotiations that made the deal acceptable. One was that the Senate would aim for health coverage of at least 94 percent of Americans. The other was that it would contain no public health plan. His group didn't want it, arguing that hospitals already lose money on Medicare payments and the last thing they needed was another public program with low payment rates.[21] It wasn't a formal part of the deal. But already, the stage was being set for the "public option" to be dropped from the debate.

On Wednesday, July 15, 2009, the Health, Education, Labor, and Pensions Committee became the first panel in either the Senate or the House to approve a health care bill. The victory came after a month of work in which Chris Dodd methodically walked the panel through each section, title by title, to let senators from both parties have their say. This kind of approach is extremely rare in the Senate. In my eighteen years there, I don't remember any bill that was handled this way. Chris let the markup continue for days on end, allowed the Republicans to offer hundreds of amendments, and sat back and listened patiently as they made their arguments. And he had delayed adding key parts of the bill, such as the public plan and the incentives for employers to cover their workers, until he and the Republicans had thoroughly talked them through. All of the media coverage focused on the partisan nature of the debate, but it never captured just how much time and energy Chris spent to make sure both parties had a voice.

In the end, the Democrats accepted about 160 Republican amendments—mostly technical changes, but some substantive ones too, such as an amendment by Judd Gregg of New Hampshire to make sure a new long-term care program would be solvent over a seventy-five-year period.[22] The committee filled in the missing pieces and got a better cost estimate from the Congressional Budget Office after making several changes, such as tightening the subsidies to help middle-income people buy health coverage.[23] But it was a strictly party-line vote, with all 13 Democrats voting for the bill and all 10 Republicans voting against it.[24] For all of Chris Dodd's efforts, health care reform was off to a partisan start. And for all of the time Baucus would spend pursuing a broader agreement, it would always be just a little bit out of reach.

3 | THE HOUSE

Two weeks after Obama was elected president, another shift in leadership took place, this time in the House of Representatives. In a large caucus room on the third floor of the Cannon House Office Building, Henry Waxman of California, an accomplished lawmaker who had also built a reputation as one of Capitol Hill's most effective investigators, ousted John Dingell of Michigan as the chairman of the House Energy and Commerce Committee.

Henry rose to the top job on one of the most powerful committees in the House in a secret ballot of the Democratic caucus, after mounting a challenge that had been building through years of clashes. The two simply could not come to terms over environmental policy. Waxman's district is based in Hollywood, and his constituents want strong environmental controls. Dingell's is in southeast Michigan, near Detroit, and he has to worry about what the economic impact might be on the auto industry. At a time when Congress was likely to take up legislation to reduce global warming, Waxman argued that it was time for a change in leadership on the committee.

It was a raw power struggle, and their colleagues in the House cringed at the sight of it. When George Miller of California, the chairman of the education committee, walked out of the showdown that day, he said it was like "watching Zeus and Thor hurling lightning bolts at each other." For me, it was especially painful to watch. Both men are friends, but more than that, they are both legislative giants in their own ways. The clash may have been inevitable, but that did not make it easier for anyone.

Henry Waxman is one of the most skillful lawmakers I know. He is not physically imposing, and he has a great sense of humor about himself, but he also has a tough demeanor that signals to everyone, "Don't mess with me." He is a persistent negotiator who doesn't give up, but also a pragmatist who understands the value of compromise in the pursuit of a worthy goal. In congressional hearings, he asks the smartest and bluntest questions, and he knows how to make the witnesses sweat—as he did in 1994, when he organized the hearing in which top tobacco executives claimed they did not believe nicotine was addictive. He had decades of experience with health care policy, and he would prove his skills with a remarkable performance in overcoming deep disagreements.

But in many ways, John Dingell was the soul of health care reform in the House. At the beginning of every new Congress, he introduced the same national health care bill his father had introduced when he held the same House seat. Dingell had served in the House since 1955, when he was elected to replace his father, and he had presided over the House in 1965 when it passed the bill creating Medicare. A large, lumbering figure, Dingell has been slowed a bit by age, but still remains a powerful and even intimidating presence. During his years as chairman, he often used his physical fearsomeness to his advantage, especially in pressuring his colleagues relentlessly until they did what he wanted. Waxman himself later wrote about Dingell's approach, which Dingell called "diddling"—as in, "I want to diddle that guy a little longer."[1] He still has the gavel he used to preside over the Medicare vote in 1965, and he displayed it during the health care debate at every chance he got.

Waxman and Dingell later made peace of sorts, when the two agreed that Dingell would be the lead sponsor of the health care reform bill. But it was Waxman who would lead the negotiations needed to get a bill out of his committee. This was a big change from the 1990s health care debate, and we all hoped that the change would be another factor to prevent history from repeating itself. Waxman would need every bit of his formidable legislative skills to help his committee straddle a divide between progressives and centrists that easily could have stopped the entire effort.

The House health care bill would be the product of work by the leadership and the chairmen of three committees: Energy and Commerce, Ways and Means, and Education and Labor. But of the three committee chairmen, it was Waxman who had the hardest job. Eight Democrats on his committee were members of the Blue Dog Coalition, a group of fiscally conservative House Democrats that worried about the cost of health care reform—and shared some of the Republicans' concerns about how much it might expand the federal government's role. This was by far the biggest faction of moderates on any of the three committees.

Energy and Commerce has had an unusually large number of moderates for many years, and this was also the case during the last health care effort, before the Blue Dog Coalition was created. Despite Dingell's own legendary political skills, he was unable to bridge the Democratic divide on his committee in 1994, as the moderate Democrats fought against the proposal that year to require all employers to cover their workers.[2] Dingell had to abandon his effort to get a health care bill through the Energy and Commerce committee—a development that earned his committee the unfortunate reputation of being the "graveyard" for the Clinton health care reform plan. If reform was to succeed this time, Waxman could not let the committee be the graveyard again.

He had one advantage, however, and all of the other Democrats knew it. Henry Waxman had the confidence of a fellow Californian: Speaker Nancy Pelosi. Whatever tactics Waxman used to get the bill through his committee, or whatever trade-offs he made to win enough support, it was likely to have the support of the most powerful Democrat in the House.

Nancy Pelosi is the most effective House Speaker in a long time. She is tough and focused, but also fair to all members of her caucus. She also shows incredible discipline and never seems to sleep. I served with her in the leadership for two years, when she was the House minority leader and I was the Senate minority leader. But our friendship went back to the days when she was my California finance director during my first Senate race in 1986, the year before her first election to the House.

In just over two years as House Speaker, Pelosi had defied all of the critics who had tried to dismiss her as just a "San Francisco liberal." She had shown her sense of pragmatism about what it takes to have a broad House majority: you have to let some of your members from conservative districts go their own way. She even drew a challenge from the left, from antiwar activist Cindy Sheehan, in her 2008 reelection race when she refused to simply cut off funds for U.S. troops to force George W. Bush to end the Iraq war.

But on health care, Pelosi was relentless. She pushed full speed ahead, holding out for the most comprehensive and most progressive bill the Democrats could get, even when some of the moderates in her caucus were nervous that the party was taking on too much. She never backed away from the goal, even during the days when the votes seemed out of reach and when the entire effort seemed to be collapsing. When she wasn't out selling the bill in public, she was working quietly, behind the scenes, to find the best way to keep a comprehensive health care bill alive. The Senate was the big hurdle for much of the health care debate, because of its filibusters and the need to find sixty votes. But by the end of the debate, it was Nancy Pelosi who would have to provide the final push to make health care reform a reality.

In the spring, the House leadership assembled a group to start working on an ambitious project: a health care bill that would have broad enough support that it could be approved by all three of the main health care committees. This in itself would be a big advance over the 1994 effort, which broke down before the House committees could reach any kind of consensus.

The project was led by House Majority Leader Steny Hoyer of Maryland, the second most powerful Democrat in the House behind Pelosi. Courtly and serious, Steny had more centrist views than Nancy on many issues, particularly on foreign policy, and he was the House leader moderate Democrats viewed as the most sympathetic to their concerns. This difference in style was the source of ongoing tension between the Pelosi and Hoyer camps. When the moderates got nervous about the health care bill, fearing that their party was overreaching, those close to Nancy saw Steny—rightly or wrongly—as more receptive to scaling the bill back. To his credit, however, Steny never did so. And every time he and I talked, he sounded determined to keep pushing ahead through the darkest hours.

The group included the chairmen of the three health care committees and the chairmen of each panel's health subcommittee. For Energy and Commerce, the negotiators were Waxman, the chairman, and Frank Pallone of New Jersey, the health subcommittee chairman. Charlie Rangel of New York, then the chairman of Ways and Means, represented his committee along with Pete Stark of California, the subcommittee chairman. And George Miller of California negotiated for his committee, Education and Labor, along with Rob Andrews of New Jersey, the subcommittee chairman. Dingell was there, too, as the lead sponsor of what would become known as the "tricommittee bill." Their mission was to write a bill that would achieve four goals: cover as many Americans as possible, slow the out-of-control growth of health care costs, pay for itself, and rein in the worst practices of the health insurance companies.[3]

Early on, it became obvious that their Republican counterparts did not share the same goals as the Democrats. At first, Waxman got some encouraging signs from the top Republican on his committee, Joe Barton of Texas. Barton had suggested on a couple of occasions that it might be possible to get a bipartisan agreement. But when Waxman probed further, to see what Barton had in mind, all of his ideas were the standard Republican fare—such as selling insurance across state lines and limits on medical malpractice lawsuits—that were unacceptable to most Democrats.[4]

In April, Andrews met one-on-one with several Republicans he knew well, hoping to sound them out about what they could accept in the bill. None of them were willing to support any of the steps—revenue increases, spending reductions, or mandates—that would be needed to cover most of the uninsured. And if health care reform didn't cover most of the uninsured, it would defeat much of the purpose of what Democrats wanted to do. It wasn't just that the two parties had different views on how to achieve the same goals. They didn't even share the same goals.[5]

The other Democrats in the group came to the same conclusion. So they went ahead with their talks, determined to at least unify their own party on how to achieve their goals. If it had not been for his earlier meetings, Andrews says, he would have been happy to urge the other Democrats to invite top Republicans into the room. "But I knew what the answer would be," he said. "From the people I had met with personally, I knew what they were going to say."[6]

It might have been unrealistic to expect a bipartisan agreement to emerge from the House, because there is a big difference in the cultures of the House and the Senate. In the House, the atmosphere is much more polarized and heated, because most of the members represent districts that are carefully drawn so that their voters are either mostly Democrats or mostly Republicans, leaving them with no incentive to do anything but please their base.

But this was about more than just political calculation. Most House Democrats genuinely thought their efforts would be worthwhile only if the bill covered all Americans (or at least came close), helped them with their struggles with insurance companies, and gave private insurance real competition. And however they paid for the bill, they wanted it to be fair to the middle class. If they could not convince Republicans to take the necessary steps to achieve those goals, they had to move ahead themselves.

In the broader picture, this was what they needed to do to end up with the strongest possible bill. Compared to the Senate, the House is more like a legislative assembly line. With a strong front manager, you can move a lot through. And in doing so, you put more pressure on the Senate, where many Democrats are more cautious, not to give away too much. Nancy Pelosi is as strong a front manager as the Democrats could want. But in order for her to be able to prove her skills, the committee chairmen would have to deliver for her first.

The House Democrats spent months hashing out crucial details: how a requirement for everyone to buy health insurance would work, how generous the subsidies would have to be, how much people should be protected from out-of-pocket costs, and how much employers should be required to do.[7] By July 9, 2009, the Democrats were closing in on a health care bill they could release to the public. It was a Thursday, which is often the busiest day in Congress before members fly back to their states and districts. The tricommittee group had already circulated a discussion draft of the bill in mid-June, and if they could lock down the final details, they could release the official bill as early as Friday.

The Blue Dogs, however, stopped that plan. They released a letter, signed by forty of their fifty-two members, warning that they could not support the bill unless significant changes were made from the discussion draft.[8] That night, they delivered the same warning in person in a meeting with the leadership.[9] If that many Democrats were truly prepared to vote against the bill, it would not pass the House. The rollout was postponed.

For Mike Ross of Arkansas, the chairman of a fifteen-member Blue Dog health care task force, the issue was simple. He and the Blue Dogs had deep concerns about fundamental issues—the public option, the bill's impact on employers, and the cost of the bill—and didn't think the chairmen were taking them seriously enough. That was why the group went public with its concerns by releasing the letter. Ross was particularly worried about a public option that might base its payments on Medicare rates, since the doctors in his rural district claim that Medicare doesn't cover their costs. "You can go to many doctors' offices in my district," he said, "and there will be a big sign on the door saying, 'We no longer take Medicare patients.'"[10]

But Ross also thought it would be a mistake, in the middle of the worst economic crisis since the Depression, to require employers who provide health coverage to pay for at least 65 percent of the premiums for family coverage, as the tricommittee group wanted to do.[11] And the group didn't think the discussion draft included enough measures to bring down health care costs, as they argued in their public letter to Pelosi and Hoyer.[12]

I was enormously skeptical of how serious the Blue Dogs were about cost control. If they really wanted to bring down health care costs, it was hard for me to understand why they were so opposed to a public plan to compete with private insurance, a powerful tool that could have given the health insurance companies a real incentive to waste less money. And they certainly undermined their goal of cutting costs by deferring so much to health care providers, such as doctors, who were fighting to keep any payment cuts as small as possible. But the House did need to do more in other ways to bring costs down. After all, cost control was the main goal the president had set out in his public case for health care reform.

Nancy Pelosi was fully aware of the cost problem. Even before the Blue Dogs aired their complaints, she told Waxman, Rangel, and Miller to "wring every possible dollar out of the health care system . . . in order to help cover the cost."[13] But there wasn't enough time to negotiate major changes to the bill. To stay on schedule for the House to pass a bill before the August recess, the bill had to be unveiled early the next week. So Nancy decided to move ahead. The bill would be released, and then the committees would keep working on it as they held their markups, where Democrats and Republicans would have their chance to make changes.

On Tuesday, July 14, the Democratic leaders and the committee chairmen released the House tricommittee bill. Already, they had advanced the health care reform initiative well beyond the 1994 effort, simply by writing one bill that could be supported by all three committee chairmen. At the press conference, Pelosi called it "a starting point and a path to success." John Dingell, whose father had pushed for national health insurance with Harry Truman in the 1940s, said that "my old dad would be pleased." And Henry Waxman declared that health care reform could not be delayed again: "We, quite frankly, cannot go home for a recess unless the House and the Senate both pass bills to reform and restructure our health care system."[14] Mike Ross, however, saw little in the bill that had been changed to win over the Blue Dogs.[15]

By the end of the week, two of the House committees had produced health care bills as well. Working in grueling, all-night markup sessions, both the Ways and Means Committee and the Education and Labor Committee approved their versions of the tricommittee bill the Democrats had negotiated. In both cases, all of the Republicans voted against the bills, just as they had in Ted Kennedy's committee. But this time, there were a few Democrats who were dissatisfied as well. In the Ways and Means Committee, three Democrats voted against the bill, including two Blue Dogs and one member of the centrist New Democrat Coalition, which had also registered concerns. And in the Education and Labor Committee, three Democratic centrists voted against the bill, including one Blue Dog and one member of the New Democrat Coalition.[16]

Those votes were a warning of the troubles Henry Waxman would face in his committee, which had the biggest concentration of Blue Dogs. In their eyes, the bill still had a public plan that would pay providers based on Medicare rates, it still would have required employers to pay 65 percent of the premium for family coverage, and it still did not have enough cost containment to satisfy them.

So on the first day of the Energy and Commerce markup—Thursday, July 16—seven Blue Dogs on the committee all read the same opening statement, word for word. They were committed to passing a bill that lowered costs and improved health care quality, and they were prepared to work with Waxman, but "we cannot fix these problems by simply pouring more money into a broken system." They wanted the bill to save more money in public programs, create more innovative ways to deliver health care at lower costs, and help people and small businesses get health coverage "without bankrupting the federal government."[17]

It was a show of solidarity, carefully choreographed to show the Blue Dogs' power as the swing votes on the committee. In case anyone missed it, they delivered a stronger message the next day. On Friday, as the committee began considering its first amendments, the Blue Dogs provided the winning votes for an amendment by Republican John Sullivan of Oklahoma to get rid of duplicative programs.[18] It was not a make-or-break issue. But by siding with the Republicans against most of the committee Democrats, Ross said, the message was clear: We can stop the bill if you don't listen to us.[19]

The leadership and the committee chairmen had wrestled with many of the most complicated health care problems. They had tried to find solutions to the runaway growth in health care costs, the uneven quality of the medical care we get, and the vulnerability people face when they can't get decent health coverage. And they had tried to find reasonable ways to pay for the changes, a challenge they would struggle with until the end of the process.

These were all necessary challenges to take on. In some ways, the bills didn't go far enough. But at a time of deep skepticism about government—and an economy that caused seemingly endless suffering for millions of Americans—they tested the limits of what our political system can accept.

4 | HOLDING DOWN COSTS

If Congress didn't find a way to keep health care costs from rising out of control, the public would never consider health care reform to be a success. So the authors of the health care bill had to grapple with ways to address the root causes of the spending that makes health care more expensive for all of us. Lawmakers had to find a way to do that without angering the stakeholders who would have had the most to lose, and without being so disruptive that patients would get hurt in the process.

By the time the committees got to work, there was a lot of consensus among health care experts about what kinds of solutions had the most promise. Unfortunately, there wasn't enough evidence on any of them—yet—to justify trying them out across the nation. They were too new for Congress to have more than a general idea of how well they'd work, and there wasn't enough experience to let the bill writers know what might go wrong. So the committees went as far as the members thought they could go. They wrote in lots of pilot projects for the most promising ideas and laid the groundwork to expand them if they went well. And by trying most of them in Medicare, which has a lot of influence on the practices of private insurance, they hoped to have enough leverage to spread the ideas more broadly.

The key was to find ways to start paying for value rather than volume. Rather than just paying doctors and hospitals every time they perform another test or procedure, we have to start rewarding them for helping their patients recover as quickly as possible. They should do that without spending more money than necessary, but also without rushing things so people have to come back for more treatment. There are different ways to do that—by simply changing the way we pay the providers, and by changing the way the providers are organized and deal with each other. By trying just about all of them, the bill writers hoped to find out what would work best and then make a bigger commitment to the best ideas later.

One way to get away from paying for every service is to move to a system called bundled payments. The idea is to set a fixed amount of money for an entire course of treatment—including, say, surgery and all of the follow-up care—rather than paying separate bills for every step. The money is set at a level that should be high enough to cover a whole episode of care, which is why it's also sometimes called episode-based payments.

The way it works now, if you have to go to a hospital for surgery, the hospital may or may not talk to the doctor who's going to take care of you afterwards, and they may or may not make sure you know how to take care of yourself. But under bundled payments, if no one is going to get paid more if you have to go back to the hospital, they all have a lot more reason to talk to each other and make sure you actually get better. Under the Senate version, for example, a pilot program would have tied the payment "bundle" to the entire set of services a Medicare patient gets from hospital care. So there would have been one payment to cover any doctors' visits before the patient went to the hospital, the hospital care itself, any readmissions to the hospital, and the first month of follow-up care.[1]

Another way is to tie the payments to how well providers treat serious conditions without spending an excessive amount of money. That's called value-based purchasing, and it became a big part of the reforms proposed in the Senate. The Department of Health and Human Services would set up a value-based purchasing program for hospitals, in which they would get rewards for doing well at treating conditions such as heart attacks, heart failure, or pneumonia, or for skillful handling of events such as surgery or infections.[2] It's another experiment that Health and Human Services would have to design on its own, figuring out what else to measure and how to rate the hospitals' performance.

A different way into the problem is to take a fresh look at how doctors' offices and clinics are organized. Here, both the Senate and the House bill writers tried to set up tests that might teach us some important lessons. One idea was to encourage health care providers to share responsibility for a patient's care, from beginning to end. They would do it by forming "accountable care organizations," which would be partnerships between different kinds of providers—such as primary care physicians, specialists, nurse practitioners, and hospitals—that would take care of patients across all settings. If they coordinate their work well enough to heal their patients quickly and without spending too much, they'd get to share the savings.[3]

Another way of reorganizing how people get their health care is to beef up primary care in a way that would let one doctor's office or clinic arrange all of your medical care. These would be called medical homes, and as the name implies, they would be the place where you could go whenever you have medical needs. They would use a team approach—typically a doctor, a nurse, a pharmacist, and maybe other medical staff—and they would get to know you and your needs. You would get your basic care there, and they would make the arrangements if you needed to go to a hospital or a specialist. They would have enough staff that you would be able to get appointments when you needed them. You would be able to reach somebody on the phone twenty-four hours a day, seven days a week, and you might be able to reach your doctor by e-mail. Your doctor might even be able to send your prescription to the pharmacy electronically.[4]

Finally, there was an idea that became increasingly popular with the Senate—a way to bypass at least some of the usual political pressures that make it so hard to cut health care costs. The idea, proposed by Democratic Senator Jay Rockefeller of West Virginia, was to create an independent board that would recommend other ways to slow the growth of Medicare spending. If the program's spending rose beyond certain targets, which would be tied to the rate of inflation, the fifteen-member board would have to recommend ways to throttle it back. In this way, the board would act as a kind of backstop to keep Medicare spending from rising too much. Its suggestions would go into effect automatically unless Congress voted to block them, and even then, Congress would have to come up with other ways to achieve the same amount of savings.

The catch, however, was that the bill writers took a lot of cost-control tools away from the Medicare board. Clearly concerned that the bill's opponents might label it an antidemocratic way to take health care away from vulnerable people, the bill writers declared that the board wouldn't be able to change anyone's benefits, premiums, taxes, or eligibility for the program. That's a pretty big list of exceptions, and while it left the board with some options, it didn't leave a lot. The bill suggested the board could look for solutions such as coordinating care better and making medical care more efficient. Of course, a lot of the best ideas on how to do that were already being tried elsewhere in the bill.

There were other approaches to controlling costs that didn't involve as much political risk, but the results were likely to be a lot more mixed. One important step was to put a new emphasis on preventive health care. We've discussed how we don't treat prevention with the seriousness it deserves, which probably inflates our health care costs as a result, since a big share of the costs is due to preventable illnesses such as cancer and cardiovascular disease. So it seems common sense that if we encouraged more people to get the screenings and counseling sessions that could help them avoid those illnesses, we could save a lot of money and keep people healthier, too.

The Senate, for example, proposed a permanent source of support for those efforts, the Prevention and Public Health Investment Fund, which would get a guaranteed stream of federal money to invest in prevention and public health programs. This was the creation of Senator Tom Harkin of Iowa, who wrote the prevention fund in a way that would provide the money automatically, rather than depending on Congress to live up to its commitments every year.[5]

The bill writers also wanted to give people more generous coverage so they would seek out the preventive services. Both the House and the Senate would have let people in private health plans get preventive services without having to pay copayments or other cost-sharing.[6] Seniors on Medicare would have been able to get recommended preventive services—such as cancer, diabetes, and glaucoma screenings—without paying copayments or any other cost-sharing. As an added incentive, the Senate also would offered a free annual wellness visit under Medicare, where seniors could have gotten a personalized plan for their preventive care.[7]

The other way to control costs without taking on big political risks is to modernize our health information technology so our doctors' offices no longer have to wade through file folders full of outdated paper records. As of 2008, only about 13 percent of American physicians were using electronic medical records—way behind the curve compared to most other developed countries.[8]

By helping health care providers shift to electronic medical records and electronic billing, we can save money, make these offices more efficient, and cut down on the kinds of duplicate tests that waste both money and patients' time.

The main investment in health information technology had already taken place, with the $20 billion Congress had included in the stimulus package to help doctors, hospitals, and other providers convert to electronic medical records. Physicians get as much as $65,000 if they can show they're making a real commitment to modern health information technology, and hospitals can get millions of dollars. Eventually, the incentive payments stop. And if providers still aren't using modern technology by 2015, they'll start to lose part of their Medicare payments.[9] In this round, the Senate added to the effort by requiring new standards so federal and state health programs can talk to each other—using the new electronic systems—and setting up a demonstration program to test the use of the technology in nursing homes.[10]

But this is one issue that will need more attention in the future, and there's no reason for it to break down because of partisan fights. This should be one of the easiest health care issues on which Democrats and Republicans can find common ground. If it's encouraged in the right way, with proper standards to make sure the new systems can talk to each other, modern health information technology has so much potential to improve quality and reduce costs that we need to stay on the case. It won't solve the health care cost problem by itself, but if we want to start down the road toward a more efficient health care sector, it's a basic first step.

5 | IMPROVING QUALITY

It would never be enough just to crack down on all health care spending. To approach the problem in a thoughtful way, Congress had to find ways to target the waste—the $800 billion the United States spends every year on health care that doesn't make us better. To do that, it had to come up with measures that would improve the quality of the care we all receive. If it could do that, we could save money in the right way so the patients would never know what they were missing—and save people from bad experiences at the same time.

We had already taken an important first step by putting $1.1 billion in the stimulus bill to support comparative effectiveness research, the study of what works best when you compare two or more different ways of treating the same condition. Now it was time to make a bigger commitment. Since comparative effectiveness research is expensive and takes a long time, it needed a big boost from the federal government. But members of Congress also had to find better ways to let providers know about the findings, since they're so busy that it's hard for them to stay up-to-date on the latest research.

There was a split over whether the job should be handled by a new government agency or an independent entity. The House bill would have created a government agency, a new office within the Agency for Healthcare Research and Quality. The Senate, however, decided to make it a nonprofit corporation instead. To be called the Patient-Centered Outcomes Research Institute, it would have an independent board of governors with members representing different health care interests, including patients, physicians, insurers, and researchers. It would hire the staff of the institute, who in turn would set the research priorities and contract with federal and private researchers to do the actual studies.[1]

The Senate went with an outside entity because the Finance Committee wanted it that way. It was partly a political decision. Max Baucus knew that conservatives loved to use horror stories from the British national health board—the National Institute for Health and Clinical Excellence (NICE)—to scare people about how the federal government might use the research. If the Senate could accomplish the same goal by putting the research in the hands of a nonprofit, rather than a government agency, Baucus figured there was no point in picking an unnecessary political fight. In addition, this was the model that had been suggested by the Medicare Payment Advisory Commission, an independent agency that advises Congress on Medicare issues. With an independent board of experts setting the research agenda, the commission argued, people would have more confidence that there would be no political bias in the choice of research topics.[2]

There also had to be a way to learn more about best practices, and to make sure doctors and hospitals know about them and use them. It's one thing when we don't know as much as we should about which treatments work better than others. It's another when we know, for example, that hospital staffs can keep infections to a minimum by using checklists for their procedures and simply by washing their hands—and yet hospitals are still struggling to get infections under control.

The House would have created a new research center to handle the task. The Senate, however, decided to build on an existing agency, the Center for Quality Improvement and Patient Safety, which mainly focuses on preventing medical errors. Under the Senate bill, the center would set the research agenda, find the providers who do the best jobs, and spread the word about their best practices in ways that providers and patients can understand.[3]

With any issue as serious as health care quality, any good public policy should have rewards and consequences. Both the Senate and the House would have cracked down on hospitals that have high rates of readmissions that we know how to prevent. They would have lost part of their payments if patients had to return for additional treatment of conditions such as heart attacks, heart failure, and pneumonia.[4] The other way to approach the issue was to focus specifically on infections, since that is such a deadly, and preventable, problem for hospital patients. The Senate, for example, would have taken away 1 percent of a hospital's Medicare payment if it ranked in the top 25 percent of facilities where the patients get "hospital-acquired conditions."[5] Those can include infections, but they can also be the results of basic mistakes such as leaving a medical tool in a patient after surgery, giving them the wrong blood type, or letting them develop pressure ulcers.[6]

Perhaps the biggest key to better quality, however, was to make health care more transparent than it is today. If you can't see the problem, you can't fix it. Health information technology will help us do this, as we learn to keep better track of, for example, which patients are getting the preventive care they need and which are not. When two-thirds of all people with asthma have not gotten a flu vaccine—putting themselves at serious risk of complications if they get the flu—health information technology can alert their doctor that they need the shot.[7] And it will help us keep better track of hospitals' performance as they face penalties for preventable readmissions and infections.

But our health care needs better transparency at all levels, from the performance of doctors and hospitals to the prices of their services to the details of how much health coverage we actually have. The Senate bill took some good steps in this direction. Hospitals would have to post the prices of their services. A new federal Web site would help people on Medicare look up how physicians have scored on different quality measures. The public would be able to learn more about payments to physicians from drug and medical-device makers. And, for the first time, health insurance plans would have to illustrate how their coverage would work under an example of an expensive illness—what it might actually cover and what you, the patient, would have to pay.[8] The message was clear: our health care will not get better until all of the stakeholders accept the need for more openness.

Of all of the quality ideas Congress considered, the comparative effectiveness research became the biggest lightning rod for those who wanted to scare the public about health care reform. If you don't already know what the research is, and what it isn't, it is very easy to distort it into a big-government scheme to ration health care. And that's exactly what several of the Republicans did as the committees debated the bills—backed up by outside interest groups that conditioned the public to be deeply suspicious of how the research would be used.

Comparative effectiveness research isn't about rationing health care. It's not about government bureaucrats telling grandma that she's too old to save, or a person with a disability that their health care is costing too much money. It's about finding out, based on scientific evidence, whether one particular way of treating a disease gets better results than others. Yes, the researchers might consider the cost as one factor in comparing the different options. If you find out that the more expensive way of treating an illness isn't any more effective than cheaper ways, you can't ignore that discovery. It's telling you something important. But it's not the reason you do the research. You do it to find out whether the most common way of treating a disease or condition is really the best way, or whether you'd be better served by trying something else.

Here is a vivid example. In the 1990s, doctors treating women with breast cancer started to move away from the old standard of care, which was conventional chemotherapy. Instead, it became more common to treat them with a new combination: high-dose chemotherapy and then a bone marrow transplant. At first, a lot of health insurance companies refused to pay for the new approach, because they considered it experimental. Most backed down, however, when patients sued to force them to cover it and some states began requiring insurers to pay for it. It also became a covered procedure for all federal workers.[9] In 1999, however, five clinical trials all came to the same conclusion: breast cancer patients who got the treatment didn't get any better results than those who had conventional chemotherapy. The side effects were worse, and it cost about twice as much.[10]

If we had more scientific research that made those kinds of comparisons, we could give people better health care—and, yes, less expensive health care—without having to go through so many years of trial and error. That is the point of comparative effectiveness research. But the way some Republicans described it, it came out sounding like a sinister plot, a way to give government bureaucrats a scientific-sounding excuse to second-guess every decision your doctor makes.

As the House Energy and Commerce Committee worked on the bill in July, Representative Mike Rogers of Michigan charged that the legislation "creates an entire new federal regime" to conduct the research and warned that "we cannot allow the federal government to use a calculator or a bureaucratic standard to get in the middle of patients and doctors."[11] Representative Tom Price, a physician from Georgia, declared on Fox News, "There may be abuse, but the question is, who is going to be deciding what that abuse is and how we're going to cut down on it? If it's politicians and bureaucrats in Washington, then that's a bad idea."[12]

So the Democrats tried to write in assurances that the powers of any new comparative effectiveness research entity would be limited, and that there was no "slippery slope" to worry about. For example, the Patient-Centered Outcomes Research Institute would circulate its research findings, but it wouldn't be able to make any recommendations about what to do with them. The Health and Human Services secretary would be able to use them to make coverage decisions in federal health programs, but only after all of the different health care stakeholders had a chance to give feedback, and only after considering other studies that might show a medical procedure or treatment works better for some patients than for others.

The department would not be able to make coverage decisions "in a manner that treats extending the life of an elderly, disabled, or terminally ill individual as of lower value than extending the life of an individual who is younger, non-disabled, or not terminally ill." And in any case, it would not be able to "deny coverage of items or services under such title solely on the basis of comparative effectiveness research."[13] That is about as far as Congress could reasonably go.

And if the federal government didn't step in, we would never get enough research to learn about what really works. The private sector doesn't do enough on its own, and what it does produce, mostly in the form of industry-sponsored trials, is either biased or not available to the public.[14] Health care reform could make a major contribution to the public good by making objective research more widespread than it is now. But that would only happen if lawmakers could convince Americans, once and for all, that Big Brother would have nothing to do with it.

6 | REACHING (NEARLY) EVERYONE

The third part of the policy challenge for Congress was the one that matters most to people on an emotional level: how to help the uninsured and the underinsured. It's also the part that lawmakers had the least ability to solve in small steps. People had to be able to get health care without being locked out by the worst practices of the health insurance companies.

But unfortunately for Congress—which works best when it can pass small, easily understood, and popular measures—there was no way to solve this problem with only the charges that are easy to pass. Everyone would cheer if Congress banned insurance companies for rejecting people with preexisting conditions, or from charging higher premiums for people with health problems. But if that was all lawmakers did, everyone's health insurance premiums would go through the roof because health insurance companies would not simply take on the added risks without covering their costs. So to spread those costs around, Congress would have to find a way to get everyone to participate, including relatively young and healthy people who don't have health insurance now.

The only way to do that, as Obama reluctantly concluded, was to require everyone to get health insurance. That way, there would be enough healthy people paying premiums to offset the higher costs of less healthy people. But if you simply make everyone get health insurance without helping low-income people pay for it, you're just saddling them with an enormous financial burden. So Congress had to provide subsidies to help the people who truly couldn't afford health insurance. It could reach some of them by expanding Medicaid, the health care program for low-income people, to include people slightly over the poverty line and fill in the gaps in its coverage. But the rest would need federal help to make their private health insurance premiums less expensive.

To give individuals and small businesses an easier way to find and compare health plans, there had to be a new "exchange" similar to the one in Massachusetts. That way, there would be more standardized rules and a broader pool of customers so people could be insured as part of a group, with more stable prices than they would get on their own. And to protect people from the indignity of going bankrupt because of a serious illness, lawmakers had to set an absolute limit on what patients should have to pay out of pocket when they have health insurance.

It may seem like a lot for Congress to take on in one package. But the health care sector is full of interconnected parts. If you tried to break up the reform bill into bite-size pieces, you might pass them with broad bipartisan support, but you would set off a chain of events that you probably wouldn't be able to control. And you wouldn't really help the uninsured and the underinsured. To do that, Congress had to pass the popular pieces and the unpopular pieces together. And it had to relearn the art of doing big things.

The first step was to shut down the practices insurance companies use to deny coverage to people who need it. Congress would require insurance companies to give health insurance to everyone who applies and ban them from rejecting people with health problems. The insurers would have to renew people's coverage automatically, unless they hadn't paid their premiums. The insurers would be required to cover preexisting conditions, ending the infamous practice of denying the health care people need the most.

And in the individual market, health insurers would be banned from canceling people's coverage retroactively, the practice known as rescission, in which insurers look for a reason to stop covering you if you get sick. Both parties agreed on the need to do this. The only way insurers would be able to cancel your coverage is if you had committed fraud or lied about an important part of your medical history.[1]

If this was all Congress did, though, insurance companies still would have been able to steer away the less healthy people by charging them much higher premiums than everyone else. This wouldn't be the same thing as rejecting them, but it would have the same effect. So all of the bills would have banned insurance companies from charging premiums based on how healthy you are. They would have been able to vary the premiums only for other reasons, such as your age, the size of your family, and where you live.[2]

Finally, Congress had to tackle the problem of annual or lifetime limits on what an insurance company will cover. Most people will never deal with those practices, but if you have a disability or a serious illness, they can leave you exposed to devastating medical debt. The solution was to ban insurance companies from capping what they'd pay for your benefits over your lifetime.[3] It was harder to end annual limits, however, because the Senate leadership was worried that health insurance companies would raise their premiums too much to cover the costs.[4] Eventually, the Senate settled for restricting annual limits for a few years and then eliminating them completely starting in 2014.[5]

All of these measures were necessary, and all would have corrected serious injustices. But by themselves, all would have raised people's premiums, because they would have left the insurance companies with more costs to cover. To keep that from happening, Congress needed something else that could lower premiums enough to offset those increases. What was needed—not only for moral reasons, but also for practical reasons—was to get as many people insured as possible. When people have good health insurance, they're protected against costly illnesses, but they're also paying premiums that help cover other people's costs. So the next step had to be the "individual mandate"—the requirement that everyone get some kind of health coverage.

It is a big step to require people to buy anything as expensive as health insurance. It is not a step any elected official would want to take if they could get the desired result any other way. But nothing else we have tried over the years has covered everyone or come anywhere close.

Most uninsured people lack coverage because it would be too much of a financial burden to get it, not because they've chosen not to get it. About two-thirds are poor or just a bit over the poverty line, and the age group that is most likely to be uninsured is young adults, because their incomes are usually so low. But there is also a group that should be able to afford insurance: the people whose incomes are more than four times the poverty line.[6] About one out of ten uninsured people is in this high-income category. So the bills had to address both groups.

All of the bills provided subsidies to help people with low-to-moderate incomes pay for health coverage, as Congress hoped to take the sting out of the individual mandate. However, it quickly became clear that the Finance Committee bill's subsidies would be the least generous of all for the people with the lowest incomes. Over time, the Democrats made the subsidies more generous as the bill moved to the Senate floor, and then increased them once again, at the insistence of the House, in the final version. This would be a constant tension throughout the debate, as Democrats tried to make sure the reform bill didn't just force people to buy coverage they couldn't afford.

All of the bills also would have exempted some people from the individual mandate, just as Massachusetts allows people to get a "hardship exemption" if they can prove they truly can't afford health coverage. In the Senate, the Democrats struggled with that policy. The original bill would have required people to pay up to 10 percent of their income before they were exempt. But Senator Chuck Schumer of New York thought that was too much, and amended it to lower the threshold to 8 percent. Even that much, he said, was "still a lot for a lot of families."[7]

At the same time, though, the bill needed penalties strong enough to convince people to get health insurance. Otherwise, some might decide it would be cheaper to pay the penalty and stay uninsured, even if their incomes were high enough that they should be able to afford it. The House took a straightforward approach, declaring that people who did not get coverage would pay a fine of 2.5 percent of their adjusted gross income unless they got the exemption.[8] The Senate proposed flat fees instead, but it reduced them as senators from both parties worried that the bill would punish people too harshly for struggling with the expense of health insurance.[9]

Congress also wanted to give employers a share of the responsibility, too, by giving them an incentive to cover their workers. The lawmakers didn't want to go so far, however, that they could be accused of hurting businesses and killing jobs. In the Senate, the solution was to stop short of actually requiring employers to cover their workers, but to fine larger employers if they didn't. The fine was originally set at $750 per worker, but the House insisted that was too low, and it was later raised to $2,000. Small businesses with fifty or fewer workers would be exempt from the fines, and in fact would get tax credits as an incentive to provide coverage.

Through all of this, there was an easy and efficient way to help the poor and the near-poor get health coverage. It was to expand the Medicaid program. Ever since it was created in 1965, as a health care program jointly run by the federal government and the states, Medicaid has helped millions of low-income people get health coverage they might not have had otherwise. But it has also been a patchwork, with major categories of people who aren't eligible. To reach such a big group of the uninsured, Congress had to allow more of them into the program. All states would have to give Medicaid coverage to people with incomes up to 133 percent of the federal poverty line, roughly $14,400 a year for an individual or $29,300 for a family of four.[10] The federal government would cover most, but not all, of the costs.

There was one big political problem: some states' governors didn't want more people in their Medicaid programs. The states would have had to pick up some of the extra expense at a time when the economic collapse was already putting enormous strains on their budgets. The states' requests for help, and the Democrats' desire to ease their burden, would create one of the biggest political headaches of the entire health care debate.

The markets for individual and small business health coverage have always been the most dysfunctional parts of our health insurance industry. If you're trying to get health insurance on your own, you will face a world with few rules, wildly different standards for what is covered and what is not, and loopholes that you may not discover until it is too late. You can buy low-cost health insurance, but its benefits are so limited that it is barely worthy of the name *insurance*. And small businesses and individuals share another problem: they can't join pools big enough to share their costs with others. So if you have individual insurance and one family member gets sick, or you're in a small business and one of your coworkers gets seriously ill, you can end up with sky-high health premiums.

The answer, as Obama proposed on the campaign trail, was to set up health insurance exchanges that would serve as a new marketplace for health coverage. They would provide an easy place for people to research and apply for coverage, certify individual and small business health plans to participate, standardize the categories for different levels of coverage, give people a place to apply for subsidies, and provide enough information on the different health plans so they could make an informed decision. Once you joined a plan in the exchange, you would become part of a broader pool of insured people, so your premiums would be a lot more stable than they'd be if you were on your own.

This was the approach Massachusetts used when it set up its Health Connector, and Congress studied the Massachusetts experience closely as it drew up its own plans for a new health care exchange system. There was a big difference, however, in the way the House and Senate designed their exchanges. The House bill would have created one national exchange, to be run by a new agency with standard rules throughout the country.[11] The Senate, however, would have let all of the states set up their own exchanges, with separate exchanges for individuals and small businesses, and with more authority to run their own operations as long as they followed the national eligibility rules.[12]

The Senate went with the state version because the Democrats thought they had to, in order to win the crucial votes of their moderates. But a national exchange would have worked much better. If you let all of the states run their own exchanges, you have to have a lot of faith that they will set them up quickly and well, because it becomes a huge challenge if the Department of Health and Human Services has to correct their failures. And you have to hope that no state will run a sloppy exchange to try to undermine national health care reform. Even Jon Kingsdale, who runs the Massachusetts exchange, warned that this is exactly what could happen in states where people didn't support the reform effort.[13] This would be a sticking point between the House and the Senate until the end—because a well-run health exchange system would be absolutely critical to the success of health care reform.

Most people will judge the success or failure of health care reform by whether their own costs go down. At the least, their personal costs have to stop rising so fast that health care eats up their paychecks. It was not just a matter of making the overall health care sector less expensive. Congress also had to protect people in more direct ways: by shielding them better from devastating medical bills, by making sure health plans don't have major loopholes in their benefits, and by getting rid of the notorious gap in Medicare's coverage of prescription drugs.

One of the strongest arguments Obama and the Democrats made for health care reform was the national disgrace of people going bankrupt because of medical bills. To end that disgrace, Congress had to limit the amount of out-of-pocket expenses any American should be required to pay. Under the Senate bill, no health plan could make you pay more than $5,950 a year out of your own pocket if you had individual coverage, or $11,900 if you had family coverage. If your income was low enough, you would get subsidies that could help you cut your costs down to as little as a third of those amounts.[14] That's still a lot of money, if you're living paycheck to paycheck and struggling to pay your other bills. But it would be more protection than a lot of people have now.

Congress also wanted to set some basic standards for what kind of coverage people would get through the exchanges. The plans would have had to cover such basics as hospital care, doctors' services, prescription drugs, preventive services, mental health, maternity care, and pediatric services.[15] And, most importantly, the bills ensured that "limited benefit" health insurance plans—the kind that put unrealistically low limits on what they'll pay, or don't put any limit on how much you'll pay out of your own pocket—would not be offered through the exchanges.[16] That's the best way to protect people from seriously inadequate health plans.

Finally, there was a chance to close a major gap that millions of seniors on Medicare face: the "donut hole," which leaves a wide range of prescription drug expenses uncovered. When Congress passed the Medicare legislation in 2003 that created the drug benefit, the Republican majority set a limit on how much could be spent on it. As a result, there wasn't enough money to go around, leaving a big "hole" in their coverage. For example, in 2010, after someone on Medicare has had $2,830 in total drug costs—paying $940 out of pocket—Medicare will not pay for any more prescription drugs until the person has reached $6,440 in total costs. By that point, if people get that far, they have spent $4,550 of their own money.[17] At the time, my Democratic colleagues and I tried to close that gap, but we did not have the votes to do it.

This time, Congress could correct that injustice. The House bill would have gradually phased out the gap, so that by 2019, there would be no hole in seniors' drug coverage.[18] Unfortunately, the Senate wouldn't go that far. This was a high priority for seniors' groups, and ending the notorious gap could have helped secure the crucial support health care reform needed from senior citizens. It also happened to be the right thing to do. Before the debate was over, this was a big area the House and the Senate would have to work out.

7 | THE PUBLIC OPTION

Of all of the reforms Congress tried to accomplish, nothing captured the fight over the role of government as powerfully as the public option. This was the Medicare-like public plan that would be available in the new exchange—and only in the exchange—as an option for people who wanted to try an alternative to private health insurance. For Republicans, it was Exhibit A in their charge that the Democrats were trying to impose "government-run health care." For centrist Democrats, it was a worrying sign that their party had too much faith in government solutions.

But for liberal and progressive Democrats, it became an absolutely essential element of reform—and a test of whether their party really wanted to change the equation. Why did the public option dominate so much of the debate? Because it deserved all of the time and attention it got. The public option would have done more than any other single measure to bring health care costs under control, by putting pressure on private insurers to follow its lead, and to give people a place to go if they could not get affordable health insurance anywhere else.

It was not the only way to accomplish these goals, and some of my friends on the left oversimplified the health care effort by implying that nothing else mattered. But the public option definitely would have been the best way to accomplish these goals. When we lost that part of the health care bill—despite numerous polls that showed the majority of Americans supported it—we proved how tough it is for Democrats to propose even a modest expansion of the government's role in health care, even at the peak of their political strength.

The power of the public option was that it combined elements of costs, quality, and access—the three broad problems that health care had to solve. It would have been more cost-efficient than private health insurance, because it would have had lower administrative costs and wouldn't have been under pressure to make profits. It also would have been a testing ground for some of the cost-control ideas the reform bill was only going to try as limited demonstrations elsewhere, such as medical homes, accountable care organizations, and value-based purchasing.

It would have promoted quality by gearing these kinds of experiments, and others, toward the goals of making people healthier and making the quality of health care more consistent throughout the country.[1] And it would have given people better access to health care by giving them a more reliable source of health insurance than they usually get in the individual health insurance market—with better coverage and more stable premiums, thanks to its ability to spread costs across a large pool of people.

The main argument for the public option was that it would have provided real competition for the private health insurance companies, and a real choice of health plans for people who used the health care exchanges—a choice that would be distinctly different from all the others. Compared to insurance companies that look too hard for excuses to deny claims, the public option would have provided a new source of coverage that wasn't so driven by profits. For those that spend too much of your premiums on overhead or high executive pay, the efficiency of the public option could have pressured them to become more efficient themselves.

And for those plans that don't bargain hard enough with doctors and hospitals, the public plan could have used its national clout to set payment rates that would allow providers to charge only what they really need. This is one aspect of our current market that is often overlooked. As John Holahan and Linda Blumberg of the Urban Institute have pointed out, private health plans haven't used their bargaining power to challenge providers very aggressively on payment rates.[2] If they had, our premiums might not be rising so fast.

All of this was built on the premise that Medicare, which has provided dependable and efficient health care to senior citizens for more than four decades, could be the model for a new way of providing health coverage to individuals and small businesses that don't have good options now. Instead, the fact that the public option would have been a true "government-run" health care program—just like Medicare—sent the bill's opponents into a frenzy.

It started with fairly mild objections. Chuck Grassley, the top Republican on the Senate Finance Committee, brought up the public option at the White House health care forum, during a question-and-answer session with Obama at the end: "There's a lot of us that feel that the public option, that the government is an unfair competitor, and that we're going to get an awful lot of crowd-out. And we have to keep what we have now strong and make it stronger." He was referring to the concern that the private plans wouldn't be able to compete and would lose customers to the public plan.[3]

But it didn't take long before the opponents began making breathless claims about the dangers of the public option. In June, all but one of the Republican members of the Senate Finance Committee sent Obama a letter warning that private plans would not be able to compete, because public health plans can impose price controls and shift costs to other plans. "The end result would be a federal government takeover of our healthcare system, taking decisions out of the hands of doctors and patients and placing them in the hands of a Washington bureaucracy," the senators wrote. The one Republican who didn't sign the letter was Olympia Snowe of Maine—who didn't like the public option, but was serious about negotiating a compromise plan with the Democrats.[4]

At times, the Republicans clearly were being egged on by outside interests, including providers and small businesses, and sometimes by conservative pundits and talk-show hosts. The South Carolina Medical Association reached a new low in June, with a letter to its members warning that "the federal government is kicking us down the road toward indentured servitude."[5] In July, the Medical Association of Georgia sent an alert to its members claiming the House bill "could result in the end of private practice medicine in the U.S."[6] And the National Federation of Independent Business circulated a letter that said the public option "would further compromise the viability of private insurance and would restrict choice to a single plan: the government-run plan."[7]

Meanwhile, Frank Luntz, the same Republican pollster who wrote the memo about the best antigovernment phrases to use against the bill, was coaching prominent conservatives on the best language to use to turn people against the public option. "If you call it a public option, the American people are split.

If you call it 'the government option,' the public is overwhelmingly against it," Luntz told Fox News commentator Sean Hannity in an August appearance on Hannity's nightly show.[8]

A lot of these critics were simply trying to scare the public about the government again—nothing more. The more serious theme in these criticisms, however, was the fear that private health plans wouldn't be strong enough to compete with the public option. It was a strange argument, because if the public option really turned out to be that popular, doesn't that mean people actually like government-run health care? The other political problem, however, was the way many Democrats and grassroots progressives started treating the public option as the only thing that mattered in health care reform. "Everything hangs on it," Charles Chamberlain, the political director for the progressive group Democracy for America, said during the height of the debate.[9]

Much of the fervor arose because some of the public option's most vocal supporters really would have preferred a single-payer system. In their minds, the public option was already a big step down from what they actually wanted. "We have compromised. We can compromise no more," Representative Lynn Woolsey of California, the cochair of the Progressive Caucus, said at a July rally at the Capitol.[10] Others were tired of the tactics of private insurance companies and wanted an alternative. And as polls throughout the summer showed the majority of Americans supported the public option, some Democrats insisted it was only a vocal minority that opposed the idea.

With all of the attention the public option got, it is easy to forget how few people ever would have dealt with it. The public option was only for people in the new health insurance exchanges—meaning people who couldn't get health coverage through the workplace or, in a few cases, people whose workplace coverage was too expensive. Even if you were excited about the public option and wanted to try it, you wouldn't have been able to if you already had coverage. And if you were scared that you would be forced into the public option, you had nothing to worry about. This was mainly for people who didn't have another source of health insurance. But for those people, the public option would have made their choices better than they would have been otherwise.

In all four of the committees that approved bills with the public option, Republican committee members tried, and failed, to eliminate the measure. For the Democrats, however, the bigger problem was the concerns coming from their own side. In the House Energy and Commerce Committee, for example, the centrist Blue Dogs had a strong presence, and they were worried about the public option because of their own experiences with Medicare. Many represented rural districts, and they thought Medicare's payment rates were too low for rural providers. Mike Ross, for example, said his district's providers had their Medicare payments cut so much that some were refusing to treat Medicare patients.[11]

In the Finance Committee, meanwhile, the Democratic side included a large enough group of centrists with their own concerns about the public option—including Kent Conrad of North Dakota, Blanche Lincoln of Arkansas, Tom Carper of Delaware, and Bill Nelson of Florida—that it had virtually no chance of getting through the committee. Instead, Kent tried to bridge the divide with a new idea: a system of federally chartered co-ops to compete with the private insurance plans.

There are examples of successful health care co-ops such as the Group Health Cooperative, a well-regarded, nonprofit health care system based in Seattle. But it was not an idea that had been circulating widely in the health care discussions before. Kent and his staff simply thought about North Dakota's experiences with cooperatives and came up with the idea of applying the model to health care.[12] This way, Kent argued, private health plans would still have new competition, but the competitors would not be run by the government.

It was a good effort, and a thoughtful way to try to find middle ground in an increasingly polarized fight. But it was no substitute for the public option. If health care co-ops had been the only element of competition in the final health care bill, as they ultimately were in the Finance Committee bill, they would have worked out reasonably well. But they would not have been strong enough competitors to bring down costs, improve quality, and give people better access to health care in the same way as the public option. In fact, the Congressional Budget Office concluded that the co-ops "seem unlikely to establish a significant market presence in many areas of the country."[13]

If it was not possible to pass the public option, there were other compromises that might have had a better impact. But that search would have to go on a while longer.

8 | PAYING FOR IT

From the beginning, Obama placed one major condition on health care reform: it had to be fully paid for. It could not just be an expensive new social program that added to the federal deficit. This was partly a matter of political necessity, because much of the country would likely ask the same question we asked of ourselves in those early transition discussions: Could the nation really afford to reform health care in the middle of an economic crisis?

If Americans thought the president was simply spending their money on a longtime Democratic goal, so soon after Congress had spent $700 billion to bail out Wall Street and $787 billion on the stimulus package, he would lose the broad support he had won in the election. But if the president and Congress could find a credible way to pay for the costs of expanding coverage, the public would be a lot more likely to support the package. And it would be a notable contrast to the way the Republicans handled the creation of the Medicare prescription drug program in 2003. They didn't offer a single dollar of savings or new revenues to pay for it.

The committees rose to the challenge, and they came up with ways to make sure the early costs of expanding coverage would be funded by the end of ten years. But the different political leanings of House and Senate Democrats were obvious in their choices of how to pay for the bill. Senate Democrats were more willing to raise money by taxing generous health care benefits, a step that could help control health care costs, but would put them in direct conflict with the labor unions. House Democrats preferred to fund the bill by raising taxes on high-income people, a step that Senate Democrats thought would make their party vulnerable to the old charges of "class warfare."

To raise the money for reform, the Senate relied heavily on a new, 40 percent tax on health insurance plans that are more generous than most people have—the so-called Cadillac health plans. This would be the first time that Congress would seriously confront the way the tax code has treated health insurance since World War II, in which health insurance through the workplace isn't taxed as income. Because of this tax break, the federal government is giving up roughly $133 billion each year in tax subsidies for employer-based health insurance.[1] In effect, the Senate was asking, should the taxpayers subsidize health plans that have more frills than most people need?

There is a very good argument to be made for taxing the Cadillac plans. Everyone needs to be protected from huge medical bills that would put health care out of their reach. But once you get above a certain level of coverage, you are basically just shielding people from the consequences of overusing health care. After all, the average workplace health plan in 2009 cost $4,824 for individuals and $13,375 for families—way below the levels that would have been exposed to the tax.[2]

Most of the people with the rich coverage will use their benefits wisely, but there will always be some who go to the doctor too many times, or don't ask enough questions about whether they really need that extra test. They're not thinking about, or may not be aware of, how the overuse of health care can drive up costs for everyone else. And, of course, many of the people who have the most generous health plans are the well-paid executives and investment bankers who don't need any more help from the taxpayers.

However, a lot of the people who have these plans aren't wealthy at all. They're union workers who have rich health benefits because their unions couldn't win pay raises for many years and started negotiating for better benefits instead. That's why labor leaders viewed the "Cadillac tax" as a tax increase on the middle class. And most House Democrats agreed with them, since they're generally more receptive to labor arguments than Senate Democrats. So the House didn't include the Cadillac tax in its bill, but more importantly, it made the Senate bill utterly unacceptable to House Democrats. Over the long run, the issue would become one of the biggest divides between the House and the Senate as they struggled to close in on a final deal.

The House, meanwhile, would have raised much of its money for reform by taxing Americans with the highest incomes. To most House Democrats, this was a better way to pay for health care reform than getting money from the middle class. They thought that people at these income levels should be easily able to carry the load. There were predictable attacks from House Republicans, but a sizeable group of Democrats also expressed concerns about paying for reform in this way. In a July letter, twenty-two first-term House Democrats warned House Speaker Nancy Pelosi that the tax would have hurt small businesses more than the bill writers had assumed, because small businesses owners often report their business income on their individual tax returns and nearly two-thirds of all taxpayers with incomes over $250,000 are small business entrepreneurs.[3]

The House leadership tried to lessen this problem by making the tax kick in higher up the income scale. By the time the bill came to the House floor, it had a flat 5.4 percent tax that applied only to individuals with incomes over $500,000 and couples with incomes over $1 million. It still would have been, by far, the major funding source for the House bill, raising $460 billion over ten years.[4]

Just as the Cadillac tax was a nonstarter with House Democrats, the tax on the wealthy was a nonstarter with their Senate counterparts. In part, this is because the balance of power among Senate Democrats is closer to the political center than it is in the House. Senate Democrats have always been more worried about Republican charges of "class warfare," especially those who have to depend on Republican support to get elected. But they were also right on an important point: the Cadillac tax was a better funding source if Congress was concerned about reducing health care costs. It would have raised money, but it also would have encouraged employers and employees to look for lower-cost health coverage that wouldn't be taxed.

The other major political battle, this time between Democrats and Republicans, was over the decision to fund a lot of the reform bill with spending reductions from Medicare. It's a political nightmare when opponents can accuse you of cutting Medicare and hurting senior citizens. That is exactly the charge that Republicans made, over and over again. But in reality, the savings were carefully designed to come from places where senior citizens never should have noticed a difference.

The Senate, for example, would have saved $182 billion over ten years by increasing Medicare payments to doctors, hospitals, and other providers more slowly. The idea was that the providers should be expected to become more efficient in how they provide many of their services.[5] The danger in reducing provider payments, however, is that if you cut too deeply, they might stop seeing your patients. That is what has happened with Medicaid, and while it's not true to the same degree with Medicare, the complaints that Medicare doesn't pay providers enough—particularly in rural areas—were the reason so many of the House Blue Dog Democrats were so skeptical about the public option.

But the Medicare Payment Advisory Commission has found that Medicare's payment rates are actually high enough for most providers, with little evidence that large numbers of seniors have trouble finding doctors. And while the payments are not covering the costs of all hospitals, the chairman of the commission told a House subcommittee that they are "adequate to cover the costs of efficient hospitals"—the ones that do the best on controlling costs while still providing high-quality health care.[6] In other words, there should be room to tighten the payments without making seniors' health care worse.

There definitely was room to tighten the payments in another area of Medicare: the private plans known as Medicare Advantage, which contract with the federal government to provide Medicare services and often extra benefits. The thinking behind allowing private plans to provide Medicare services was that they should be able to do it more efficiently than the usual fee-for-service system. But as the use of private plans has expanded, it hasn't proven more efficient at all. In fact, in 2009, the federal government's payments to Medicare Advantage plans cost about $11 billion more than it would have spent to provide the same services under traditional Medicare.[7]

The idea was to go after the wasteful payments, not to deprive seniors of basic health care. But it was portrayed as an assault on senior citizens. Republicans and outside interest groups charged that the Democrats wanted to "cut Medicare" to pay for reform. "How can we justify dipping into funds for seniors' care," Senate Minority Whip Jon Kyl of Arizona asked in a July radio address, "to pay for a new government plan?"[8]

Cutting wasteful payments, however, is not the same thing as "dipping into funds for seniors' care." It's possible, as the Congressional Budget Office would later conclude, that the lower payment rates would have forced the plans to offer fewer extra benefits that aren't covered by traditional Medicare. So if seniors were worried about these extras, such as vision or dental care, they might feel that they were losing something under the new payment system. But they would not have lost their basic Medicare benefits. They certainly would not have faced "long waits for care" or expensive tests such as MRIs and CT scans, and they would not "lose their own doctors," as the 60 Plus Association, a group that bills itself as the conservative alternative to AARP, charged in one TV ad.[9]

Another big source of savings was possible only because of the agreement the hospitals had reached with the White House, in which they would accept payment cuts in return for expanded coverage (and no more cuts down the road). Both the House and the Senate would have scaled back on the special payments to safety-net hospitals that are known as "disproportionate share hospital" payments. As the name implies, these are hospitals that serve an unusually large number of low-income patients. They get extra payments to make up for all of the uninsured patients they treat. But because the hospitals expected health care reform to cut way down on the number of uninsured patients who would need their help, they agreed to accept lower payments. The cuts would only happen after the number of uninsured people had actually fallen under certain levels, a measure to reassure the hospitals that they wouldn't be hurt in the process.

One can find flaws with any of the measures the Senate and the House proposed to pay for health care reform, and many critics have. But it was a remarkable accomplishment that lawmakers were able to rise to the challenge at all. For all of their efforts to create a health care reform bill that paid for itself, though, Obama and Congress never quite escaped the suspicion from much of the public that they were spending too much on health care reform, at a time when the nation could not afford expensive new programs. This suspicion would add to a growing sense of public unease about the effort—even as the president and Congress were getting closer to the goal than anyone ever had.

9 | ONE BIPARTISAN SOLUTION

With so many complex health care issues at stake, and so many multilayered solutions in the House and Senate bills, it might seem impossible that Democrats and Republicans could ever find common ground. But that's only true if you looked at the hard-line positions lawmakers were staking out in Congress. Outside the halls of the Capitol, there was a unique project, which I was privileged to be involved in, that fit all the pieces together in a way that both parties could support. It produced exactly what the White House and Congress were struggling to achieve: a health care reform plan that was both comprehensive and bipartisan. And for all of its political trade-offs, the proposal wasn't all that different from the bills the Democrats were trying to pass.

It was the reform plan negotiated by four former Senate majority leaders, including myself, for a health care project organized by the Bipartisan Policy Center. This was an organization I had cofounded back in 2007 with the other three former majority leaders—Bob Dole and Howard Baker, both Republicans, and George Mitchell, a Democrat—to produce consensus solutions to difficult policy problems. By June 2009, we had a health care plan to recommend to Congress and the public. As frustrating and difficult as it was at times, it was also a truly satisfying project because it proved that, when experienced lawmakers from both parties truly want to solve the health care problem, no disagreements are too great to stop them.

In April 2008, we had launched the Leaders' Project on the State of American Health Care, an effort to find bipartisan solutions to the problems of cost, access, quality, and financing in our health care sector. We held four forums around the country to gather ideas from health care stakeholders, and our goal was to propose a plan that could be a model for Congress. I had left the project when I became the Health and Human Services nominee, but it was a satisfying project to return to when I rejoined the private sector. We had two of the best policy advisers both parties had to offer: Chris Jennings, who had been Bill Clinton's health care adviser in the 1990s, and Mark McClellan, who had headed the Medicare and Medicaid programs and the Food and Drug Administration under George W. Bush.

Best of all, we had four experienced legislative leaders, all of whom had been through the same kinds of negotiations Congress now faced, and who were determined to prove that a bipartisan solution was possible. On the Republican side, Bob and Howard were both genuinely committed to finding a package all of us could recommend to Congress. And while George could not stay until the end of the project—he joined the administration in January 2009 as the special envoy to the Middle East—his help was invaluable in getting us far enough to negotiate the final package.

The plan had four "pillars": promote high-value and high-quality care, provide health coverage that's affordable and easy to get, emphasize personal responsibility and healthy choices, and come up with a sustainable way to pay for all of it. Of these pillars, the one about access to health coverage probably would have been the most recognizable to members of Congress. It would have set up health care exchanges in each state, or in regional groups of states in some cases, with the Department of Health and Human Services setting up exchanges in any state that didn't do so. Health insurance companies would have been required to accept everyone who applies for coverage, regardless of how healthy he or she was. And to make sure people didn't take advantage of that rule by skipping coverage until they were sick, the plan would have required everyone to buy health coverage.[1]

To promote high-value and high-quality care, the plan called for more investments in health information technology. It suggested boosting funds for the development of better quality measures, especially those that can be narrowed down to a particular patient or one "episode" of care, such as an illness or an injury. The plan called for phasing in bundled payments, once there was enough evidence that they worked, and setting up accountable care organizations that would get to keep some of the money they saved. And it suggested ways to use and refine comparative effectiveness research—the very subject that caused so many cries of "rationing" during the congressional debate.[2]

To encourage people to be responsible for their health, the plan offered ways to enforce the requirement that everyone get health coverage. These included tax penalties for people who didn't buy health insurance, which was the mechanism Congress used. But there were also other suggestions, such as automatically enrolling people in basic coverage when they started a new job and creating a "fair share" fee to help pay for the uncompensated care for people who chose not to get health coverage.[3]

Finally, we wanted to suggest ways to pay for the long-term costs of expanding health coverage, just as Congress had to design a reform package that would pay its own way. Although the Finance Committee bill would not be released until about three months after we had announced our plan, there were a lot of similarities between the committee's solutions and ours. For example, the Bipartisan Policy Center plan would have trimmed the Medicare Advantage payment rates to make them closer to traditional Medicare, scaled back Medicare provider payments as the providers became more efficient, and cut back on payments to disproportionate-share hospitals as more people gained health coverage.

In any real negotiation between the two parties, both sides have to give things away. I certainly did to reach an agreement with Bob and Howard. The Cadillac tax was one major example, given how strongly labor unions opposed it. Another was the nature of the exchanges. I had a strong preference for a national exchange, not a series of state-based ones. If you want to make sure people in every state have a well-run exchange—with enough health insurance options, adequate benefits, and regulators who are committed to making the arrangement work—you can do that much more easily with a national exchange.

A national exchange is also likely to have lower administrative costs than a collection of state-based exchanges, and it would be easier for consumers to find and use. But as Republicans, Bob and Howard wanted to keep a stronger role for the states, which have usually regulated health insurance. So we agreed to let the states run the exchanges, with some regional exchanges if that was their preference.

We also included a nod to one of the Republicans' top goals: reforming medical liability laws to limit lawsuits. This isn't likely to have a huge impact on containing health care costs. At most, the Congressional Budget Office believes it could make a small contribution, reducing U.S. health care spending by about 0.5 percent, or $11 billion.[4] But because it was so important to Bob and Howard, we threw in a carefully worded statement that medical liability reform "is an important part of improving health care value, and should be carefully considered in the context of health care reform."[5]

The biggest trade-off, from my end, was the public option. This led a lot of progressives to accuse me of giving up too much, especially when some of the early coverage erroneously suggested that I was pushing the administration to drop it.[6] In reality, I felt so strongly about the need for the public option that it was the last issue we decided. I held out as long as I could, trying to convince Bob and Howard that a national public plan was the key to making so many other things work. But the public option was too much to ask of them. They believed, as virtually all Republicans did, that the public option would lead to too much federal involvement in health care.

Instead, we endorsed the best compromise we could come up with. The states would be able to set up plans to compete with private insurers, and if the states had not improved their health coverage rates or costs after five years, the president would send Congress a proposal for a federal plan, which it would consider under special fast-track rules.[7] It was not what I wanted, by any means, but it would have at least preserved an element of competition with private insurers. And it was better than letting the entire effort die because of one issue.

So what did the Democrats get for these concessions? Remarkably, we won a plan that accepted the basic framework of Obama's campaign plan, and of the bills that were starting to emerge in Congress—particularly in the Finance Committee. In our plan, the Republicans endorsed new federal rules requiring insurers to accept everyone who applies, forcing them to cover pre-existing conditions, and banning them from charging higher premiums for people with health problems.

The Republicans agreed to require everyone to get health insurance—the step needed to make those other rules work—and to provide tax credits to help low-income and middle-income people pay the premiums. And they signed on to the approach of setting up health care exchanges, with standardized coverage options and minimum benefits, so individuals and small businesses would have a more rational market where they could get their health insurance.

Until the very end, it was not clear that we would be able to reach an agreement at all. Even so, it seems that it was still easier for Democrats and Republicans outside of Congress to reach an agreement than it was for those who were in Congress. Part of the reason, I believe, is that we were free from a lot of the political pressures you face when you're serving there. It is hard to overstate the amount of peer pressure you feel from your colleagues, whether you are in the majority or in the minority, not to give an inch to the other side. If you're in the majority, you believe you were given the majority for a reason, and anyone who concedes too much to the other side is a bad negotiator. If you're in the minority, you think that helping the other side is a sure way to stay in the minority.

But there was also a broader reason, one that says a lot about why the debate in Congress took the direction it did. When we released our plan, the bipartisan Gang of Six talks were getting underway in the Senate Finance Committee. Our recommendations were very much along the lines of what the Democrats and Republicans in that group were discussing. And if those talks had succeeded in producing a bipartisan plan, it might have looked even more like our proposal than the bill that eventually emerged. But as the summer dragged on, the protests on the right would become louder, and the Republicans in the Finance Committee would feel enormous pressure not to cooperate with any effort that might lead to "rationing" or "government-run health care."

When the Gang of Six talks began, the political environment might have allowed them to reach the same kind of bipartisan bill that we did. But by the end of the summer, the environment would change—and the goal of a bipartisan bill would be completely out of reach.

10 | ROADBLOCKS

By mid-July, three committees had approved health care bills in rapid succession—one in the Senate, two in the House. But it appeared that this might be the only progress we would see for a while. The other two committees were getting bogged down, with no quick resolution in sight. In the Senate Finance Committee, Max Baucus and the Gang of Six were still talking through ways to trim the cost of their health care bill and find the elusive balance that both parties could accept. And in the House Energy and Commerce Committee, Henry Waxman faced the real possibility of a rebellion within his own party if he could not satisfy the concerns of the Blue Dogs.

Waxman had started talking to the Blue Dogs on his committee, headed by Mike Ross, the leader of the group's health care task force. Ross and the other Blue Dogs thought the bill went too far in expanding the federal government role, particularly with the public option, and didn't do enough to cut costs. To me, these arguments contradicted each other, since the public option would have cut costs. And in Waxman's view, the Blue Dogs simply wanted to wait for the Senate bill, which they expected to be more moderate, and bypass the House entirely.

According to Waxman, the Blue Dogs' biggest concern was that they didn't want to be "Btu-ed." Among House Democrats, this is shorthand for saying they don't want to take a risky vote and then be abandoned by the president. It refers to an incident during Bill Clinton's presidency, when the House, at Clinton's urging, passed a budget bill that included a Btu tax, an energy tax based on the heat content of fuels. It was a politically unpopular tax that would have hit many middle-class people, and it was dropped from the final version of the bill, largely because the Senate didn't want it—making many House Democrats feel that they had gone out on a limb for nothing. This time, the Blue Dogs didn't want to vote for politically controversial proposals, such as the public option, that they believed would not be in the final bill anyway.[1]

Soon, Waxman got help from the highest levels. On Tuesday, July 21, Obama met with Waxman and the Blue Dogs at the White House to try to talk through the sticking points. Obama was "like a referee," Ross recalls, trying to listen equally to both sides' points and help the compromise come faster. He also thought Obama and Rahm Emanuel, who also participated in the meeting, both understood how hard it would be to sell such an ambitious health care plan in rural districts. But there were a lot of sticking points, and Obama was closer to the Blue Dogs on some issues and to Waxman on others.

The president, for example, liked the idea of an independent board to suggest ways to hold down Medicare costs. The Blue Dogs had strongly favored the board as an additional mechanism to put the brakes on health care spending, but Waxman thought the board would take away too many decisions that should be made by Congress. He told Obama, however, that he would be willing to give ground on the issue if the Blue Dogs really wanted it. (By that point, the Blue Dogs were less interested, because providers were complaining that it could force cuts in their payments.) However, both Obama and Waxman wanted a public option, and they wanted its payments to be based on Medicare rates. Ross didn't want a public option, and if it was necessary to keep it in the bill, the last thing he wanted was for the payment rates to be as low as Medicare's.[2]

During this time, the Energy and Commerce Committee stopped its work on the bill. Waxman and the Blue Dogs met with a rotating cast of leaders and White House officials, including Nancy Pelosi, Steny Hoyer, and Rahm Emanuel. By the end of the week, they seemed to be closing in on an agreement that might include a public option, but with payment rates that were negotiated with providers, and possibly the independent Medicare board. The Medicare board dropped out of the proposal quickly, though, after provider groups lashed out because they didn't want their payments cut.[3] To me, the episode proves why the cost-control decisions need to be taken out of the hands of Congress. If providers can get their way every time they're worried about lower payments, we will never get the escalating costs of health care under control.

On Friday, the talks nearly collapsed. Waxman, frustrated at the seemingly never-ending talks with the Blue Dogs, threatened to bypass his own committee and take the bill straight to the House floor if the Blue Dogs continued to oppose it.[4] He was annoyed at the Blue Dogs, who were still publicly threatening to side with the Republicans against the bill, and he thought their increasingly hard-line negotiating tactics weren't getting the talks anywhere.[5] It was the kind of breakdown that can happen at the end of a long week in Congress. But it was also an ominous sign that history might repeat itself—that Energy and Commerce, once again, might be the "graveyard" of health care reform. And most, if not all, of the fifty-two Blue Dogs would have been more likely to retaliate by voting against the bill on the floor. Pelosi could not afford to lose that many votes.

Fortunately, both Waxman and Ross took a breath and realized they could not let health care reform end that way. Toward the end of the day, they got back together, shook hands, and promised to keep talking. The experience gave the two a better understanding of each other's concerns and pressures. "I get it. I couldn't get twenty percent of the vote in his district, and he couldn't get twenty percent of the vote in mine," said Ross.[6] But the Energy and Commerce Committee had lost a week of precious time, with more difficult talks still to come, as Democrats tried to find common ground on their own top priority. The biggest impact of the delay went almost unnoticed at the time. It was now virtually impossible that the full House would be able to vote on a health care bill before the August recess, which would start in just one week.

In fact, it would be enough of a challenge just to get Energy and Commerce to approve a bill before the recess. But the next week, on Wednesday, July 29, Waxman and the Blue Dogs finally struck their deal. The Blue Dogs would accept a public option in the bill, but in return, Waxman agreed that its payments would not be based on Medicare rates. They would be negotiated with the providers just like private insurance payments. This would lessen the concerns the Blue Dogs had about providers being underpaid, though it also meant the public option probably would have less leverage to bring costs down.

The Blue Dogs did not get the independent Medicare cost-cutting board, but they did get a change that would free more small businesses from the requirement to provide health coverage. Under the original bill, they would have had to cover their workers or pay a fee—the "play or pay" rule—unless their annual payroll was less than $250,000. Now, Waxman agreed to exempt all businesses with payroll under $500,000.[7] In practical terms, that meant most businesses would not have to worry about the coverage requirement.[8]

Finally, Waxman seemed to have found a way to get past the wall of opposition in his committee. Unfortunately, it wasn't that simple. The liberal Democrats on the committee had to sign off on the agreement, too, and they didn't like what they saw. They thought the public option had been so watered down that it would not have been of much use. They didn't like the Blue Dogs' efforts to tighten the subsidies for people who needed help buying insurance.[9] And they wondered why the Democrats, whose health care priorities had been endorsed by the voters in two back-to-back elections, needed to bend so far to accommodate the views of a small group of centrists. The practical reality, though, was that Waxman's committee would not have been able to approve anything without the Blue Dogs. The only way to hold all of the Democrats together, Waxman decided, was to add some more progressive priorities so the liberals would be happier with the rewritten bill.

Late that Thursday, July 30, Waxman and Dingell met with several of the progressives to see what could be done to bring them back on board. It was Dingell who made the most impassioned plea to the progressives. Don't let this opportunity slip away, he said. You may not like some of the trade-offs, but there are only going to be more down the road when the House negotiates with the Senate. If anything, he said, this bill is the high-water mark. And Dingell reminded the progressives of the failure that still haunted him from his days as chairman. It was right here, in the Energy and Commerce Committee, where Bill Clinton's health care reform effort fell apart in 1994. That could not happen again.[10]

By Friday, the last day before the House was scheduled to leave before the August recess, Waxman had reached his deal with the progressives. They would get to add new restrictions on how much health insurance plans could raise premiums. And, in a significant victory, the bill would be rewritten to use the federal government's purchasing power to negotiate lower drug prices in the Medicare program. The savings would be used to restore some of the subsidies for buying health insurance.[11] The changes infuriated the Pharmaceutical

Research and Manufacturers of America, because the drug negotiation language was a violation of its deal with the White House—in which it would contribute $80 billion in savings over ten years and support the reform effort, but only if the bill didn't include negotiated drug prices. The group demanded, and received, an acknowledgement from the White House that it had made the deal with PhRMA.[12] But Henry Waxman's view was that since he wasn't there at the bargaining table, he had no deal with PhRMA.[13]

On Friday, July 31, the Energy and Commerce Committee approved the health care bill. The vote was 31–28, with five Democrats joining all of the Republicans in voting against it. Three Blue Dogs opposed the bill, but the rest—including Mike Ross—supported it. Henry Waxman had done what he needed to do. This time, the Energy and Commerce Committee had not been the "graveyard" of health care reform. It overcame its differences and produced a bill—a crucial milestone that proved Congress was already closer to achieving the goal than it had been in the 1990s.

There was, however, one last committee that had to approve a health care bill, and it did not seem to be getting any closer to the finish line. The Senate Finance Committee was still holding its Gang of Six talks, the closed-door negotiations to try to produce a bipartisan bill. Max Baucus, Jeff Bingaman, and Kent Conrad were negotiating for the Democrats, while Chuck Grassley, Mike Enzi, and Olympia Snowe were representing the Republicans. There was one significant absence from the group: Jay Rockefeller of West Virginia, the Democratic chairman of the Finance health subcommittee. Rockefeller was annoyed that he wasn't invited, and as the subcommittee chairman, he probably had a right to be annoyed. But Baucus had decided that the other Democrats were more likely than Rockefeller, an outspoken progressive, to be able to work successfully with the other side.

Other progressives, however, thought Rockefeller's absence spoke volumes about the direction the talks were taking. One of them was Sherrod Brown of Ohio, a down-to-earth populist who thought the Democrats' best chance for success on health care was to "show whose side you're on." His view was that the Democrats should push hard for progressive priorities, including the public option, and apply whatever pressure was needed to make sure the centrist Democrats supported them. Brown was a member of the Health, Education,

Labor, and Pensions Committee, which had pushed the envelope to make its bill as progressive as possible—including generous subsidies to help newly insured people pay their health premiums.

But as Brown looked at the makeup of the Gang of Six, he was convinced that nothing good could come out of the talks. Without Rockefeller? With Republicans such as Chuck Grassley, Mike Enzi, and, at one point, Orrin Hatch? Brown just didn't see it. To him, the way Max Baucus and Chris Dodd talked about their goals was telling. In meetings of the Senate Democratic caucus, Baucus would say, "My first goal is a bipartisan bill." Dodd would say, "My first goal is a good bill." Baucus could chase the bipartisan bill as long as he wanted, in Brown's view, and the Republicans would never give it to him unless they got everything they wanted.[14]

That was not Olympia Snowe's view. If the public could have seen what went on inside the Gang of Six talks, she said, they would have been heartened by the process. The senators got deep into the weeds of the policies, getting staff briefings and PowerPoint presentations on what was likely to work and what was not—focusing on the policies rather than the politics, just as Americans say they want their public servants to do. They held conference calls with governors about how an expansion of Medicaid would affect their states and talked with other stakeholders about the likely impact of other proposals. There were many factors Snowe wanted to consider: how to make sure people could really afford health insurance, what the impact on small businesses would be, how to make sure the new health exchanges worked, what kind of budget burdens the states would face if they had to add more people to their Medicaid programs. When outsiders criticized the Gang of Six for taking so long, Snowe would just laugh: "Well, then, people don't really understand the nature of health care."[15]

The longer the talks went on, however, the more obvious it became that the Senate—like the House—was not going to make Obama's deadline of passing a bill by the August recess, much to the president's private frustration. This is where Harry Reid proved his commitment to letting committee chairmen work on their bills at their own pace. Harry and I had different styles as Senate majority leader. I tried to give committee chairmen as much freedom as possible, but I did step in and force action when I felt that time was running out. Harry's preference, however, is to give the committee chairmen the time and space that they feel they need. And I believe the committee chairmen appreciate Harry for not imposing heavy-handed instructions on their work.

However, the result was that on July 23, Harry had to acknowledge the Senate would not make the August deadline. The Republicans in the Gang of Six had asked for more time, he told reporters, and "I don't think it's unreasonable. This is a complex, difficult issue. . . . It's better to have a product that is one based on quality and thoughtfulness."[16] It was hard to argue with the logic of the decision. No one wanted a rushed health care bill. And yet, it meant that the entire month of August would be a news vacuum, with no forward movement on health care—just lots of cable news airtime to be filled by the opponents of reform.

The talks continued. The public option was clearly out, to be replaced by Kent Conrad's co-ops idea. The six were spending much of their time talking about other topics: how to be sure the benefit levels in the health exchange plans were adequate, how to make sure they were affordable, what insurance market rules needed to be fixed, and how to pay for the package. But on July 29, two events set off a brief round of speculation that the gang might finally be close to a deal. One was a front-page headline in *The Washington Post* that declared, "Senators Close to Health Accord"—a level of optimism that went a bit farther than the actual story.[17] The other was an interview Chuck Grassley gave on NPR that morning, in which he suggested the group was "on the edge" of an agreement. "Will we get it done so we can get a bill to the other members by this weekend, because there is a certain time you've got to give people to study it? We're on the edge, and almost there."[18]

If there was any doubt about the pressure within the Republican Party not to reach a deal, their reaction to those news reports erased it. The Republicans complained so loudly that Baucus, at their request, knocked down the stories. "While progress has been made in recent days, neither an accord nor an announcement is imminent," Russ Sullivan, the Finance Committee's Democratic staff director, wrote in an e-mail to Finance Committee senators.[19]

Grassley even backtracked a bit on a conference call with reporters later that day: "You could have a hundred or two hundred or three hundred subsets of Medicare reform, and we've probably got ninety-five percent of them decided," Grassley said. "But I mean, I'm saying out of the total number of things you've got to make decisions on, but the five percent that are left are very difficult, and I can't say that we're on the edge of getting them decided, but we're making some progress by inches."[20] If there were a true desire to get a bipartisan agreement—not just by Grassley and Snowe, but by the rest of the Senate Republicans as well—no one should have been defensive about how close the deal was.

Just before the August recess, Baucus finally set a deadline for the Gang of Six. By September 15, he told the group, the full Finance Committee would get started on the bill—with or without Republican support. This irritated Snowe, who thought it was more important to sort carefully through the bill's complexities than to be pressured by "arbitrary deadlines."[21] But even by letting the talks go on this long, Baucus was allowing the bill to slip way past Obama's original deadline of holding a vote in the full Senate before the recess.

He was also making other Democratic senators nervous. The Democrats now had the sixty votes they needed to break a Republican filibuster. But every day made it obvious how fragile their hold on those sixty votes was. Two senators, Ted Kennedy and Robert Byrd of West Virginia, were in failing health, and others were elderly and could be stricken by serious health problems at any time. "You can't act like you've got forever," said Sherrod Brown.[22]

Obama, however, was unable to speed the talks along. During the last week before the recess, he met with Senate Democrats at the White House and later got a briefing from the Gang of Six. At both sessions, the president encouraged the senators to keep at it. But just as the Democrats had allowed health care reform to stall out in 1993—giving its opponents time to confuse and scare the public—they were allowing it to stall out once again, throughout the entire month of August.

The opponents were ready.

11 | AUGUST

On the first weekend in August, viewers of cable news saw a disturbing sight. Representative Lloyd Doggett, a fiery progressive from Texas, was being chased down by angry, shouting crowds after a meeting with constituents in his Austin district. It was supposed to be an "office hours" meeting, where Doggett would answer questions one-on-one at a Randalls grocery store in southwest Austin. In the past, these kinds of sessions only drew a handful of people.

This time, however, Doggett was surrounded by protesters loudly attacking the health care bill. They shouted questions that clearly weren't designed to get answers, such as "How in the world can you sign and pass bills without ever reading them?"[1] When he tried to leave, they followed him out to the parking lot and surrounded him again. "Just say no!" they chanted, and waved signs with antigovernment slogans: "No Government Counselor in My Home!" "No Socialized Healthcare!" One woman held up a photo of Doggett defaced with a pair of devil's horns. Another protester carried a tombstone with his name on it.[2]

It was an intense scene, but also a strange one, given where it took place. Austin is not exactly a hotbed of antigovernment activism. It has Republicans and libertarians, but it is better known as the most Democratic city in Texas. In Travis County, where Austin is located, Obama won 64 percent of the presidential vote in 2008, and John Kerry won 56 percent in 2004 against Texas's own former governor, George W. Bush.[3] So it was a bit suspicious that the citizens of Austin would suddenly rise up in protest against health care reform.

Sure enough, a blog post by the chair of the Travis County Republican

Party had encouraged people to show up for the Doggett gathering.[4] "BE LOUD! NO GOVERNMENT HEALTHCARE!" Rosemary Edwards, the Travis County Republican Party chair, wrote on her blog. "Get the word out to all your Patriot friends to SHOW UP, STAND UP and SPEAK UP!"[5] The bigger role, however, may have been played by the Austin Tea Party, which runs a Meetup group and continues to display videos of the Doggett showdown on its Web site. According to the Web site, the group is affiliated with Americans for Prosperity, a conservative advocacy group that urged its members to attend town hall meetings throughout the country.[6] The group's foundation also launched an organization called Patients United Now, which tells its supporters that the health care bill could deny care to the old and sick and could force them to lose their private insurance.[7]

Soon, the airwaves were filled with images of loud, disruptive protests against the bill at Democratic town hall meetings throughout the country. Representative Frank Kratovil, a Maryland Democrat, was hanged in effigy at one rally. In Florida, fights broke out at a forum where Representative Kathy Castor tried to speak.[8] Poor Arlen Specter, who had just switched from the GOP to the Democratic Party, got the treatment twice. He got it once at a forum with Kathleen Sebelius, where audience members howled and booed as he listed the problems with the current health care marketplace, and once at his own town hall meeting, where a man screamed in his face, "One day God's going to stand before you and he's going to judge you and the rest of your damned cronies up on the Hill, and then you'll get your just deserts."[9] Even John Dingell—the man who had presided over the House when it passed the original Medicare bill, had seniors turn their backs on him at a town hall where he promised that "Medicare will be here to take care of you."[10]

Much has been written about these town halls and what they really represented. Were they real grassroots anger, or were they "AstroTurf"—manufactured anger organized by political operatives? My own view is that there were elements of both, and each reinforced the other. Yes, most of the people at these town halls probably were constituents with real, if misinformed, fears about the health care bill. Even if the local Tea Party organizers helped to round up bigger crowds—as they did with Doggett's meeting in Austin, and as they did with Dingell's town hall in Michigan[11]—they themselves are constituents and had the right to be heard. Often their behavior did not help their case, but even people with no manners have the right to take their frustrations to their elected officials.

And yet, it is hard to escape the conclusion that far-right activists and operatives were egging them on. Americans for Prosperity claimed it always urged its supporters to be courteous, but it definitely encouraged its members to bring their health care protests to town hall meetings and House and Senate members' offices. It even organized a "Hands Off My Health Care" bus tour that visited Bristol, Virginia, in July to protest as Obama gave a health care speech there.[12]

The other group that was actively encouraging turnout was FreedomWorks, a conservative advocacy group that promotes tax cuts and limited government. FreedomWorks posted an interactive map on its Web site to help supporters find town hall meetings, as well as a downloadable "August Recess Action Kit" full of false talking points. It claimed, for example, that "Proposed cost controls are another way of saying rationed health care"—when the true goal, of course, was to cut down on the wasteful spending that is driving up costs for all of us.[13] One activist even circulated a memo encouraging town hall audience members to "yell out and challenge the Rep's statements early" to "make him feel uneasy early on" and "rattle him."[14]

Representative Steve Kagen of Wisconsin, an allergy specialist whose family has been in medicine for seven generations, concluded that at least some of the anger was manufactured when he was booed and shouted down during a town hall meeting in Green Bay. "There were operatives in there who were trying to confuse people and disrupt the meeting, and they succeeded," Kagen recalls. But he also thought that many people had been told for so long that government was incompetent that they didn't question it anymore.

So Kagen gave them a quick refresher course. He asked the audience to raise their hands if they knew anyone who had polio. No one did. Then he asked them if they knew anyone with smallpox. No one did. Both diseases, of course, have been wiped out in the United States—and smallpox has been eliminated worldwide—because of government vaccination programs. These were examples, he said, of how good government can accomplish tasks that are far too big for people to take on themselves.[15]

There was also an element of media hype to the protests. Yes, there was real and disruptive anger at many events. But at others, a few protesters dominated the coverage far beyond their actual numbers. I saw this firsthand when I took part in a panel discussion on the health care effort at Northern State University in Aberdeen, South Dakota, on August 18. Our discussion inside the theater, sponsored by South Dakota Public Broadcasting and AARP, was completely civil. I fielded complaints about the complexity of the bill, but we also talked about serious issues such as end-of-life care. Outside, though, there was a handful protesters who complained about "socialism," and one woman even carried a sign: "Tired of Tom." Sure enough, it was the protesters who dominated the news coverage.[16]

Still, by that point, we had reached an ominous turning point in the debate. Those who supported health care reform, in the White House and in Congress, were on defense. In my experience, you only win big political changes when you stay on offense. Once you are on defense, success becomes much harder. The reform side certainly had its own organizers who were mobilizing supporters to go to the town halls. Organizing for America, the mass mobilization operation that had begun as the organizing arm of Obama's presidential campaign, notified its supporters of town halls in their area. And Health Care for America Now, a coalition of progressive groups that had been formed to back the reform effort, ran pro-reform television ads and helped supporters find local events.[17] Overall, the supporters of health care reform had better mobilization efforts than they did in the 1990s.

But somehow, the energy and excitement on the pro-reform side seemed to have been lost. Sherrod Brown argues that progressives had become so turned off by the Gang of Six talks, and the likely compromises that would come as a result, that they lost their enthusiasm.[18] Whatever the cause, we were losing the battle for public opinion. People were hearing so many misleading statements, and even flat-out lies, that their confidence in health care reform had been shaken.

The most notorious, of course, was the claim that the House bill would have created "death panels." The term came from Sarah Palin, but the claim itself came from Betsy McCaughey, the former lieutenant governor of New York, who declared that the House bill called for a "required counseling session" for everyone on Medicare that would "tell them how to end their life sooner."[19] McCaughey had pulled this kind of stunt before, circulating misinformation about the 1990s health care plan, but somehow her newest charge still caught on. In reality, the original House bill simply said that people could talk to their doctors about end-of-life care and Medicare would pay for it.[20]

Because of all of the controversy, the House later rewrote that part of its bill to include the word *voluntary* in as many different places as possible.[21] And the Senate chose not to deal with the end-of-life-care issue at all. But somehow, the charge stuck, even though it was thoroughly debunked as soon as it came out. Olympia Snowe discovered, to her dismay, that some of her constituents thought the Gang of Six bill would include death panels and tax increases. She had to explain to them that the Gang of Six was writing a completely different bill, regardless of whatever they might have heard about the House bill. "That was a prescription for disaster," she said. "It eroded, I think, the foundation of credibility for the direction we were taking."[22]

This could not continue. If the reform effort was to get back on track, I believed we needed a resetting of the debate, complete with an effective debunking of the lies. On August 21, I met with Obama for lunch at the White House and took up the issue with him directly. After all that had happened during the summer, you might think the president would have been worn down. Actually, though, he struck me as fairly upbeat under the circumstances. He joked that August just wasn't his month. After all, in August 2007, he was down in the polls and looking for a way to salvage his race for the Democratic presidential nomination. At the end of August 2008, John McCain got a boost in the polls from the Republican convention and his selection of Sarah Palin as his running mate. In both cases, the situation turned around in September—especially in 2008, when McCain quickly lost the ground he had gained. This year, Obama said, things will get better in September, too.

Behind the scenes, in the heat of the media coverage of these town hall meetings, Obama had been talking with his closest advisers about how to get the effort back on track. There was no disagreement with his assessment of the need for bold reform. But some of his advisers were arguing for cutting his political losses and seeking consensus on a smaller bill. Obama rejected that advice. "That may be where we have to end up," he told his advisers, "but we do not have to make that decision now." He was not prepared to give up the fight for comprehensive reform.

My general message to Obama that day was that it was time to reset the debate, and that he had the most power to do that, through an address to a joint session of Congress when it returned in September. I don't believe this advice was unique. I believe lots of people in his inner circle were telling him the same thing. It was the conclusion many people were coming to at that time. And to his credit, this is exactly what he did. It would be just what the debate needed.

There was one more event in August that seemed to symbolize the mood of the health care debate. Late in the night of August 25, Ted Kennedy died at his home in Hyannis Port. The man who had led the Senate battles for better health care for so many years, and who had called health care "the cause of my life," had lost his long battle with brain cancer. The fact that we all knew this day would come did not make his death any less devastating. I felt especially bad for Vicki Kennedy, knowing all she must have gone through in his last months. And I will always be grateful for the generosity she and Ted showed by helping Greg in his own time of need.

We will never know what difference his presence might have made if he had been able to help lead this last health care debate. But I can tell you that his life held lessons for those who had to carry on the fight. At his funeral in the Basilica of Our Lady of Perpetual Help in Boston, Ted Kennedy Jr. told a story of how he and his father decided to go sledding after Ted Jr. had lost a leg to cancer. As they got close to the hill, Ted Jr. fell on the ice and decided he would never be able to climb the hill. It's too hard, he told his father. I'll never make it.

Gently, Ted Kennedy told his son not to give up. "I know you can do it," he said. "There is nothing that you can't do. We're going to climb that hill together, even if it takes us all day."

It was a powerful message at this moment in the health care debate. Those who were fighting for reform were trying to climb a hill, too—a hill so steep no one had managed it in seventy years. It would have been easy for members of Congress to decide it was too hard, especially after all of the grief they had taken at the town halls. And yet, we all knew we had an escalating health care crisis, and it would not get any better if Congress simply gave up. To achieve the goal of meaningful health coverage for all Americans, and to spend more wisely so we could finally get our health care costs under control, we had to climb the hill together.

No matter how long it might take.

This was the spirit Obama captured when he returned to Congress on September 9 to address the joint session. He told lawmakers, and the nation, not to listen to the tall tales like the "death panels" charge—and not to be scared away from giving Americans the health care protection they deserve. He quoted from a letter Ted Kennedy had written—to be delivered after his death—saying this should be the year that health care reform, "the great unfinished business of our society," should finally pass. "I understand that the politically safe move would be to kick the can further down the road, to defer reform one more year, or one more election, or one more term. But that is not what this moment calls for," Obama said. "I still believe we can act, even when it's hard."[23]

His speech almost got overshadowed by one final, ugly reminder of the town halls, when Republican representative Joe Wilson of South Carolina shouted, "You lie!" as Obama debunked the false claims that health care reform would help illegal immigrants. The last thing we needed was one more reminder that some people have no common decency. Still, Obama had performed a valuable service by reminding the public what health care reform was and was not about. And he took ownership of the issue in a way that he had not done since the campaign, by outlining the best ideas in the various bills and referring to them as "my plan."

On the morning of the speech, House Democrats held a caucus meeting to talk about the events of August. Leonard Boswell of Iowa stood up and told his colleagues that if the events taught him anything, it was that they had to pass the health care bill. Others quickly echoed him. They had all seen the protesters, but many came to see the demonstrations for what they were: a made-for-reality-TV spectacle. When they talked to the "regulars"—the constituents they knew, the ones who always come to the town hall meetings—they heard a different message. You have the best opportunity in generations to solve the serious problems we're all having, these constituents said. Don't miss the chance.

And hours before the speech, another significant event occurred on the Senate side of the Capitol. After three months of talks with the Gang of Six, Max Baucus announced the Finance Committee would begin work on a health care bill the week of September 21, with or without Republican support. It was a milestone in its own right, given how the effort had deteriorated since the August recess began. Internally, the group may not have felt the pressure of the town hall events. Olympia Snowe said the group continued to talk by conference call during the recess and never lost their commitment to reaching a bipartisan deal. The six never would have spent so much time on the negotiations, she said, if they were not serious about it.[24]

Unfortunately, some of the statements made outside of the talks by two of the Republicans—Chuck Grassley and Mike Enzi—made it appear that they did not take the effort seriously at all, or at least took it less seriously than they used to. In Iowa, Grassley told a crowd that "you have every right to fear" the House end-of-life-care language, because people "should not have a government-run plan to decide when to pull the plug on grandma."[25] Later, the *Washington Post* uncovered a fund-raising letter in which Grassley asked for "immediate support in helping me defeat 'Obama-care.'"[26] Grassley faced the threat of a possible conservative challenge in the Republican primaries when he ran for reelection in 2010, though it was not clear how serious the threat was and the challenge never materialized.[27]

Mike Enzi, however, had no such worries. And yet, when he delivered the weekly Republican radio address at the end of August, he warned that the comparative effectiveness research in the bills would be "used to limit or deny care based on age or disability of patients."[28] It was a deeply irresponsible statement. Enzi had been on the two health care committees long enough to know what comparative effectiveness research really is. The only logical explanation is that the events of August increased the pressure on Grassley and Enzi not to cooperate. After that, it became a game of running out the clock.

On September 16, Baucus released his proposed bill. The three Republicans were not ready to sign on to it, but many Democrats were not thrilled with it, either. They thought it was too stingy with the tax credits that were supposed to help people pay their health insurance premiums.[29] Since the bill would require all Americans to have health insurance, it would be a political disaster if the coverage was not affordable. Snowe, too, wanted to do more to make cheaper coverage options available to individuals and small businesses. And since she was the Democrats' best candidate to provide even the slightest Republican support, she had a lot of leverage.

So by the time the committee markup started on September 22, Baucus rewrote the bill to try to address the cost concerns. He increased the tax credits so people would not have to pay as much of their income for health insurance premiums. At Snowe's request, he added a "young invincibles" insurance policy as one of the options, where young adults could buy a cheaper plan that only covered catastrophic expenses and basic preventive care. Snowe also won a change that would provide high-deductible plans to make coverage less expensive for small businesses.[30]

As expected, the Finance Committee bill did not include a public option—only the co-ops idea. Two Democrats, Jay Rockefeller of West Virginia and Chuck Schumer of New York, decided to test the committee to see if it really would reject a public option, despite all of the polls showing most Americans supported it. Rockefeller offered an amendment to add a "pure" public option, with the payments based on Medicare rates, while Schumer tried to add a public option where the payments would be negotiated with the providers, just like Henry Waxman's compromise with the Blue Dogs. Both failed, though Schumer picked up two more Democratic votes than Rockefeller.[31]

Snowe got one more victory before the markup was over. Working with Schumer, she won an amendment reducing the penalties for people who don't get health coverage and making it easier for them to escape the penalties. They would be exempt from the penalties if they couldn't find coverage that cost less than 8 percent of their income—a change from the original bill, which would have made them spend up to 10 percent of their income.[32] Snowe's choice of amendments proved that, even though she shared other Republicans' worries about government's role in health care, one of her biggest priorities was simply to make sure people could afford coverage. "If you fail to achieve affordability," she asked, "what have you accomplished?"[33]

The changes were enough, barely, to convince Snowe to vote for the bill. In her closing statement, she made it clear that she would only support it as a way to keep it moving and make more improvements when the bill reached the full Senate. "My vote today is my vote today," she said, with no guarantees about how she would vote on the Senate floor.[34] It was a far cry from the substantial bipartisan support that could have given a nervous public more confidence in the bill. But given the amount of pressure Snowe faced from the right—just months after she had been one of only three Senate Republicans to vote for the stimulus bill—it took enormous courage for her to do even this much.

On October 13, the Senate Finance Committee approved its version of the bill 14–9, with Olympia Snowe casting the lone Republican vote. Unfortunately, hers was the only Republican support the Finance Committee won after spending three months of valuable time on the bill. And Snowe was looking for a chance to make more changes in the full Senate. She wanted to open up the "young invincibles" policy to anyone who wanted to apply, as a way to make low-cost health insurance available to even more people. And she wanted to revisit the plan to expand Medicaid coverage, to make sure it didn't put too much of a financial burden on the states.[35] Either change, however, would have been in direct conflict with two central Democratic goals for the bill: providing meaningful benefits and using Medicaid to provide the quickest expansion of coverage to low-income Americans.

With virtually no prospects for other Republican support, the Democrats had little reason to make more trade-offs to keep their single Republican vote. The August recess had killed whatever hope there might have been for a bipartisan bill. Now, Snowe would lose her leverage.

12 | BREAKTHROUGH

In late October, the House was getting ready to move ahead into uncharted territory. Never before, in the nearly one hundred years since Theodore Roosevelt had called for national health insurance, had a bill to cover nearly all Americans actually made it to the House floor. Now, the Democrats were within reach of that goal. But just as they were preparing to release the bill, with lots of fine-tuning to win as many votes as possible, a dispute from three months ago came back to threaten the entire effort.

It had happened on July 31, the last day of the Energy and Commerce markup. It was the Friday right before the August recess, and the Democrats were exhausted after the weeks of talks that finally allowed the progressives and the Blue Dogs to move forward together. The final deal had come together in the early-morning hours the night before, and the Democrats could see victory in sight at last. So it didn't get much notice when Bart Stupak of Michigan, an antiabortion member of the committee, tried to amend the bill to ban the use of federal funds to pay for abortion for anyone who got coverage through the new health exchange.

The committee had already added a measure by Lois Capps of California that would have walled off the public funds but allowed the health plans to pay for abortions with private funds. Most Democrats thought that would take care of any abortion concerns. But Stupak, a former police officer with the direct manner of an investigator, wasn't satisfied. He saw her amendment as defining abortion as a covered benefit for the first time, since at least one plan in the exchange would have to cover it.[1]

The issue, for Stupak and his allies, was the subsidies people would get to help pay for their health insurance premiums. Stupak wanted ironclad assurances that none of those public funds would pay for abortions. He argued that unless the bill specifically excluded abortion, the Department of Health and Human Services, or possibly the courts, would order plans to cover it in all cases. Most of the other Democrats disagreed, and they voted down his amendment.[2]

Now Stupak was warning that he and other antiabortion Democrats would join forces with Republicans to block the health care bill if it didn't have stronger antiabortion language. He claimed that there were about forty Democrats who would vote with him.[3] House leaders didn't believe he really had that many votes, or anywhere close to it. But there was no point in ignoring the threat. If Stupak had even a small group with him, they could bring the entire bill down.

I was astounded that the debate had come down to this. The fate of health care reform seemed to hang in the balance, not because of any of the bill's experiments to control rising costs, or because of the way it addressed the uneven quality of our health care, or because of its hundreds of pages of new rules for the insurance companies and protections for consumers. It wasn't even because of the public option, the one issue that had commanded all of the press attention. It was because of one of the oldest issues in the culture wars.

Over the last few years, the Democrats had worked hard to achieve a kind of truce between its members who supported reproductive rights and those who wanted more restrictions on abortions. In my view, this was not the place to revive the old wars. The chance to improve health care for millions of Americans should not have been derailed because of this. In Stupak's view, however, he was not the one who had raised the abortion issue. When Waxman met with committee Democrats in March to ask for their views on the bill, Stupak told him: Whatever you do, keep abortion out of the bill. He saw the Capps amendment as injecting the issue into the bill, not settling it.[4]

To most supporters of reproductive rights, including me, it appeared that Stupak was pushing his point way too hard and putting the entire health care bill at risk. By the end of the debate, however, it became clear that Stupak and his allies were not trying to kill the bill. In fact, Stupak was under tremendous pressure from both sides of the debate—from progressives who thought he was undermining reproductive rights and jeopardizing the entire reform effort, and from antiabortion people who thought he wasn't pushing hard enough. You don't put yourself through that if you're not fighting for a deep and sincere view of morality, even if it's a view of the world that many of the rest of us don't share.

The abortion dispute proved that even a large majority in the House is no guarantee of success with an issue that touches on as many emotional flashpoints as health care. Once you decide to require all Americans to get health insurance, you have to help them pay for it. And once you help them pay for it, you raise the question of what the public funds can pay for. Antiabortion lawmakers and their supporters do not want public funds to pay for abortion. Medicaid is banned from covering abortions in most cases for the same reason. And yet, if the Democrats went too far in prohibiting the coverage, they would have faced a revolt from the pro-choice majority of their caucus. In this country, pro-choice lawmakers constantly reminded their leaders, abortion is supposed to be legal.

This was the balance that Nancy Pelosi and the rest of the House leadership had to find as they got ready to bring the bill to the House floor. The price of a broad majority is that you have to live with a caucus of diverse views, especially if you want to hold on to conservative districts. But you also can't lose sight of what reform is supposed to be about. This was not the issue that should have taken up so much of Nancy's time, and she certainly never wanted to give ground on her own deeply held views about a woman's right to choose. But she did what she needed to do to pass the bill. And somehow, she did it without losing votes from her progressive members. I doubt that anyone could have handled it better.

Building enough votes to pass any major bill in the House is a long, slow, methodical process. The challenge is the sheer numbers. In the Senate, you're looking for sixty votes, whether it's with one party or with both parties. But in the House, you have to get to 218 votes. You have so many members with so many different interests, each one juggling other issues that need their immediate attention, that you don't have a fix on exactly how many votes you can expect. Many members won't take a position until they absolutely have to. Until you put the final bill in front of them, and they have the time to focus on it, they will not say which way they'll vote.

There was also another complication in the fall of 2009. House Democrats had already been through a tough vote on another high priority of Obama's agenda: climate change legislation. The vote in June was also close and difficult, with plenty of lawmakers under attack from opponents and worried about the economic impact on their districts. Some House Democrats were already exhausted from that experience. Even if the House bill had been ready before the August recess, many Democrats might not have been ready to vote on it. That may come as a surprise, since health care reform has been so high on my party's agenda for so many years. But people in Congress get emotionally drained after they've worked on an issue that subjects them to so much powerful opposition. And many House Democrats felt that the White House had not given them enough political cover from those opponents' attacks.

Still, they knew they could not simply walk away from the health care bill. So throughout the fall, the House Democrats went through a lengthy series of meetings to walk through every aspect of the health care bill. They broke up into working groups to look at the different issues at stake: health care costs, hospitals, the public option, the uninsured, paying health care providers for value instead of volume, and promoting wellness. Lawmakers and staff members shuttled back and forth between one room and another, often meeting into the evenings.

One key issue that was still in play at this point was the public option. It was sure to be in the bill, but many of the progressives didn't like Henry Waxman's compromise. They wanted to return to a public option that would pay providers based on Medicare rates, not on rates negotiated with the providers. They argued that their version would do more to bring down costs. But when the leadership surveyed all of the House Democrats, they found that they could not get to 218 votes with the version based on Medicare rates, even though it would have saved more money. This was a clear example of how the Blue Dogs' antigovernment mood undermined their case that their main goal was to control health care costs.

By late October, the leadership was ready to release the bill—and the House majority whip, Jim Clyburn of South Carolina, was ready to send out the survey known as the whip question. This is the official survey of the Democratic caucus to determine how many members will vote for the bill. It includes a packet of information about the bill, such as an explanation of the legislation, background documents, and lists of organizations that support it. But the most important part is the simple question: Do you plan to vote for this bill? Many caucus members respond immediately with a yes or a no. Others don't answer at all.

Then, it's time to round up votes from the ones who didn't answer. First, the twelve regional whips call those members or talk to them on the House floor to find out what the holdup is. If they don't get answers, the nine chief deputy whips try the same thing. If a lawmaker's concerns are serious enough, the job of talking to him or her goes higher up the leadership chain, with Pelosi taking the toughest cases. The leadership can't wait until it already has 218 votes in hand. But when a bill seems to have the support of most of the Democratic caucus, close enough that the rest of the votes are within reach, that's when it's time to "start the clock." By releasing the bill and scheduling a vote, the leadership can give the holdouts an incentive to declare which way they'll vote.

It was time to start the clock on the health care bill.

On Thursday, October 29, Nancy Pelosi and a group of House Democrats stood on the west front of the Capitol in a big ceremony to announce the release of the House bill. They all took turns giving their speeches, but it was John Dingell who really rose to the occasion. Holding up a gavel he used when he presided over the passage of the Medicare bill in the House in 1965, he promised to lend it to whoever presided this time, "because a good piece of wood doesn't wear out with one great event." And he noted that since Harry Truman's presidency, Congress had tried to pass comprehensive health care reform only about once every twenty years. "That's just a little bit too doggone long," he said.[5]

This was not a view all Democrats shared, though. When the whip count came back, it showed the leadership could not yet count on 218 votes. At a time when the Democrats controlled 258 seats, it would be hard to explain to the public why the party could not come together on an issue that was so central to its identity. Clearly, Pelosi and the rest of the leadership had a lot of work ahead. By the middle of the next week, it was obvious the House would not be ready to vote by the end of the week. It would have to stay in session on Saturday and hold a rare weekend vote.

Many of the holdouts were Blue Dogs who didn't like the public option or the cost-containment measures. When the Blue Dogs reached their agreement with Henry Waxman back in July, their only commitment was to help him fight off Republican amendments and vote for the bill in committee. They did not promise to vote for it on the floor. Mike Ross was one of the ones who decided he could not vote for it again. He had gotten an earful about the bill from his constituents over the August recess, he said, and "I represent my constituents." He also thought his party did a poor job of explaining that the bill wasn't going to cut off Medicare for seniors, but was just going to make sure the spending grew more slowly. "People across the country never got that message," he said.[6]

And once again, some of the Blue Dogs argued that the bill didn't do enough to bring down health care costs. At Pelosi's request, I reached out to Stephanie Herseth Sandlin, the House member from South Dakota and a cochair of the group, to see if she could be convinced to vote for the bill. Unfortunately, on the day before the vote, Sandlin told me she could not vote for it because there was not enough cost containment in the bill. As she explained in a public statement later that day, the bill "misses a critical opportunity to address access, quality and costs on the one hand, and solidify our fiscal future on the other hand."[7]

I couldn't argue with her on the merits. The bill certainly could have done more to bring down health care costs, although a stronger public option would have helped. In my view, though, this was not a reason to vote against the bill. We were on the verge of a breakthrough that no other Congress, and no other administration, had ever achieved. The best strategy at this point was to keep the bill moving and try to make it stronger on cost containment toward the end.

Some of the other holdouts were antiabortion Democrats who shared Stupak's concerns. And there were some who thought the bill did not take a tough enough line against undocumented immigrants. The bill said people could only get health insurance subsidies if they were in the country legally and could prove it. But it did not say anything about keeping undocumented immigrants from buying health coverage through the exchange with their own money. Some of the more conservative House Democrats wanted to do what the Senate did: ban undocumented immigrants from participating at all, even if they paid the entire cost of the coverage themselves. If Pelosi had taken that language to please the conservatives, though, she could have lost the votes of any number of members of the Congressional Hispanic Caucus.[8]

Pelosi also had a policy of not wasting time making concessions to wavering Democrats if they were likely to vote no anyway. At one caucus meeting in October, she cut off Earl Pomeroy of North Dakota as he raised a list of concerns about the cost of the bill. Is there any chance, she asked, that you will actually vote for it? In the end, he did, despite his concerns. This was not a small matter for Pomeroy, who decided that this was the kind of thing members of Congress were elected to do, even if the vote meant the end of his political career. Still, Pelosi's determination not to spend time on likely no votes was a good policy. It saved her a lot of time and allowed her to concentrate on the members who could truly be swayed.

Throughout the week, other votes fell into place. The American Medical Association and AARP endorsed the bill, giving undecided House Democrats a measure of confidence that two of the most powerful stakeholder groups—doctors and seniors—would not attack them if they voted for it. And a potential political threat turned out not to be much of a threat at all. House Republicans introduced their alternative health care reform plan, which they would offer as a substitute on the day of the vote to replace the Democratic bill. If it had been a strong, attractive package, it might have peeled away lots of Democratic votes. Instead, it was, as Lloyd Doggett put it, "as skimpy as a hospital gown."[9]

The House Republican alternative turned out to be just a rehash of the standard ideas the party has offered in the past, each of which has substantial problems. It would have allowed people to buy health insurance plans from other states with fewer rules, creating a "race to the bottom" where health insurers would all try to set up shop in the states that allow them to offer the skimpiest coverage. The plan would have sent people with preexisting conditions into high-risk pools, a solution that, in the absence of bigger reforms, simply dumps everyone with health problems into health plans with high premiums. And it would have put limits on medical malpractice lawsuits, an idea that would hurt too many deserving patients in its response to the real problem of defensive medicine. If this plan had become law, the Congressional Budget Office said, it would have covered 3 million Americans—a drop in the bucket when 46 million Americans have no health insurance.[10]

But by Friday, November 6, Pelosi still could not count on the 218 votes she needed to pass the bill. Bart Stupak may have had only a small group of House members with him, but she needed their votes. She would have to deal with Stupak personally. And, most likely, she would have to do something that went against her years of support for abortion rights. She would have to give Stupak what he wanted.

For most of the week, Stupak had not even been in Washington. His mother-in-law had died, and he had to fly back to Michigan for the funeral. The man who held so much power over the fate of the health care bill was not around for Pelosi to negotiate with. He had, however, spent the week phoning and e-mailing antiabortion Democrats from his BlackBerry, pleading with them to stick with him. On Friday, he flew back to Washington. As he rushed into the Capitol and headed to the House chamber for a series of votes on minor bills, he ran into Pelosi in the hallway.

Pelosi told Stupak she was sorry to hear about his mother-in-law. And, she said, "We need to talk."[11]

Most of the leadership did not believe Stupak actually controlled forty votes. He got that number, however, from an earlier abortion showdown. In July, he and his allies nearly defeated a spending bill after the Rules Committee, which sets the terms for every debate on the House floor, refused to allow antiabortion lawmakers to offer an amendment restricting abortion funding in the District of Columbia. On that day, he had nearly forty Democrats with him.[12] After the vote, he confronted Pelosi and Steny Hoyer on the House floor. "This is a warning shot," he told them. "You can't keep doing this."[13]

So on Friday night, after a long week of preparing for the floor debate and lining up votes, Nancy Pelosi shuttled back and forth between meetings in her Speaker's suite on the second floor of the Capitol. First, she met with Stupak and his allies to figure out the most painless way to bring him on board. Then, Pelosi met with a group of House Democrats, all strong supporters of abortion rights, to break the news to them.

Stupak wanted an ironclad guarantee that federal funds wouldn't be used to pay for abortions through the new health care structure. That meant making sure the federal subsidies for health insurance premiums did not pay for abortions, and it meant banning the public option from covering them except in cases of rape, incest, or danger to the mother's life. To achieve that goal, his amendment would have allowed women in the health exchange to get abortion coverage only if they bought it separately, with their own money.

Stupak argued that this was the same principle that we use in Medicaid, which doesn't cover abortions except in the same three cases. To those who support reproductive rights, though, what Stupak proposed went well beyond current law. For all practical purposes, the National Women's Law Center concluded, it would be "a de facto ban on insurance coverage of abortion" in the health exchange because insurance companies would not bother to offer the separate abortion coverage.[14] The antiabortion Democrats, however, were taking their cues from the United States Conference of Catholic Bishops, which was sending flyers to parishes throughout the country claiming that the bill would have expanded abortion rights.[15] It wasn't true, but the antiabortion Democrats were listening to the bishops. And unfortunately, Pelosi needed their votes.

At first, Pelosi and Stupak hit on a strategic compromise to try to soften the blow for the House Democrats who opposed the change. Stupak would get a milder version of his language. The ban on abortion coverage would apply only to the public option. For the exchange, it would be renewed year to year. There would not be a direct vote on this language. Instead, it would be added to the bill automatically. It would wrapped into the rule that would set the terms for the debate, and once the House adopted the rule—a step that takes its own, separate vote—the Stupak language would become part of the bill.[16]

In return, Stupak had to promise not to leave Pelosi's suite until he had phoned all of his allies to ask them to support the agreement, which he did. But later that Friday night, when Pelosi called in the House Democrats who support reproductive rights, they were furious. They wanted nothing to do with the Stupak language. But if it had to come up at all, they insisted on a separate vote on it. That way, they could vote no, making it clear they did not simply accept it. Some of them thought they could defeat it.[17]

One of the Democrats who clashed with Pelosi over the compromise that night was Louise Slaughter of New York. She was the chair of the powerful Rules Committee, which sets the terms for every debate on the House floor. She and Pelosi had been elected to the House at around the same time—Slaughter in 1986, Pelosi in 1987—and both had fought for reproductive rights throughout their careers. It was Slaughter who had been in charge when the Rules Committee refused to allow the antiabortion amendment to the spending bill in July.

On this day, the Rules Committee had been meeting all day, but it could not finish writing the rule for the health care debate until the abortion issue was resolved. Now, Slaughter was stunned when Pelosi proposed compromising with Stupak. The group of lawmakers argued for hours. To Slaughter, it was a betrayal of the cause she and Pelosi had fought for. The only saving grace, Slaughter decided, was that Stupak's abortion language probably would not survive a court challenge.

By now, it was close to midnight. The House was set to vote on the health care bill the next day, and the House Rules Committee was about to meet to write the rule for the floor debate. The plan was to allow no amendments, to save time and keep lawmakers from creating mischief by offering changes that might weaken the bill. But now, it was clear to Pelosi that there would have to be one amendment: Stupak's. She told Slaughter to write a rule that would allow a vote on the amendment. Pelosi had proposed to Stupak that they use the compromise language, but Stupak believed the compromise would not get enough votes to pass. Since the original deal was off, he said, he would insist on his original language.

Slaughter did as she was asked. But she did not have to take part in the public proceedings. When the Rules Committee voted on the rule, well after midnight, she and the other two Democratic women on the committee—Doris Matsui of California and Chellie Pingree of Maine—skipped the vote. They sat in her office, with a fire roaring in the fireplace, and watched it on C-SPAN.

On Saturday morning, the weary House members headed to the Capitol to begin the debate, which would last all day and end in a vote that night. The Democrats gathered in the spacious caucus room in the Cannon House Office Building to hear a final plea from the one person who could close the sale: Obama. He had revived the momentum for the bill after the disastrous August recess, and he was the one Democratic leader who could give everyone the true sense of the historic accomplishment that was at hand.

He did that by invoking the biggest and most meaningful accomplishments of past generations: Social Security in the 1930s, Medicare and the civil rights legislation of the 1960s. Every generation or two, Obama told the House

Democrats, Congress has the chance to pass a law that leaves a lasting impact as big as those laws, and that forever changes people's lives for the better. This was one of those times. Rob Andrews felt the atmosphere shift during that speech. He believes at least a few undecided Democrats became yes votes that morning.[18]

The House Democrats needed that sense of history to overcome the frustration many of them felt over the abortion compromise. When Stupak brought up his amendment that night, Diana DeGette of Colorado, one of the nine chief deputy whips and the cochair of the Congressional Pro-Choice Caucus, was visibly angry as she led the debate against it. The amendment was a "wolf in sheep's clothing," she said. Women would not be able to get a medical procedure in the public option at all, even with their own money.

And it was "offensive to women," DeGette said, to expect that women could plan far enough ahead to buy separate coverage for abortion. "Why would we expect to have people buy supplemental insurance for cancer treatments," she asked, "just in case maybe they might get sick?"[19] Louise Slaughter's conclusion was grim. For herself and other House members who had fought to make the days of back-alley abortions for low-income women a thing of the past, she said, "It means thirty or forty years of our life is being canceled out."[20]

But when the amendment passed, shortly after 10:00 p.m., those House members had to make a choice. They could have turned against the bill and let it go down to defeat. Instead, their message to Pelosi was that they would vote for the bill despite the abortion language, but that she would have to fight to take it out when the House and Senate negotiated the final version. If Nancy Pelosi had not had such strong credentials as a supporter of reproductive rights, she might not have been able to hold on to their votes.

Instead, as the House began voting on the health care bill just before 11:00 p.m., Pelosi managed a monumentally difficult task: she won the antiabortion Democrats without losing the other side. As tough as it was for Pelosi to let Stupak have his way, she did the right thing. She did not let the culture wars jeopardize the chance to make lives better for millions of Americans.

At 11:07 p.m. on Saturday, November 7, the Democrats in the House chamber burst into applause as the electronic vote tally for comprehensive health care reform reached 218 votes.

13 | SIXTY VOTES

Harry Reid had a nearly impossible task ahead. In his third year as Senate majority leader, he had his biggest majority yet, and the biggest our party had had in the Senate since the 1970s. After Al Franken was declared the winner of the Minnesota Senate seat in June, Reid effectively had control of sixty votes. This was the number many of us who served in that job could only dream of: the number needed to break the other side's filibusters.

If you looked more closely at the senators behind sixty votes, however, you would have seen just how fragile Reid's coalition was. Only fifty-eight of the senators were Democrats. The other two were independents who "caucused" with the Democrats. One was Bernie Sanders of Vermont, a self-described socialist who was to the left of many Democrats, but generally voted with the party. The other, however, was Joe Lieberman of Connecticut, the man many Democrats wanted to strip of his chairmanship of the Homeland Security Committee for supporting John McCain in 2008. Joe had always been a moderate, but in recent years he seemed to have drifted farther to the right, especially on foreign policy. He mostly voted with the Democrats on domestic policy, but lately, even that was no longer a sure thing.

Reid's next task was to merge two very different Senate health care bills—the progressive one produced by Chris Dodd, and the centrist one written by Max Baucus—into one bill that could win enough votes to pass the full Senate. It would have to be progressive enough to win the votes of senators such as Sanders, Sherrod Brown, and Jay Rockefeller. But it also would have to satisfy the more conservative leanings of senators such as Joe Lieberman, Blanche Lincoln of Arkansas, and Ben Nelson of Nebraska. Nelson, a former insurance company executive, was widely considered the most conservative Democrat in the Senate, and he would be an especially hard sell.

Harry and I have been close ever since our six years working together in the Senate leadership. He was the whip for most of the time I was the Democratic leader, and he was tough and incredibly loyal. One day in 2002, when I was the majority leader and Republicans were attacking me for "obstructing" George W. Bush's agenda, he held a press conference without my knowledge to come to my defense. He became one of my best friends and confidants, and we remain close to this day.

Although he's soft-spoken, Harry has always been a fighter, blunt about his likes and dislikes. But he also shows a lot of deference to the wishes of the committee chairmen and invites dissenting opinions from rank-and-file senators. Those qualities have earned him fierce support within the Democratic caucus. And they put him in a good position to lead the sensitive negotiations that would be needed to pull the caucus together behind a health care bill.

By the fall, the Democrats knew they would have to pass the bill themselves. Some still held out hope that they could win the support of either Olympia Snowe or Susan Collins, the two moderate Republicans from Maine, to get them to sixty votes in case they lost someone like Nelson or Lieberman. But in reality, Collins never showed much interest. And Snowe became increasingly alienated from the process. She was concerned that the merging of the Senate bills would produce a package to the left of the Finance Committee bill, which was true, since it had to win the support of progressive Democrats. And Snowe thought that by merging the bills in closed-door meetings, Reid and the other Democratic leaders undermined the bipartisan support they could have built by adding features to the bill openly, through amendments on the Senate floor.[1]

Unlike the other Republicans, Snowe always struck me as being a potential yes vote. But it would have taken a lot of time and attention from Reid, and probably from the president as well. I told Reid she might be persuadable, and he recognized her importance and tried to reach out to her. So did Obama, who had a series of discussions with Snowe, including phone conversations and private meetings in the Oval Office. But in the end, they did not win her vote.

Reid could not even pin her down on exactly what it would take. And in hind-sight, it may have been too much to ask. Since both Snowe and Collins took a lot of heat from the right for voting for the stimulus package, it would have taken a lot to persuade them to go out on a limb again.

But without them, the Democrats had to go it alone. To most Americans, once the Democrats had sixty votes in the Senate, they lost any excuse for not being able to pass whatever they wanted. And the Republicans did everything they could to encourage that view, even as they vowed to fight the health care bill with everything they had. The Senate Republican leader, Mitch McConnell of Kentucky, was especially adamant that the bill had to be stopped. A strongly ideological conservative who was known for waging stubborn fights—as he did against campaign finance reform for several years before he lost the battle in 2002—McConnell went to the Senate floor almost every day that fall to stir up opposition to health care reform. In one October floor speech, he claimed the Senate bill would "slash Medicare for seniors by about a half a trillion dollars over the next ten years," even though he admitted that no one had seen it yet.[2]

Without the Republicans, Reid would have to do what it took to win the votes of everyone on the Democratic side. Even Joe Lieberman. And even Ben Nelson.

Many people on the progressive side, including some House Democrats, won-dered why the Senate did not just use the budget reconciliation process to pass its bill. If there was a way Senate Democrats could pass it with fifty-one votes rather than sixty, people asked, why didn't they just do it? The truth, however, was that Reid knew reconciliation was not a serious option—at this point in the debate. Because reconciliation can only be used to pass measures that have an impact on the budget, the Republicans would have been able to strip out large and important pieces of the health care bill.

Most of the insurance reforms, such as requiring health insurers to cover people with preexisting conditions, would have been gone. The health exchanges—the centerpiece of the plan to help Americans get better coverage—would have been gone, too. The public option could have been in jeopardy, and the preventive care and wellness measures probably would have been stripped out. Some Democrats worried that even the pilot programs to control health care costs might have been vulnerable to a challenge, since they're so new that the

Congressional Budget Office could not predict exactly how much money they would save. If you lost all of those pieces, the bill that was left would hardly be worth passing.

Those were big factors as Reid and the other Senate Democratic leaders debated the best strategy for moving forward. But there were other reasons not to turn to reconciliation just yet. For one thing, you only use reconciliation as a last resort. Reid didn't think they were there yet—not before the leadership had actually tried to get to sixty votes. And if they had tried reconciliation this early, it would have been seen as such a heavy-handed move that some rank-and-file Democrats, especially the centrists, might not have gone along with it. In some ways, Reid believed, it might be easier to get to sixty votes in a normal debate than it would be to get to fifty-one votes through reconciliation.

So Reid, the other Democratic leaders, the committee chairmen, and their staffs met throughout October to merge the committee bills in a way that would have the best chance of winning sixty votes. They included virtually all of the cost-containment strategies the Finance Committee had included in its bill. They accepted Jay Rockefeller's independent board to review Medicare costs, as well as the experiments with bundled payments, accountable care organizations, medical homes, and value-based purchasing. They also included the comparative effectiveness research, to be run by a nonprofit organization rather than a government agency.

The Senate bill would also take the Finance Committee's version of the health exchange, making it a series of exchanges based in every state, rather than one national marketplace. I wasn't happy about this decision. A national exchange would have been much more effective, because it would have been easier to make sure it was well run and gave the same level of service to people in every state. But this was another way to make the centrist Democrats less fearful of an expansion of federal power.

To make the progressives happier with the new Senate bill, however, the leadership did agree to make the tax credits more generous for people buying health insurance through the exchanges. At most income levels, people would have gotten more help than they would have under the Finance Committee bill—though that was not true, unfortunately, for the people with the lowest incomes.[3] The Senate bill also narrowed the reach of the Finance Committee's "Cadillac tax"—the penalty on unusually generous health insurance plans—by raising the limits of the benefits people could have before the plan would be taxed.[4]

It also included a new long-term-care coverage program Ted Kennedy had proposed: the CLASS Act, which would create new, optional coverage people could get through the workplace. It would be self-financing, and it would give people a cash benefit they could use to help with nursing home expenses or the costs of personal assistance at home if they became disabled. And the Senate bill took some of the preventive care measures that the liberals on the Health, Education, Labor, and Pensions Committee had championed, including the Prevention and Public Health Investment Fund that Tom Harkin had created.[5]

One of the biggest decisions Reid had to make was whether to include the public option, and if so, what limits should be placed on it so the moderates would be satisfied. There was no easy middle ground on this. Chris Dodd's committee put the public option in its bill, but Max Baucus and his committee left it out of theirs. Reid's decision, which he announced to the public on October 26, was to include the public option in the bill that would go before the full Senate. But it would have a crucial compromise: states would be able to opt out of it if they didn't want to participate.[6] This way, moderate Democrats would have less reason to fear the public option as a big expansion of federal power over the states.

But in Reid's view, the public option had to be in at the beginning. He believed in it, so he wanted it to have the best possible chance to succeed. And strategically, it would be harder for the opponents to take it out than to block it from being added on the Senate floor. Besides, Reid wanted to show the liberals in his caucus that he was doing his best to pass the most progressive bill possible. In return, he could tell the liberals: You've got to help us find the votes to pass this.

There was one more bit of strategy that had to be worked out. No matter how hard the leadership tried to satisfy the entire Democratic caucus, they would not be able to win sixty votes right away. That would take a lot more negotiating with the holdouts—sure to be the centrists such as Lieberman and Nelson—who would bargain for everything they could possibly get. So Reid's strategy, once the Senate debate began, would be to wrap up all of the deals with those holdouts into a "manager's amendment" at the end. This massive amendment would include every agreement with the holdouts, including, if necessary, yet another compromise on the public option.

But there would be a price. Every senator who got an agreement in that manager's amendment, whether they were moderates or progressive Democrats, would have to promise to vote for the amendment at the end. And they would have to vote for the final bill. This way, the negotiations could continue while the Senate debated the bill—a process that could take weeks. And it was Reid's best chance of building to sixty votes.

By the time Reid was ready to bring the bill to the Senate floor, he was already getting worn down. On Wednesday, November 18, I met with him, Vice President Joe Biden, and Interior Secretary Ken Salazar to hear him describe the high points of the Senate bill, which he was going to release later that day. Reid looked tired and drawn and clearly had not slept much. He had been trying to win over the moderates in his caucus, who were still making noises about opposing the bill, and the stress of trying to win them over was taking its toll.

We agreed to talk to some of the moderates ourselves. Biden would talk to Blanche Lincoln, Salazar would talk to Mary Landrieu of Louisiana, and I would talk to Ben Nelson. The immediate concern was the first procedural vote, which Reid wanted to hold just before the Senate left for the Thanksgiving break. The vote would only allow the Senate to start debating the health care bill. It had nothing to do with passing it, a vote that would come much later. But even now, the Democrats needed sixty votes to get past the wall of Republican opposition.

That vote took place on a Saturday. No senator likes to work on a weekend, especially right before a holiday, when everyone just wants to get out of town. So by scheduling a vote for a weekend, or even threatening to do so, a Senate majority leader can put subtle pressure on the holdouts to give up their fight. To his credit, Ben Nelson voted to begin the debate. I had told him there was nothing more at stake in this vote—that it did not commit him to voting for the final bill—and this was the argument he made in his own public statement.[7]

Finally, on the day of the vote, Landrieu and Lincoln announced they would be yes votes, too. Landrieu was defensive about the circumstances; the leadership had just added about $400 million in Medicaid funding to help

Louisiana, and Landrieu had to insist on the Senate floor that it was not related to her vote.[8] But by the end of the day, the bottom line was that Harry Reid had put together the sixty votes to begin the debate.

Getting the sixty votes to end the debate and pass the bill, however, would be another matter entirely. On the Sunday talk shows the next day, both Lieberman and Nelson said they would vote against the bill if it included a public option. Lieberman called the idea "radical." Nelson labeled it "a big-government, Washington-run operation" that would undermine the private insurance of millions of Americans.[9] The senators all headed home for Thanksgiving. But when they got back, there would be a lot of work for Reid to do.

On Monday, November 30—the first day the Senate returned—I was invited to a strategy session at the Capitol with Reid, the rest of the leadership, and top administration officials. We gathered in the leader's conference room—room 217 on the Senate side of the Capitol. Rahm Emanuel, Kathleen Sebelius, Nancy-Ann DeParle, and Ken Salazar were all there, as were Phil Schiliro, my former aide and now the top White House liaison to Congress, and Jim Messina, the White House deputy chief of staff. Reid's leadership team—Majority Whip Dick Durbin of Illinois, Caucus Vice Chairman Chuck Schumer of New York, and Conference Secretary Patty Murray of Washington State—were there as well, joined by Baucus and Dodd.

I was starting to attract a bit of unwanted public attention. Reporters had spotted me at the Capitol during my meeting with Reid before Thanksgiving, leading to a new round of stories about my continued involvement in health care. Now, my presence at the strategy meeting triggered more stories and questions from watchdog groups about whether I should have been at the meetings, given my role in the private sector.[10] (I had just joined DLA Piper, my current firm, as a senior policy adviser and member of the global board.) I must confess that I felt a bit uneasy about it, too. I wanted to help Reid and my friends in the administration pass health care reform, and if they thought my feedback was useful, I wanted to give it. But I did not want to provide more ammunition to the critics of health care reform. After it was over, I told Reid I should stay out of meetings like that.

The meeting, however, was mostly just a state of play. We talked about the three main issues that would determine the success or failure of the bill: the public option, the ways the bill would pay for reform, and—once again—abortion. There were about a dozen senators whose votes Reid could not yet count on, including progressive Democrats as well as moderates. Everyone was in reasonably good spirits, considering how far the road ahead still looked. But over the long run, of course, the moderates would make that road even longer.

Ben Nelson was the biggest challenge of all. He had a lengthy list of concerns, so lengthy I wasn't sure he ever actually wanted to resolve them. At one point, the list included the public option, which he opposed under any circumstances; abortion, on which he wanted to duplicate Stupak's total ban on funding; the new long-term-care program, which he thought would become a new government entitlement; the penalties for not having health insurance, which he thought were too low; new taxes on medical devices, which he thought were too high; and cuts in Medicare payments to nursing homes, which he thought were too tough.

As the debate dragged on, Nelson would shift his focus from one issue to another, settling on abortion, Medicaid funding for the states, the long-term-care program, and the Medicare payment cuts as his main concerns.[11] It was hard to tell how Reid could ever do enough to bring him on board. Somehow, however, he had to do it. Just as Nancy Pelosi had to make compromises she hated in the pursuit of a larger goal, Reid would have to do the same.

On the Senate floor, Republicans offered amendment after amendment to highlight issues where they thought they could stir up concerns among the public. Here, John McCain, back in the Senate after his White House run against Obama, found a new niche as a critic of the bill's Medicare provisions. "The message to the 330,000 Americans in Arizona who are on Medicare Advantage is that they are out to get you," McCain said as he tried, unsuccessfully, to amend the bill to take out all of the Medicare savings.[12] It was a shame to see John resorting to those kinds of scare tactics. Of course no one was out to "get them." If the Medicare Advantage plans are overpaid, that's a valid source of savings that can be used for reform. At worst, the seniors would lose their extra benefits, such as eyeglasses and gym memberships, not the program itself.

Behind the scenes, meanwhile, some of the Democrats were trying to solve the public option deadlock. At Reid's request, ten senators, evenly divided between progressives and centrists, met for days in a meeting room in the Capitol to work out the compromise plan. The senators crowded around a small conference table, and their aides had to stand against the walls for hours as the talks went on. Chuck Schumer became the day-to-day leader of the negotiations. Jay Rockefeller, Tom Harkin, and Sherrod Brown represented the progressives, as did Russ Feingold of Wisconsin. Ben Nelson, Blanche Lincoln, Mary Landrieu, Mark Pryor of Arkansas, and Tom Carper of Delaware were the centrists. The new group became known as the Gang of 10.

It came up with a novel solution, one that seemed to offer something to both centrist Democrats and progressives. Instead of a government-run public option, their idea was to offer a choice of private, but national, health insurance plans that would be available in every state. At least one of the plans would have to be a nonprofit. They would be administered by the Office of Personnel Management, which runs the health insurance program for members of Congress and federal workers. In that program, the Office of Personnel Management negotiates the contracts, including the premiums the plans can charge, but the plans are run by private companies. That is the way the new, national plans would work.

This was a good compromise for the centrists, but it had little to offer to the progressives. To satisfy them, the compromise also would have allowed people between the ages of fifty-five and sixty-four to buy Medicare coverage if they didn't have any other source of health insurance. This would have addressed the unique problems of people in this age group, who are usually starting to have health problems and have more trouble getting coverage than people in younger age groups. But it also represented an attractive fallback position for the liberals. If they couldn't have the public option—originally designed as a Medicare-like plan for younger age groups—they could let a new age group into Medicare itself. The idea had been around since the Clinton presidency, but in this case it came from Howard Dean, as a suggestion on how to cushion the blow for progressives if they lost the public option.

The Office of Personnel Management idea quickly took hold. In fact, Jay Rockefeller believed progressives might support it more strongly if they realized that one of the national plans would have to be a nonprofit. In his view, a national nonprofit plan might accomplish many of the same goals as the public option, including the main one: providing for-profit health plans with real competition. He was even more enthusiastic about another concession to the progressives. Health insurance companies would have to spend more of their premium revenues on actual medical care, rather than profits and overhead.[13] If an insurer spent less than 85 percent of the premiums on clinical services for large group coverage, or less than 80 percent for small group or individual coverage, they would have to give rebates to their customers.

The Medicare buy-in idea, however, lasted less than a week. Reid announced the deal on Tuesday, December 8, and the details began to circulate throughout the Democratic caucus the rest of the week. On Sunday, December 13, Lieberman announced on CBS's *Face the Nation* that he would not vote for the bill if the Medicare buy-in was included. "It has some of the same infirmities that the public option did," Lieberman said. "It will add taxpayer cost. It will add to the deficit. It's unnecessary." The underlying bill was a good one, he said, but "we don't need to keep adding on to the back of this horse because we're going to break the horse's back and get nothing done."[14]

It was a huge setback. The progressive Democrats were furious. They had given ground on the public option, and now Lieberman—who had supported the exact same Medicare buy-in idea as the vice presidential nominee in 2000—was threatening to jump ship after giving virtually no warning that he had problems with it. These Democrats paid close attention to an interview Lieberman had given to the *Connecticut Post* just a few months earlier, now circulating in the political blogs, in which he had defended his support for the Medicare buy-in idea and said it would be "less expensive" than expecting the fifty-five-to-sixty-four age group to buy private health insurance. He expressed not a word of second thoughts about it.[15]

Sherrod Brown could barely hide his exasperation. In his view, the Democrats never should have had to compromise on the public option to begin with. Yes, there were centrists in the caucus who didn't like it. But Brown believed that if Obama and Reid had come down hard on the centrists, making it clear that this was a Democratic priority and they were expected to support it, they would have.[16] I'm sure Reid was frustrated, too, but it is hard for me to see how much harder he could have pushed. Reid understands the importance of keeping Lieberman in the caucus, and as such, he gives Lieberman a lot of leeway.

The big, unanswerable question, however, is whether the president could have made a difference if he had pushed the moderates harder. When you are the president, anything you say carries more weight than it would coming from any other party leader. But that does not mean you can make individual senators do anything you want. In fact, Obama had held numerous conversations with Democratic senators and concluded that no matter how much progressives wanted him to insist on the public option, there never would be enough moderate votes to support it. Without the moderates, the bill could not pass the Senate, and the reform effort would be dead. Instead, Obama insisted there might be other ways to achieve the same goals.

So now, the public option was out, and Reid had no choice but to scuttle the Medicare buy-in. In the end, the compromise gave a big concession to the centrist Democrats, but the progressives lost theirs. The Lieberman story, however, is a classic example of how a Senate majority leader sometimes has to cut deals in the pursuit of a larger, worthy goal. Reid had to keep building to sixty votes to help millions of Americans get better health care. Although he paid a big price for it, he now had Lieberman's vote.

Now, Reid had to deal with Ben Nelson.

There was one week left to go before Christmas. That was Reid's deadline for passing a bill out of the Senate, and after lawmakers had missed so many other deadlines, he had to at least make this one. But Nelson still would not commit to voting for the bill. He was under intense pressure from Nebraska's other political leaders, including Republican governor Dave Heineman, who argued in an open letter to Nelson that the bill was "a substantial unfunded Medicaid mandate" and would be "bad news for Nebraska."[17]

And like Stupak, Nelson thought the bill was not written tightly enough to prevent public funding of abortions through the health exchanges. But when he and Orrin Hatch tried to amend the bill to include Stupak's abortion language, the Senate voted it down. After that, Nelson warned, once again, that he would have a hard time voting for the final bill. So Reid sat down with him to try, with infinite patience, to work through his many concerns.

After a long day of negotiations in Reid's office that nearly broke down several times, Nelson suggested a "two check" solution to break the abortion impasse. They would let the states pass laws banning abortion coverage in the exchanges. And for any plans that did cover abortions, the money would be kept strictly separate. If someone wanted to sign up for a plan that covered abortions, she would have to write two checks— one for the abortion coverage and one for the rest of the benefits.

And there would be one more concession. The federal government would pay the full cost, for Nebraska alone, of the bill's expansion of Medicaid. Every state, starting in 2014, would have to cover people up to 133 percent of the poverty line. For most states, the federal government would pay most of the costs. But only Nebraska would have its expenses covered completely. Around 10:15 p.m. that Friday night, December 18, Reid and Nelson shook hands and got their deal. After months of round-the-clock meetings and late-night haggling, Reid finally had his sixtieth vote for health care reform.

On Saturday morning, as a heavy snowfall began to bury Washington, Nelson trudged to the Capitol and announced he was on board. Reid filed the manager's amendment with the Gang of 10 agreement and the Nelson language. The countdown began toward the first of a series of votes the Senate would have to take to end the debate. With the Republicans determined to run out all of the debate time allowed under Senate rules, that meant the first vote would take place around 1:00 a.m. on Monday. It was the only way to get all of the procedural votes out of the way and hold the final vote by Christmas.

But the Nebraska Medicaid deal immediately became an enormous public relations disaster, quickly overshadowing the fact that the Senate was now on the verge of making history. To much of the public, the Nebraska provision was proof that the Senate relied on shady deals to pass the health care bill. Nelson was stung especially hard by the criticism. He told everyone who would listen that he had not, in fact, wanted Nebraska to get special treatment. He wanted the federal government to pick up the extra cost for all states, he said, so they would not have an extra burden as they struggled with the effects of the recession.

The talk of all of the "deals" hurt the health care effort a lot. But in my experience, this is nothing new. Every major piece of legislation in Congress requires deals to win the support of the last holdouts, and they're never pretty to look at. What has changed in recent years, though, is that there is more transparency in the legislative process, so we know more about them. We heard about not only the Nebraska Medicaid agreement, but also the extra Medicaid funding Mary Landrieu won for Louisiana.

And there was another one that got less attention. Under the bill, the recommendations of the independent board to control Medicare costs—now renamed the Independent Payment Advisory Board—wouldn't apply to hospitals. The Finance Committee agreed to leave them out because of the deal they had already struck, in which they had accepted the $155 billion in payment reductions. The hospitals didn't want to get hit again, so they were rewarded for supporting the reform effort. Rockefeller didn't think it made sense to leave anyone out if you really wanted to bring Medicare costs down. And the White House was concerned enough about losing Rockefeller's support that the president himself called to ease his concerns. The carve-outs, Obama told him, will come out. But they never did—proving that when Congress cuts deals, it is hard for a president to knock them out.[18]

None of these deals were pleasant to look at. But in the pursuit of a higher goal—health care for millions of Americans—they were the price that had to be paid. As Rockefeller put it, "We all walked around with our heads bowed down" after the Nebraska deal. But at that moment, to get sixty votes for comprehensive health care reform, it had to be done.

Shortly after 1:00 a.m. on Monday, December 21, the bleary-eyed senators assembled on the Senate floor for a rare spectacle. Under Reid's orders, all of the senators sat at their desks, and each senator, when called by the clerk, stood up to announce his or her vote on ending debate on Reid's manager's amendment. It was a far more formal scene than the usual Senate vote, where everyone walks around the floor and chats with each other while the votes are taken. It was a perfect way to capture the historic nature of the moment. Each senator would have to stand up and be counted. Each Democrat voted "Aye," and each Republican voted "No." At about 1:15 a.m., Nelson stood up and voted "Aye."

Reid had won his sixty votes on the first procedural vote. There would be others, and the Republicans were threatening to use every bit of debate time on all of them. That would have forced the Senate to take the final vote at about 7:00 p.m. on Christmas Eve. But as the Democrats kept winning sixty votes on each one, the Republicans decided there was no point in keeping everyone that late. After all, they had planes to catch, too.

Instead, the exhausted senators gathered at 7:00 a.m. on Thursday, December 24. It was like the end of a marathon. With Vice President Joe Biden presiding, they sat at their desks once again and stood up to vote—this time on the bill itself. Once again, every Democrat voted "Aye," and every Republican voted "No." Reid, so tired he could barely think straight, accidentally voted "No." As he heard the laughter of the other senators, he threw up his hands, leaned his head down on his desk, and corrected himself. The count stalled out at fifty-nine for a few agonizing minutes—until Bernie Sanders ran in late, rushed to his seat, and voted "Aye."

At 7:15 a.m., Biden announced that the Senate had passed comprehensive health care reform.

We were getting so close. After so many years of failure, both the House and the Senate had passed health care reform bills. That did not mean it would be easy to get to the finish line. The House and the Senate still had to write a final bill that both chambers could accept, and they had deep differences to overcome. They would have to settle their disagreements on the public option, on the amount of subsidies to help people buy insurance, and on whether there should be one national health insurance exchange or separate exchanges in all of the states. And the dispute over how to pay for reform had the potential to be the biggest of all.

Still, they had come so far that the ending seemed inevitable. They would work out their differences, pass a final bill, and Obama would sign it into law early in 2010. The House had proven it could get 218 votes for health care reform. And the Senate had proven it could get sixty votes, as long as the Democratic caucus stuck together once again.

Everyone assumed the Democrats would still have sixty votes on the final round. In just a few weeks, however, that assumption would be shattered. The health care reform effort faced its biggest threat yet, a blow that was nearly fatal. And it came from the last place the Democrats ever expected.

It came from the state that provided the model for the health care bill. The state Ted Kennedy, the man who called health care reform "the cause of my life," represented in the Senate for so many years.

Massachusetts.

14 | THE RESCUE PLAN

The rumblings started around the second week of January 2010, as members of Congress returned to Washington from the holiday break. The special election to fill Ted Kennedy's Senate seat was coming up on January 19, and Martha Coakley, the Massachusetts attorney general and Democratic Senate nominee, was losing her lead. Scott Brown, a Republican state senator who was campaigning as "the forty-first vote" to stop the health care bill, was closing in on her.

On January 9, just a week and a half before the election, a survey by Public Policy Polling gave Brown a one-point lead.[1] Three days later, a Rasmussen poll had Coakley ahead by just two percentage points.[2] For the first time, Democrats realized there was a real danger that Kennedy's seat might go to a Republican. Now, the consequences of all of the delays—with the Gang of Six in the Senate, and with the Blue Dogs in the House—were becoming apparent to everyone. The "go fast" strategy on health care had been the right one. The Democrats could not assume they would have sixty votes forever.

Scott Brown didn't have a problem with the Massachusetts health care reform law that had inspired the bills in Congress. In fact, he had voted for it as a state senator. He just didn't want to give it to the rest of the country. Massachusetts had taken care of its uninsured people through its own reform law, Brown said, and giving the same kind of reform to the other states would just force Massachusetts taxpayers to subsidize the rest of the country.[3] The message couldn't be clearer: We've got ours. "It's not good for Massachusetts. We already have ninety-eight percent of the people insured," he told Sean Hannity.

"Everyone is entitled to some form of insurance, but why do we need a one-size-fits-all?"[4]

Unfortunately, that appeal to selfishness seemed to be working. In Washington, Senate and House Democrats were already talking about how to bridge their differences and negotiate a final health care bill that could pass both chambers. They would have to take that last, difficult step before Obama could sign it into law. But now, the talks suddenly took on a greater sense of urgency. It seemed that the Democrats were running out of time, sooner than they had ever expected.

That week, Obama held a series of meetings with top House and Senate Democrats to try to work out the sticking points. One of the biggest was how to pay for the final bill. House Democrats wanted nothing to do with the Senate's Cadillac tax on the most generous health plans, and Senate Democrats thought the House bill's biggest source of revenue, the tax on the wealthy, was a nonstarter. Even at that time, Henry Waxman thought the biggest challenge would be to write a bill that could please Ben Nelson. But as the president and the lawmakers argued over a fairly small amount of funding for the bill, Waxman saw that Obama was more worried about what was about to happen in Massachusetts. "I'm looking at the possibility of losing my sixtieth vote next Tuesday," Obama told the lawmakers. "Can't you work this out?"[5]

By that point, however, there was no real chance of getting the final bill to the president's desk before the election. Obama and the Democratic leaders closed in on a deal, even working out a delayed and smaller version of the Cadillac tax with union leaders.[6] But they would have to get a cost estimate for the final bill from the Congressional Budget Office—because many members would base their votes on whether it added to the deficit—and the office could not possibly prepare an estimate in a few days. Even if it could, there would be holdouts in both the House and the Senate once again. And as we saw during the fall debates, you cannot hold the vote until those members are satisfied, and they will use every last minute available to them.

On Tuesday, January 19, Scott Brown won Ted Kennedy's Senate seat, defeating Martha Coakley 52 percent to 47 percent.[7] That night, the health care reform effort seemed to collapse. Obama and the Democrats in Congress had been on the verge of making history, and they were closing in on the finish line. Now, the finish line had vanished.

It is hard to overstate how grim the mood was on Capitol Hill after Scott Brown's victory. Without sixty votes, there was virtually no chance that the Senate could pass a final version of the reform bill. Some Democrats suggested that maybe they really had overreached, and that they should listen to the voters and pass something smaller. Even Representative Anthony Weiner of New York, one of the most vocal progressives in the House and a strong advocate of a single-payer health care system, was having second thoughts. He said Democrats "should take a step back and say, 'What are the things people really want out of health care, the things that are popular?' "[8]

At that point, there appeared to be only a handful of options on comprehensive reform. The simplest was for the House simply to pass the Senate bill, without any changes. If both chambers pass the exact same bill, they can send it directly to the president to be signed into law, without having to negotiate a final version. There was just one problem with that plan: House Democrats hated the Senate bill. *Despised* would not be too strong a word. They thought it had too many compromises—no public option, state health exchanges instead of a national exchange, and subsidies too low to make health insurance affordable for people who would have to buy it. They were especially adamant that the Cadillac tax had to go, because that would hit too many middle-class households. And the Nebraska Medicaid deal was pure poison to them.

Incredibly, in the first few days after Brown's election, I was getting reports that as many as seventy-eight House Democrats would vote no on the Senate bill. I was stunned that so many would reject it out of hand. I could understand their concerns, and I shared many of them, especially on the public option and the lack of a national exchange. But we were too close simply to walk away from the effort. It was a classic case of making the perfect the enemy of the good.

Another option might have been to pass a final bill, negotiated between the House and Senate, using the budget reconciliation rules that the Senate had rejected before. But that would get ugly very quickly. Once again, the Democrats would face the risk that major portions of the bill would be knocked out by rules challenges. And Republicans would accuse the Democrats of ignoring the "message" of the Massachusetts election, and they could drag out the debate for a long time. A third option would be to try again with some of the

Republicans, particularly Olympia Snowe, to see if there might be a new path to sixty votes in the Senate. But it was hard to see what incentive the Republicans would have to negotiate, now that they had put the Democrats on the defensive.

And then there was the most drastic option of all: drop it. Wait another generation to try comprehensive reform again. Amazingly, from the reports I was getting in those chaotic first few days, that option was just as likely as any of the others. It might even have been the most likely of all.

In the House, some Democrats were eager to scale back to just a few popular items, such as repealing health insurers' exemption from antitrust laws. The House eventually did pass a stand-alone bill on this, with bipartisan support, but it was no substitute for addressing the cost, quality, and access problems that were the reason for taking on health care in the first place.

Others wanted to find some way to focus on the most well-known problems people face, such as preexisting conditions. The problem, as Democratic leaders had to explain to them, is that you cannot just require health insurers to cover preexisting conditions, because they will just raise their premiums to cover their costs. To give people the needed protections and keep premiums stable, you have to require everyone, including healthy people, to get coverage. You have to do the popular things and the unpopular things together.

And then there was Rahm Emanuel's plan. He had floated the idea of scaling back even earlier in the debate, as a way of salvaging something that could pass more easily. Now he was quietly pushing for a smaller reform plan that would focus on covering all children. This was a goal that had been attempted with the creation of the State Children's Health Insurance Program, but it had never been fully achieved. To get to full coverage, the plan would have required all parents to cover their children. It may have had some appeal to the president, since his original campaign proposal called for mandatory coverage only for children, not for adults. And to Rahm, this was a practical way to get some kind of accomplishment on health care. But in the circles of people who were pushing for comprehensive reform, Rahm's idea gained a mocking nickname: Kiddiecare.

Pelosi was not a fan of Rahm's plan, or any of the other incremental ideas being floated by House Democrats. She called them "eensy-weensy spider." They were not popular with health care officials in the administration, either.

Nancy-Ann DeParle, the director of the White House Office of Health Reform, and Health and Human Services Secretary Kathleen Sebelius were especially adamant that we should hold out for comprehensive reform, now that we had come this far.

And ultimately, Obama was not prepared to give up. It was not the first time his White House chief of staff had urged him to go smaller, and it certainly was not the first time he had fought with his own advisers about attempting health care reform at all. From the earliest discussions in the transition team, including the ones that had made me so nervous, Obama had battled with his own economic and political advisers about the wisdom of taking on comprehensive reform now. He could have pulled the plug at any number of times, but he did not.

The problem now, however, was that there was no clear path forward. On the night of the Massachusetts election, Obama and Reid tried to urge Pelosi to do the simplest thing: pass the Senate bill in the House. Impossible, she said. Her caucus would not stand for it. Her suggestion was to use a reconciliation bill to fix the problems her caucus saw with the Senate bill—and to have the Senate pass it first. House Democrats simply did not trust the Senate enough to act until the Senate had passed the changes. To Obama, however, putting a reconciliation bill before the Senate first was a recipe for political disaster. It would virtually guarantee that Congress would debate health care reform for another four to six weeks. No one could afford to let that happen.

Over the next few days, however, it became clear to the White House and Democratic leaders that some form of the two-bill approach would have to be the solution. The House could not simply pass the Senate bill and leave it unchanged. But it might be able to pass the Senate bill if both the House and Senate could also pass, in a separate package, a set of "fixes." This second bill would rewrite the parts of the Senate bill that the House hated the most, and it would be passed through the budget reconciliation rules. This way, the Senate would only have to pass a small reconciliation bill, not a big one that could be vulnerable to rules challenges. And the Senate would only need fifty-one votes to pass it—not sixty.

In these early days after the election, Obama did not always send the strongest signals about comprehensive reform. In an interview with George Stephanopoulos the day after the election, Obama said the administration and

Congress should "move quickly to coalesce around those elements of the package that people agree on."[9] He still talked about broad themes, including insurance reforms and cost containment. But this was a time when Obama's choice of words mattered greatly to millions of Americans, and to a lot of people, his remarks sounded like scaling back.

In reality, though, this was not the case. Slowly and quietly, Obama, Pelosi, and Reid were working through the steps that would be needed to revive comprehensive reform. It would have to be the two-bill solution. And somehow, they would have to convince the House to go first.

During this time, I faced my own dilemma about how to talk publicly about the future of reform. A few days after the Massachusetts election, *The New York Times* asked me to cowrite an op-ed with Bill Frist—the Republican Senate majority leader during my last two years as minority leader—about smaller, achievable reforms that Congress could pass now. I did consider it, briefly. But it quickly became clear that if I wrote the piece, it would send the wrong signal at a crucial time.

The last thing the president, Pelosi, and Reid needed was more Democrats suggesting that smaller, incremental steps were a legitimate option. If I had written the piece, I could have weakened any chance of reviving comprehensive reform. The smaller steps would have taken months of new work and wasted the year of work the Democrats had already put in, and there was no guarantee they would pass any more easily than comprehensive reform. I told the *Times* I could not do it.

There was also another political factor working against comprehensive reform. After spending so much time and energy on it, many Democrats in Congress wanted to return the focus to jobs. They were getting complaints from constituents at home, who saw them spending all of their time on health care while people still struggled to find work in a dismal economy. It was exactly like the debate we had had on the transition team before Obama's presidency began. The tension between health care and the economy had never gone away.

Clearly, it was on Emanuel's mind, too. In late January, he suggested a possible new congressional agenda to *The New York Times*: a jobs bill, new fees on banks to help pay for the financial bailout program, reform of financial regulations, and then—eventually—return to health care.[10] To me, this was a sure sign that the health care effort was dying. If the White House let it lose momentum now, that momentum would never return. On the same day that story appeared, however, aides to Pelosi and Reid were talking with White House officials and meeting with the Senate parliamentarian, discussing what kinds of "fixes" to the Senate bill could be made in a reconciliation package without being stripped out by rules challenges.

It was Pelosi, ultimately, who told Obama that scaling back was not an option. The president clearly did not want to lower his sights. But he may have given some lawmakers the impression that he was open to it, because he is a good listener and he obviously was listening to those who wanted to scale back. So one day, in a meeting with Obama, Emanuel, and Reid, Pelosi laid it on the line for the president. I am only a player on comprehensive health care reform, she said. Anything less is not an option.

It was the meeting that determined, once and for all, that Obama and Congress would make one final push for the kind of reform the nation needed.

The first step was to decide the process for moving forward. Once everyone had decided that, they could move on to the substance of what would be in the "fixes" bill. By now, the process for rescuing the bill was becoming clear to Congress and the White House. It would have to be the House passage of the Senate bill, followed by the "fixes" bill that both chambers would pass through budget reconciliation.

This put much of the burden on the House, and specifically, on Pelosi. Until now, much of the focus had been on the Senate and its ability to find sixty votes. But the House did not have an easy time passing its bill, either. Pelosi and the rest of the leadership had to find the exact mix of policies that could get them to 218 votes. Now they would have to find a new path, using a different mix of policies that much of their caucus hated.

To do that, they would have to have a reconciliation bill that took care of the Senate bill's biggest problems. Pelosi knew what she would need to make the bill tolerable to the House, thanks to the lengthy caucus meetings and many hours of one-on-one conversations with her members. The Cadillac tax would have to go, and the money for reform would have to come from somewhere else. The premium tax credits would have to be more generous, to make health insurance more affordable once everyone was required to have it. The bill would have to close the Medicare donut hole, the gap in prescription drug coverage, since the Senate bill did not do that. And Ben Nelson's Medicaid deal for Nebraska would have to be shelved. Instead, the bill would have to provide more Medicaid help for all states, not single out one state for special treatment.

These were the fixes that had the best chance of getting through reconciliation without being stripped out by a rules challenge. The House could not get the state-based exchanges in the Senate bill converted into a national exchange. That provision would not have had a budget impact, so the Republicans would have been able to knock it out. And regardless of how either side of the abortion debate felt about the language in the Senate bill, that could not be changed through reconciliation either.

But the fixes that were most likely to survive reconciliation also created problems of their own. For one thing, the Cadillac tax produced $149 billion of the funding for the Senate bill.[11] If the Democrats took that out completely, they would have to fill that hole. Senate Democrats refused to do it by taking the House's tax on high-income households, because the moderates thought it was too easy a solution and had no relevance to health care. Besides, there were good policy reasons to have the Cadillac tax, in the view of some Senate Democrats, because it would be a good tool for discouraging overuse of health care. If the tax was completely eliminated, Reid would have had a hard time finding even fifty-one votes for the reconciliation bill.

The basic problem, however, was the question of who should go first. If the Senate tried it, the Republicans could stall the reconciliation bill for weeks with amendments and rules challenges. Eventually, the Democrats would have to make a move to cut off amendments, and an already ugly situation would get even uglier. There was only one real way forward: the House would have to go first. Eventually, Pelosi and the other top House Democrats came to understand this. If the House passed the Senate bill and the fixes bill first, Obama could sign the Senate bill into law almost immediately. That would take much of the energy out of the Republican opposition, giving them less of a reason to stall the Senate passage of the reconciliation bill.[12]

But it would be an enormous challenge to convince rank-and-file House Democrats to go first. They simply didn't trust the Senate. To them, the Senate was too slow and too beholden to moderates. And it had become a graveyard for important bills that the House had worked on at great political risk, such as the climate change bill the House had passed back in June. Senate Democrats had wasted valuable time on health care, in the House view, and now it had lost its sixty-vote majority. If the House took a risk and passed the Senate bill, why would anyone believe the Senate could finish the job by passing the fixes?

It was a frustrating time for Pelosi and Reid. One Saturday in early February, as Washington, D.C., virtually disappeared under two feet of snow, Pelosi and I talked for nearly an hour about the situation. After all, the snow had practically shut down the city, and neither of us could go anywhere. She was under a lot of pressure to find the votes for the Senate bill—no small challenge, even with the fixes strategy. But Reid was having his own problems finding ways to pay for the fixes the House wanted—and finding the fifty-one votes to pass them.

These were all problems that could be solved. But to find the votes, they would need the president's help. By working the phones aggressively, and asking reluctant Democrats to help him rescue the most important domestic initiative of his presidency, he could help Reid and Pelosi line up the votes and break the logjam. Had Obama done that, however, he would have gotten ahead of their efforts. It was not his style, as president, to preempt the House Speaker and the Senate majority leader.

The end of the deadlock was nowhere in sight.

There were, however, some signs that the health care effort could make a comeback. One of them was the result of a masterful political performance by the president. On January 29, Obama gave a speech to House Republicans at a retreat they held in Baltimore, and then held a lively debate with them as he took their questions. The White House had asked the Republicans to let the exchange be televised, and they agreed.

That day, Obama brilliantly deflected most of their criticisms of the health care bill and discussed the shortcomings of the Republican alternatives. He explained why selling health insurance across state lines won't work without basic standards, for example—because insurance companies would just move to the states with the fewest rules and "cherry-pick" the healthiest customers. But he made his case patiently and respectfully. And he was able to tell the Republicans: I've read your plans. I haven't ignored them.

Obama also brought up the bipartisan health care plan I had worked on with Bob Dole and Howard Baker at the Bipartisan Policy Center. He pointed out, correctly, that the basic elements of the Senate bill weren't too different from the plan our group had proposed. "Now, you may not agree with Bob Dole and Howard Baker and Tom. And certainly you don't agree with Tom Daschle on much," Obama said, to appreciative laughter from the Republicans. "But that's not a radical bunch. But if you were to listen to the debate, and, frankly, how some of you went after this bill, you'd think that this thing was some Bolshevik plot."[13] He came off as relaxed and easygoing, even as he corrected the Republicans' many distortions. And White House advisers began looking for other forums to help the president reeducate the public about the bill.

The other event was, for all practical purposes, a gift from the health insurance industry. In early February, Anthem Blue Cross, the largest for-profit health insurer in Calilfornia, announced that it would raise premiums for people in the individual insurance market by as much as 39 percent. It was a stunning move, and inexplicable at a time when the health insurance industry was under such scrutiny. This would be fifteen times faster than inflation, as Kathleen Sebelius effectively noted in a letter to the insurer, and its parent company—WellPoint Inc.—was not hurting for profits.[14] Anthem Blue Cross insisted it was being hurt by rising medical costs and the loss of young, healthy customers who went without insurance because of the recession. In April, however, California regulators rejected the plan and Anthem Blue Cross withdrew it.[15]

Obama now had an opening to explain exactly what was on the line if comprehensive health care reform failed. Reform was supposed to pool people together and stabilize costs so individuals and small businesses wouldn't be vulnerable to rate hikes like this. If reform did not happen, Obama said, the 39 percent rate hike Anthem Blue Cross wanted was "a portrait of our future."[16]

There was now an opportunity to re-engage the public, and the president quickly scheduled a new forum to do so. On February 25, he would hold a bipartisan summit at Blair House, the presidential guesthouse near the White House, to discuss health care reform with key Democrats and Republicans from the Senate and the House. There was no real expectation that the forum would present any breakthroughs, but it was a great communications strategy. It would give Obama another chance to educate the public through his televised discussions with Republicans. And it would allow him to take command of the health care debate again, in a way he had not done since his September address to the joint session of Congress.

There was just one problem. In its invitation to the summit, the administration promised to post online, well in advance of the meeting, "a proposed health insurance reform package" that would "put a stop to insurance company abuses, extend coverage to millions of Americans, get control of skyrocketing premiums and out-of-pocket costs, and reduce the deficit."[17] This would have been the perfect description of an agreement between the House and the Senate on a final bill—the Senate bill as rewritten by the fixes package. The problem was, there was no agreement yet. When the invitation went out on February 12, Reid and Pelosi, with the help of administration officials, were trading offers on what should be in the fixes and how to pay for them. But they had not closed the deal.

The White House wanted to post its proposal online about a week before the summit. If there was no agreement between Pelosi and Reid by then, according to the reports I was getting, the White House would post Rahm Emanuel's proposal instead. Even at the White House, patience was running out. They could not be consumed by health care anymore. They were under pressure to move on, to turn the spotlight back to the economy and jobs.

It is possible that Obama would have refused to do that. He had rejected the pressure to scrap comprehensive reform so many times before. And ultimately, it was his decision, not anyone else's. Still, much of the talk coming out of the administration at the time suggested that the threat was real. So the pressure on Pelosi and Reid was very real, too.

They had about a week to reach a deal. If they didn't, comprehensive health care reform might be dead.

By February 18, Pelosi and Reid were just about there—on the substance of a fixes package. The House would get the increase in subsidies, the closing of the Medicare donut hole, and more Medicaid assistance to all states instead of the Nebraska deal. The Senate's Cadillac tax would not be completely gone, but it would be cut way back, to about 20 percent of the amount that had been in the Senate bill. Instead, there would be a new Medicare tax on unearned income, such as investments.

Unfortunately, they had not yet resolved who should make the first move: the

House or the Senate. Pelosi needed assurances from the Senate that it would not leave House Democrats hanging if they passed the Senate bill. She had to have a rock-solid guarantee from Senate Democrats that they could pass the "fixes" bill. So she consulted with me and others, at the White House and on Capitol Hill, for ideas on how to bridge the trust gap between the House and the Senate.

After a series of conversations and e-mails, a three-part rescue plan emerged. First, Reid would get fifty-one Democratic senators to sign a public letter stating that they would vote for the fixes bill. Next, the bill would be introduced in the Senate, with fifty-one cosponsors. Then, House and Senate Democrats would hold a joint caucus meeting with Obama, as a big show of unity, in which the president would rally the Democrats to make one final bid for history. Once all three of those things had happened, the House would pass the Senate health care bill and the fixes bill.

The mood was finally beginning to turn more positive, in both the House and the Senate. Reid liked the rescue plan, and agreed to get to work on it. Pelosi was still getting heat from her caucus about the Senate bill, but she could finally see a path to victory in the House. And Max Baucus supported the emerging reconciliation agreement. One day, he called me—a surprise in itself—and assured me that reform was back on track: "We're going to get this done one way or another. I guarantee you, we're going to get this done."

Finally, Obama himself was on board with the rescue plan. I talked to him by phone on Monday, February 22, three days before the summit. He sounded more upbeat than he had in a long time, and was determined to see health care reform through to the end. There was never a formal deal on all three parts of the rescue plan, and ultimately, only the first part of the rescue plan took place: the letter of support for the reconciliation bill. Some Senate Democrats saw the revival of comprehensive reform as too big a risk to endorse it publicly—or reject it publicly—so the list of cosponsors became unworkable. And the lack of trust between the House and the Senate made the joint caucus too risky in its own way.

But even the idea of a three-part rescue plan changed the dynamic. The more Reid talked about how he was sure he could pull it off, the more Pelosi and the rest of the House leadership believed they could pull together the votes on their end. This growing sense of optimism was enough, in itself, to allow them to make their deadline.

That Monday, the White House posted "the president's proposal" on its Web site, giving the public three days to look it over before the bipartisan summit. Thankfully, it was the reconciliation agreement. The threat of stripping back to an incremental health care bill had passed. The premium tax credits in the Senate bill would be strengthened to provide more help for both lower and higher incomes. The "Cadillac tax" would be reduced to about 20 percent of its former size. The Medicare "donut hole" would be closed. And the Nebraska Medicaid deal would be gone. Instead, the federal government would pay the entire cost of the Medicaid expansion from 2014 through 2017, 95 percent of the cost in 2018 and 2019, and 90 percent from then on.[18]

By calling it "the president's proposal," the White House was sending a clear message: Obama was taking ownership of the reform effort. He would put his authority behind the last push for comprehensive reform, and he would stake his presidency on whatever happened. The time for leaving the details of reform to Congress had passed. It was the moment many Democrats on the Hill, and many of us who had supported reform from the outside, had been waiting for.

Anyone who watched the summit on television on February 25 would have seen just how much Obama took command of the debate. He moderated the discussion skillfully, giving Democrats and Republicans plenty of time to make their points. He listened to the Republicans' ideas and praised the most reasonable ones. He took note of Tom Coburn's suggestion to use medical professionals as undercover patients to look for fraud, and Chuck Grassley's suggestion to boost Medicaid payments to providers so they don't turn away so many Medicaid patients.[19]

Much of the news coverage focused on the shots Obama fired back against Republican attacks—such as his famous retort to his former presidential rival, John McCain, that "we're not campaigning anymore. The election's over." But the summit was also a good educational experience for any Americans who had the time and the patience to watch the rest of it. Obama explained, step by step, why the main Republican alternatives to the bill wouldn't work. He explained why high-risk pools, a big part of the House Republican proposal, tend to have expensive premiums because they attract the least healthy patients—and why the pools were "just not going to be a very useful tool" for the amount of money Republicans wanted to put into them.[20] (They proposed $24 billion in funding over ten years, but only $3 billion for the first three years.)[21]

The biggest accomplishment of the summit, however, was that Obama finally was able to make a clean break from the Republicans. He was able to show that the Democrats had tried to consider the Republicans' ideas, but that the divide was simply too great. The Republicans spent much of the day urging him not to use reconciliation, calling it a heavy-handed tactic. And once again, Lamar Alexander of Tennessee said the Democrats should "start over," as he had been saying since the beginning of the process. But the Republicans' claims that they had been shut out of the process fell flat. After all, the entire experience of the Gang of Six—and all of the problems that resulted directly from that delay—showed that if anything, the Democrats spent too much time trying to get the Republicans on board.

In fact, it was now the perfect time to use reconciliation. The Democrats could not have used it at the beginning of the process, when they had an entire bill to pass in the Senate. Too many central pieces would have been stripped out, and too many moderate Democrats would have been uncomfortable using reconciliation so early. Now, however, most of the moderates were more willing to consider it. It was not an entire bill anymore—just a set of changes to a bill that had already passed with sixty votes. It was narrow enough that there was little risk of losing pieces to budget rule challenges. And, above all else, it was clearly the only way to finish the job.

On March 3, Obama stood before an audience of friendly health care stakeholders in the East Room of the White House and made the equivalent of a closing argument. Everyone had made their points, he said. Democrats and Republicans had talked the issue to death, and they would never be able to bridge the divide completely. But the problems were too big, and the suffering was too great, for Congress to do nothing. It was time, he said, for "a final vote on health care reform."

One of the stakeholders in the East Room that day was Chip Kahn, the man behind the "Harry and Louise" ads against the Clinton health care plan. Now, as the president of the Federation of American Hospitals, he was here as a supporter of reform. The hospitals may have had their own interests in supporting reform, but Kahn's presence sent a powerful message. This reform bill would not die at the hands of "Harry and Louise," or any of the counterparts in this year's debate. This bill would make it to the finish line.

"At stake right now is not just our ability to solve this problem, but our ability to solve any problem," Obama said. "I do not know how this plays politically, but I know it's right. And so I ask Congress to finish its work, and I look forward to signing this reform into law. Thank you very much, everybody. Let's get it done."

With that, he stepped forward into the audience to greet the stakeholders. And he shook hands with Chip Kahn.

15 | THE FINAL PUSH

It was up to the House now. This had been the place where the Democrats had pushed for the most progressive bill possible. They had insisted on the public option, which was not in the bill anymore. They had asked for a national exchange, rather than the state-based exchanges that were in the bill now. They had asked for no Cadillac tax, and although it would be much smaller now, it was still in the bill.

The day after Obama's East Room speech, he started meeting with House Democrats to ask for their support. He told centrists to consider the bill a job creation measure, and he told progressives his presidency was on the line.[1] It was just the kind of personal involvement he needed to show in the days ahead. The House had won some improvements in the bill, including slightly bigger subsidies, the closing of the Medicare donut hole, and the removal of the Nebraska deal. But those would become a reality only if the Senate passed the reconciliation bill with all of the fixes.

And to many House Democrats, that was a big if. Even after Obama's East Room speech, and even after all of Pelosi's and Reid's work, most House Democrats still did not trust the Senate.

The plan was to hold the votes in time to send both bills to Obama—the Senate bill and the fixes bill—before Congress left for its Easter recess on March 26. That way, Reid would have extra leverage to prevent the Republicans from dragging out the reconciliation bill too long with amendments and rules challenges. And this time, the bar would be just a bit lower for the House to pass the bills. Because of vacancies in four House seats, mostly due to retirements, Pelosi would only have to find 216 votes.

But if anything, it would be even harder to find 216 votes this time than it was to find 218 votes in the fall. For one thing, Pelosi would have to deal with the antiabortion Democrats all over again. Even though the Senate had added stronger antiabortion language to win Ben Nelson's vote, it was not strong enough for the most vocal opponents of abortion, including the United States Conference of Catholic Bishops.[2] When Bart Stupak read it, he thought it was almost turning the clock back to the House language he had fought in November. It did a better job of separating the payments for abortion coverage from the payments for everything else, he said. But in his view, it still would have recognized abortion, for the first time, as a benefit.[3]

Pelosi was annoyed at the prospect of having to fight this emotional battle yet again, distracting the public from all of the benefits and changes the bill had to offer. This is not an abortion bill, she said repeatedly. This is a health care bill. But unfortunately, the odds were not good that she would be able to find the votes without satisfying the antiabortion Democrats.

She was going to lose most of the Blue Dogs again. They weren't much more enthusiastic about the Senate bill than they were about the House bill. They thought it had grown in size and complexity, well beyond the point where their constituents could understand it. The Clinton health care bill was 1,342 pages.[4] The Senate bill was 2,409 pages, not counting the fixes, which would be made in the reconciliation bill.[5] To Mike Ross, that was "too big, too complex. It was too easy to distort." He also thought the effort had been permanently damaged by all of the criticism of the Nebraska deal. "At this point, my mother could rewrite the bill," Ross said in early March, "and I still couldn't vote for it because the process is just too tainted."[6]

It was the lack of trust of the Senate, however, that made the bill an even heavier lift this time. Pelosi could not lose more votes on final passage, and that was exactly the prospect she faced, even as Reid worked on his end to give the House the assurances it needed. So Pelosi put her own credibility on the line. At a caucus meeting on Friday, March 12—about a week before the House was likely to vote—she got an earful from one Democrat after another. The Senate can't finish the job on anything the House does, they said. Why should we trust the Senate?

"You don't have to trust the Senate," Pelosi told her caucus. "Trust me."

That same day, Obama was feeling better about the odds of passage. I joined him at the White House for lunch, at his invitation, and we compared notes about how the effort was going. He was a bit exasperated with the Senate—which carried a certain irony, since it was where he served when he launched his campaign for the White House. But he was still hopeful that the bill was back on track.

From time to time during the debate, I would predict the odds of passage based on the political circumstances at the time. At the lowest point after the Massachusetts election, I had figured the odds were down to about 10 percent. On this Friday afternoon, the president and I both agreed on the odds of victory: 65 percent. It was still far from a sure thing, but it was looking more likely than it had at any time since Massachusetts.

By the next week, though, the House leadership still did not have the votes locked down. They also did not have a crucial element: the official cost estimate of the new health care package by the Congressional Budget Office. A sizeable number of House Democrats would base their vote on how much the reform package would cost—including the Senate bill and the fixes bill—and whether it would reduce the deficit or increase it. Until the leadership could fine-tune the reconciliation bill so it not only paid for itself, but reduced the deficit by a big enough amount, they could not release the actual reconciliation bill. And until they could do that, they could not win the votes of undecided Democrats who wanted to see the exact language.

On Tuesday, March 16, Steny Hoyer acknowledged that the Democrats didn't have the votes yet.[7] By this point, time was running out. The House had to vote sometime this week, or on the weekend, to give the Senate enough time to debate and pass the reconciliation bill before the Easter recess began. Once again, it appeared that the House would have to hold a weekend vote on health care.

Pelosi was toying with a new legislative strategy that might make it easier for House Democrats to get over their distaste for the Senate bill. Before every vote on major legislation, the House approves a rule that sets the terms for the debate. The idea was to use the rule to pass the Senate bill automatically. When the House approved the rule, the Senate bill would be declared to be passed, and the House could move on and vote for the fixes bill without ever voting directly on the Senate bill.[8] This "deem and pass" approach had been used frequently on other legislation, but not on anything this big. This way, however, Pelosi would not have to convince progressive Democrats to vote for the original Senate bill—a vote that could be easily exploited by political opponents if the reconciliation bill failed.

Unfortunately, the idea gave Republicans a new opening to claim the Democrats were using underhanded tactics to pass the bill. In truth, there was nothing unusual about the deem-and-pass procedure, and both parties had used it. But this was an argument the Democrats did not need to have. To the public, it might well have looked like an underhanded tactic. So that weekend, the leadership dropped the idea. In going through the exercise, however, they helped rank-and-file Democrats accept the inevitable. There was no way to avoid a direct vote on the Senate bill. If they wanted to finish a year's worth of work on health care—and make history—they would have to pass the bill and have faith that the Senate would pass the fixes they wanted.

Slowly, Obama's one-on-one efforts with skeptical House Democrats were beginning to pay off. On Wednesday, March 17, he won a new convert. Dennis Kucinich of Ohio, a two-time presidential candidate who had run against Obama for the Democratic nomination in 2008, had voted against the House bill in the fall. He was a strong supporter of single-payer health care, and he thought the House bill did too much to preserve for-profit health care. But now, after an intensive lobbying effort by the president—including a speech in Kucinich's district and a lengthy talk with him on Air Force One—Kucinich announced he would vote for the package.[9]

The next day, Luis Gutierrez of Illinois dropped his threat to vote against the bill for banning undocumented immigrants from buying health insurance through the exchanges. Obama gave Gutierrez his word that he would push for an immigration reform bill soon.[10] The problem, though, was that other House Democrats who had voted for the health care bill in the fall were announcing they would vote against it this time. For example, Stephen Lynch of Massachusetts said the new bill was too soft on the health insurance and pharmaceutical companies.[11] If Pelosi was going to start losing votes she had won in the fall, she would have to convert some former no votes to yes votes just to break even.

On Thursday, March 18, the leadership finally had a reconciliation bill with a good cost estimate. Both were released, giving wavering Democrats a chance to read the details they had been waiting for. And the estimate from the Congressional Budget Office was good news indeed. The final package would, in fact, reduce the deficit, not increase it. Many Americans did not understand this. All they heard were the opponents' attacks on the "trillion-dollar health care bill." They never heard that, with all of the savings in the same bill, Congress had more than paid for the cost.

According to the final estimate, the bill would cost $788 billion over ten years to expand health coverage. But after you counted all of the savings, it would actually reduce the deficit by $124 billion over 10 years. (There was also another part of the reconciliation bill, dealing with education, that added another $19 billion in savings.) Once all of the important reforms were in place, the Congressional Budget Office predicted, 94 percent of Americans would have health coverage. That's not universal coverage, but it would be much better than the 83 percent of Americans who have coverage now. In all, 32 million uninsured people would finally join the ranks of the insured.[12]

Both Obama and Pelosi met with one House Democrat after another, looking for anyone who might switch from no to yes. Now, the votes started coming in. Bart Gordon of Tennessee, a Blue Dog who had voted against the House bill in the fall, announced he would support the new bill, in part because it would reduce the deficit.[13] Betsy Markey of Colorado, another Blue Dog no vote in the fall, said she would switch her vote this time, too. The next day, Allen Boyd of Florida, John Boccieri of Ohio, Scott Murphy of New York, and Suzanne Kosmas of Florida—all opponents of the original House health care bill—announced they would be yes votes on the final package.[14] One by one, Pelosi was building up her safety margin.

It was still not enough.

Bart Stupak was looking for ways to change the abortion language. It couldn't be done, the leadership had told him. Any change in the abortion section would not affect the budget, and if it didn't affect the budget, it would not survive in the reconciliation bill. That objection, however, did not rule out a separate vote on his abortion language. So that was what Stupak wanted.

The votes on the Senate bill and the reconciliation bill were now scheduled for Sunday, March 21. As of Friday night, Pelosi had not ruled out a separate vote for Stupak's language. Once again, she had to hold a difficult meeting with the pro-choice Democrats in her office suite late Friday night. These Democrats were furious. And this time, they were firm: no more abortion votes for Stupak, or Pelosi would lose the pro-choice votes. If Stupak got his way, Diana DeGette of Colorado warned, anywhere from forty to fifty-five Democratic votes could be at risk.[15]

Besides, there were big problems with the way Stupak wanted to hold the vote. His suggestion was an "enrollment corrections" resolution, which allows technical fixes to be made to a bill after Congress passes it and before the president signs it into law. A change in abortion policy, however, is not really a technical change. And more importantly, from Stupak's point of view, the vote he wanted was sure to fail. Rahm Emanuel told him the resolution would not get more than forty-five votes in the Senate because the Republicans, most of whom shared Stupak's views on abortion, were not interested in helping him rewrite the language. To Stupak, that said it all. The Republicans didn't care about policy. They just wanted to kill the health care bill.[16]

On Saturday morning, Pelosi finally ruled out a vote on Stupak's language. By that point, however, another alternative was gaining momentum. If Obama issued an executive order promising that federal funds would not be used for abortion, Stupak and his allies might be satisfied without any need to rewrite the actual bill language.

It came up as the Democrats were kicking around ideas for presidential actions that might solve the problem. One early idea was to have Obama issue a "signing statement," an official written message the president sometimes puts out that can clarify how the executive branch interprets the law. This was a questionable idea, to say the least. George W. Bush became notorious for using the "signing statements" to claim the right to ignore parts of the new laws, as if a president can single-handedly decide which laws to obey. Obama had criticized Bush's use of the signing statements, so this was hardly the time to use one himself. Besides, Stupak thought signing statements were worthless. He wanted a presidential action that would carry actual force.

Soon, Rahm Emanuel came up with a new idea: an executive order. In Stupak's view, this would be a much better way to go. Executive orders can be overturned by the next president, but they are almost never vulnerable to court challenges. So the White House lawyers drafted an order, and on Thursday, they read the draft on a phone call with some of Stupak's allies. Stupak was not on the call, but the other lawmakers gave him their verdict quickly: It was flowery and meaningless.

Finally, one of the negotiators asked Stupak, if you're so smart, why don't you write it? Stupak thought the answer to that question was obvious: because he wasn't one of the president's lawyers. Still, the White House needed a better idea of exactly what he wanted. So he sent over a few pages of suggestions. The White House attorneys read them and liked them. Late Friday night—in the Cannon House Office Building, far away from the center of action in the Capitol—Stupak, Representative Mike Doyle of Pennsylvania, and the White House lawyers gathered to read through a new draft of the order.

By this point, many Democrats and progressives were exasperated with Stupak. They thought he was holding up the bill for no good reason, and pushing too hard even after other antiabortion Democrats were satisfied. I felt the same way. But Stupak and his family were now getting angry phone calls from both the left and the right—and the most hostile ones were from the right. They saw him as their best chance for stopping the health care bill. Now, they saw that he might actually be looking for a way to vote for it. And they were turning on him.

Stupak was losing sleep, wondering if he was doing the right thing. As the chairman of the Oversight and Investigations subcommittee of Henry Waxman's committee, Stupak had investigated the practice of rescission—canceling people's coverage retroactively when they get sick—and the problems of the underinsured. Both problems would get needed relief from the bill, and he knew the problems had to be solved. But he was sure he was right about the abortion language, and he was sure that most of his constituents were with him.[17]

There was one day left before the House vote. It was Saturday, March 20, and it was time to gather the House Democratic caucus for one final pitch. Obama would fire them up with one more call to make history. And Harry Reid would give them the word of his caucus that if they passed the bills, the Senate would finish the job.

Reid had worked hard to gather fifty-one signatures for a letter of support for the reconciliation bill. In the end, he got fifty-six Democratic senators to sign it, more than enough to guarantee that the Senate would pass the bill. Unfortunately, the politics of the bill were still so sensitive that he could not release the names. Some senators were reluctant to commit themselves in such a public way. But Reid also wanted to protect the Democrats who did not sign the letter. If he released the letter with the fifty-six signatures, it would be obvious who did not sign it, and they would face the wrath of their colleagues and reform supporters throughout the country.

Reid was so concerned about his caucus members that when Pelosi asked him to let her keep the letter, he refused. Instead, he would release the letter on the day of the House Democratic caucus meeting, but without the signatures. And he would speak to the caucus and personally promise them the Senate would not let them down.

That day, the passions unleashed by the debate spilled out into the open in an ugly way. As the Democrats approached the Capitol for the caucus meeting, protesters who opposed the bill yelled a racial slur at John Lewis of Georgia, one of the heroes of the civil rights movement. Some shouted an antigay insult at Barney Frank of Massachusetts, the chairman of the House Financial Services Committee. And in an incident captured on YouTube, one spat on Emanuel Cleaver of Missouri as he walked up the steps. All the while, an angry crowd shouted, "Kill the bill! Kill the bill!"

Jim Clyburn of South Carolina, the House majority whip and another veteran of the civil rights movement, had a tense moment of his own. After a meeting of the Democratic whips at the Longworth House Office Building, across the street from the Capitol, Clyburn and his aides waited for his car to come to the side entrance. As they waited, a crowd of protesters recognized Clyburn as a member of Congress and started to close in. With frightening looks on their faces, they broke into the same chant: "Kill the bill! Kill the bill!" Clyburn's car came before any of the protesters could get too close to him. Later, he and Lewis compared notes on their encounters. Lewis told Clyburn he had not seen anything like this since the 1960s.

The caucus meeting, however, gave the Democrats a sense of purpose. Reid appeared before his House counterparts and delivered the promise they had all waited for. "The most sweeping changes to Americans' health care will be law in a matter of days," he said, and "I am happy to announce I have the commit-ment of a significant majority of the U.S. Senate to make that good law even better." Unfortunately, he said, he could not release the names of the senators. Clyburn let him off the hook. "We don't need to see the names," Clyburn said. "Your word is good enough for us."

And when Obama appeared, he pulled out a note card that appeared to have only two words written on it: *Pelosi Reid.* For this speech, he did not need notes. He had taken his closing arguments on the road, making his final pitch in speeches around the country, and he knew what he wanted to say. He quoted Abraham Lincoln: "I am not bound to win, but I am bound to be true." This was the lawmakers' chance, he said, to end the suffering of the people who are locked out—or priced out—of the health care they need. It was the lawmakers' chance to make good on the ideals and goals they had when they ran for office.

"Every single one of you have made that promise not just to your constituents but to yourself. And this is the time to make true on that promise," Obama said. "We are not bound to win, but we are bound to be true. We are not bound to succeed, but we are bound to let whatever light we have shine. We have been debating health care for decades. It has now been debated for a year."

Now, Obama told the House Democrats, "It is in your hands."

Sunday, March 21, was a bright and unseasonably warm day in Washington, D.C. Once again, the hostility to reform from its most fervent opponents was in full display all around the Capitol. At the south end of the building—where the House meets—a crowd of protesters gathered in defiance of the votes that were now just hours away. There was a "Don't Tread on Me" sign, a symbol of the Tea Party movement. Other protesters held up signs that captured all of the fears the opponents had stirred up: "Kill the Bill." "Obama Is Not My King." "Don't Ration My Health Care." "Government Run Health Care? You Can't Be Serious!"

And there were exchanges at the Capitol that day that betrayed real hatred—not just for the bill, but for anyone the protesters thought would benefit at their expense. As one couple, a man and a woman, walked along the edge of the Capitol grounds, they passed by a group of reform supporters carry-ing "Si Se Puede!" signs. The woman shouted at the reform supporters, "We pay taxes, and we're not paying for health care for you!" One man in that group smiled and offered, "We pay taxes." The woman's response: "If you're il-legal, you don't."[18]

That day, however, the House Democrats decided to show they would not be intimidated by the antigovernment hostility, or the open racism among the worst of the protesters. After holding one last caucus meeting at the Cannon House Office Building, they marched across the street to the Capitol to get ready for the vote. Pelosi and Hoyer linked arms with John Lewis, in a scene straight out of the days of the civil rights movement. And Pelosi held a supersize gavel that Dingell had loaned to her, one of the gavels used during the House debate on the creation of Medicare in 1965. This time, the protesters still heck-led the Democrats, but they held back. When faced with this show of force among the lawmakers, there was nothing else they could do.

Even that day, however, Pelosi was not yet guaranteed of a victory. The leader-ship team was fairly confident that they would have 216 votes for the Senate bill itself, even without Stupak. If that was all that mattered, there would have been no need to keep negotiating with him on abortion. The problem, how-ever, was the mischief that might be created by the motion the Republicans planned to offer. In House debates, the minority party usually gets to offer a "motion to recommit" the bill—sending it back to committee with instructions to add some provision the minority party wants. Pelosi's team had tried to guess which issue the Republicans were most likely to raise in their motion, out of all the options that could create the most trouble for the Democrats.

It became obvious what the Republicans were going to do. They would offer Stupak's abortion language. And the Democrats might not have the votes to defeat it. If they could not, the bill would be stopped in its tracks.

So the House leadership and the White House prepared the executive order to bring Stupak around. At about 3:00 that afternoon, Obama called Stupak and told him, "We have a deal."[19] The executive order was released later that afternoon. It noted that the legislation "specifically prohibits the use of tax credits and cost-sharing reduction payments to pay for abortion ser-vices," and it told the Department of Health and Human Services and the Office of Management and Budget to put out guidelines to help states keep federal funds separate from abortion coverage.[20] When the pro-choice Demo-crats read it, they were relieved. In their eyes, it was vague and would not mat-ter much in the long run.

But it mattered to Stupak. At 4:00, he and some of the other antiabortion Democrats—including Marcy Kaptur of Ohio, Chris Carney of Pennsylvania, and Alan Mollohan of West Virginia—held a press conference to announce the agreement. Everyone in the group wanted health care reform to pass, Stupak said, but there was "a moral principle that meant more to us than anything, and that's the sanctity of life." When asked if the agreement meant Pelosi had her 216 votes, Stupak marked the decisive moment in an understated way.

"We're well past 216, yes," he said.[21]

Throughout the day, the House Republicans had tried to play to the crowds of antireform protesters, and even encouraged them. Several even stood on the balcony outside the House chamber, holding up sheets of paper with hand-drawn letters that spelled out to the protesters below: "Kill the Bill."[22] That night, however, all they could do was make their own closing arguments as they counted down the last hours to the votes. Eric Cantor of Virginia, the House Republican whip, repeated the fiction of the "trillion-dollar overhaul." Paul Ryan of Wisconsin called the bill "paternalistic," "arrogant," and "condescending."[23]

And shortly after 10:00 p.m., House Minority Leader John Boehner of Ohio gave a rousing, theatrical speech about all of the supposed dangers of the bill. Boehner knew how to work with the Democrats when he wanted to. In 2001, as the chairman of the House education committee, he worked with Ted Kennedy to pass the most bipartisan domestic initiative of George W. Bush's presidency, the No Child Left Behind education reform law. As the House Republican leader, though, Boehner simply played to the fears of the Republican base and the Tea Party movement. "Do you really believe that if you like the health plan that you have, that you can keep it? No, you can't," Boehner said. "Can you say it was done openly, with transparency and accountability, without backroom deals struck behind closed doors, hidden from the people?" he asked, building up to a red-faced shout. "Hell no, you can't!"

It was up to Pelosi to put the debate back in perspective. The exhaustion was starting to show, after working through the week and straight through the weekend, but she still managed to rally the Democrats with the call of history. With the House vote on the Senate bill just minutes away, she reminded House members that by passing the bill, they would join the ranks of the previous Congresses that passed Social Security and Medicare. And she reminded them that Ted Kennedy had called health care reform "the great unfinished business of our society." This was their chance, she said, "to complete the great unfinished business of our society and pass health insurance reform for all Americans that is a right and not a privilege."[24]

The vote began. At 10:45 p.m., the House reached 216 votes for the Senate bill. The Democrats cheered, then counted down to the end of the vote. When David Obey of Wisconsin, who was presiding over the vote, brought down the gavel, the Senate bill had won 219 votes.

But it was not over yet. The House still had to pass the reconciliation bill with the fixes it had wanted. And before it could do that, it had to deal with the Republican motion to recommit. Sure enough, it was Stupak's original abortion language.

Hoyer came up to Stupak on the House floor. Two Democrats are going to speak on this motion, Hoyer told him: you and me. Get your speech ready. Stupak had about five minutes to prepare, so he scribbled down some notes.[25] It turned out to be one of the most powerful, and memorable, speeches of the evening. The Democrats gave him a round of applause when he stood up to speak. The man many of them had seen as an obstacle to reform was now stepping in to save it.

"This motion is nothing more than an opportunity to continue to deny thirty-two million Americans health care," Stupak said. For people who value the sanctity of life, he said, the bill would guarantee that "all life from the unborn to the last breath of a senior citizen is honored and respected. For the unborn child, his or her mother will finally have pre- and postnatal care under our bill. If the child is born with mental problems, we provide medical care without bankrupting the family." The Republican motion, he said, "is really to politicize life, not prioritize life."[26]

There was one more reminder of the ugliness of the debate, as Randy Neugebauer, a Republican of Texas, shouted, "Baby killer!" He later apologized and said he was referring to the bill, not Stupak.[27] Even if that was true, it was no excuse for boorish behavior on the House floor. But Stupak's speech did the job. The House voted down the Republican motion.

And then came the easy vote: the reconciliation bill with the fixes the House wanted. It won 220 votes. Shortly after 11:30 p.m., with a smile and a determined pound of the gavel, Pelosi declared the reconciliation bill passed.

At the White House, Obama and Biden watched the vote on a big-screen television in the Roosevelt Room in the West Wing, surrounded by exhausted aides. As the 216th vote registered on the secreen, Obama, with a look of immense satisfaction and relief, turned to Biden and applauded.

By the time the Senate took up the reconciliation bill, the debate was an anticlimax. The Republicans tried their best to amend it, but the Democrats stuck together enough to vote down all of the changes. The Republicans did manage to strip out two technical provisions in the education section, forcing the House to pass the bill once again without those two provisions. But in the end, all of the health care fixes survived, and the reconciliation bill passed the Senate with fifty-six votes. Ben Nelson and Blanche Lincoln voted against it, as did Mark Pryor of Arkansas.

The reason the debate was so anticlimactic was that the main reason for the fight—the Senate's comprehensive reform bill—had already reached Obama's desk. On Tuesday, March 23, the embattled House and Senate Democrats gathered in the East Room of the White House for the signing ceremony many had wondered if they would ever see. Vicki Kennedy was there. So were Kathleen Sebelius and Nancy-Ann DeParle. So was John Dingell, the voice of history from the passage of Medicare in 1965. Obama had invited a special guest to remind them what it was all about: Marcelas Owens, a fifth-grader from Seattle whose mother had died after losing her health insurance.[28] And, of course, Nancy Pelosi and Harry Reid were there, too.

A century of talk about health care reform, Obama told them, had finally come to an end. He talked about what Marcelas Owens had gone through, and he reminded his audience that his mother had been forced to fight with her insurance company as she was dying of cancer. "We are a nation that faces its challenges and accepts its responsibilities. We are a nation that does what is hard. What is necessary. What is right," Obama said. After decades of trying, he said, the nation had finally endorsed "the core principle that everybody should have some basic security when it comes to their health care."[29]

The journey had not gone smoothly, and mistakes were made along the way. There were too many Democrats who did not fight for one of the most basic priorities our party has. Thoughtful Republicans did not show political courage at a time when the nation needed it. And there were times when the president had learned the lessons of the Clinton years too well, staying out of the congressional fight when the Democrats needed him to get more involved. But in the end, Obama always rose to the occasion. He did not give up, even during the toughest days of the fight. And when the effort almost died after Massachusetts, he went all in and saved it.

In the end, he lived up to the promise he made to me as we ended our visit at the White House in August 2009. "They won't wear me down," Obama told me. "I will wear them down."

With Nancy Pelosi and Harry Reid standing behind him, and with Marcelas Owens and a smiling John Dingell at his side, Obama signed comprehensive health care reform into law.

Part Four

THE ROAD FROM HERE

1 | HOW CLOSE DID WE COME?

It took true courage to do what Obama and the Democrats did. They may well pay a price for it, in the short term. Many Republicans are doing everything they can to stoke the public's fears about the law, hoping they can use those fears and resentments to unseat Democrats in the next elections. Conservative activists are up in arms. State officials, mostly Republicans, are mounting legal and legislative campaigns to block the individual mandate.

It's important to keep these rebellions in perspective. When Lyndon Johnson signed the Civil Rights Act of 1964 into law, he is said to have remarked that "we have lost the South for a generation." By that standard, the pressure Democrats are facing over health care reform looks less threatening than it seems right now. The point, however, is that major social change often leads to short-term political turmoil. Over time, people come to accept that it was the right thing to do. Obama and the Democrats in Congress took a big risk by taking on the health care problems that have been building up for decades. In the long run, they will be vindicated.

It may be years, however, before we know just how close we have come to solving the problems. It does not diminish the significance of the accomplishment to say that. It is simply a fact. The fate of reform now depends on how well it is implemented across the country. The Department of Health and Human Services, the states, the newly created health care boards, providers, insurers, employers, and consumers all will have important roles to play. They will have to be vested in the future of reform to make it a true success.

If this were a football game, we would not be able to say that we scored a touchdown with the passage of health reform. In reality, we are only on the thirty-yard line, with seventy yards left to go. This is not because the law falls short of what it needed to do. It does fall short in some areas, but the ground it covers is truly astonishing. For the first time, the goals of access to health coverage for everyone, lower costs, and better quality and outcomes are within our reach. Now, however, we must all do the hard work of making the law's reforms a reality. And it will take many years before we can judge whether the reality of the reforms lives up to the promise.

There will be new structures for marketing and regulating health insurance, with health exchanges in every state and four new, standard levels of coverage for their health plans. There will be experiments with new ways of paying providers, designed to reward the most efficient care and to discourage errors. Other experiments will test new ways of delivering care, from accountable care organizations to medical homes. These will require new payment and delivery systems, and a new federal research center, the Center for Medicare and Medicaid Innovation, will develop and test these models to see which ones should be expanded throughout the country.

There will be a tremendous amount of new responsibilities for the federal government and the states. The Department of Health and Human Services will have to oversee the creation of all of these new structures, launch several temporary programs to help consumers until the biggest reforms begin, and fill in important details that Congress didn't decide in the bill—from the subsidy rules for people with unpredictable incomes to the best way to help the new long-term care program pay for itself. The states will have to get the new health exchanges up and running, and they will have to make sure the expansion of Medicaid runs smoothly. If any of the states don't create the exchanges, HHS will have to do it for them—a real possibility, given how some state officials are making such a big show of fighting the law.

We will delegate big responsibilities to newly created boards, centers, and institutes, all of which have to do their jobs well and not create their own problems. The new board to review Medicare spending—the Independent Payment Advisory Board—will have to suggest ways to restrain the program's costs without hurting seniors' health care, and without violating the many restrictions

Congress placed on it. The new Center for Medicare and Medicaid Innovation will have to monitor the payment and delivery experiments closely enough to know what works, but also to know which experiments are causing trouble and should be altered or shut down. The Patient-Centered Outcomes Research Institute, which will be in charge of comparative effectiveness research, will have to be careful not to revive the charges that the government is trying to "ration" people's care.

All of these will have to work well. But at a broader level, the law will have the best chance of success if the country accepts it. We should not have to spend the next several years mediating a fight between the blue states and the red states. State leaders can continue to fight the law in the courts if they wish, but they will have to realize that the greater the uncertainty and turmoil, the more likely it is that people's health care will suffer. Within the medical community, providers can help by embracing transparency and the new emphasis on paying for value rather than volume. If they simply complain to their patients about the new ways of doing things, they will undermine their patients' confidence without doing anything to solve the problems.

And as patients, all of us can help by accepting our new responsibilities—to get health coverage, to use medical care wisely, and to keep ourselves as healthy as we can. The days of uncritically accepting every test or procedure a provider recommends, or demanding all of the latest drugs or medical products we have seen on television, have to end. We have to become more conscious of how the overuse of medical care raises costs for everyone, including us.

And unless it would be a truly unbearable financial burden, everyone who can get health coverage should do so. The more people delay getting coverage until they're sick, the more the law's most important protections, such as coverage for people with preexisting conditions, will unravel because they will become too expensive. That would be a tragedy, and not just for other people. It would be a tragedy for all of us.

The law takes on all three of the major problems that plague our health care today: the runaway costs, the uneven quality, and the difficulty so many Americans have in getting the coverage they need. However, it is much more specific on the last part—the new protections and marketplaces to help people get coverage—than it is on costs and quality. That may have been the only way Congress could handle it, at least for now. We simply don't know enough yet about what methods will work the best. There is a broad consensus on the most promising ideas for delivering better medical care and paying for it more wisely. But there is no consensus on which ones stand out from the rest.

So the law sets up ten years of experiments to find out which cost and quality methods truly work, while the most concrete reforms will be the ones that help people get, and keep, meaningful health coverage. That may be the right balance for this round. After all, Congress had to break the stalemate first. It could not hold out for the perfect reforms in all three areas. However, helping people get coverage is also the most popular thing for elected officials to do. Bringing costs down is the least popular, but it is also critical to the success of reform.

It may take years to learn how to do it right, but over the long run, Congress and the administration must show the will to do it. Otherwise, we will just be requiring everyone to participate in a health care market that becomes less affordable every day. Obama had it right when he told the transition team, "If we don't control costs, we will have failed at health reform regardless of whatever else we do." We do not have to get them under control in the first few years, but over the long term, we must get them under control.

The administration and Congress missed a big opportunity, for example, to make prescription drugs less expensive for everyone. The law does close the Medicare donut hole, and Congress was able to do so, in part, because the drug industry agreed to give seniors a 50 percent discount on the prescription drugs they buy while they are in the coverage gap. This was part of the agreement the administration reached with Pharmaceutical Research and Manufacturers of America for their support of the bill. The price of the agreement, however, was that the Democrats had to oppose two of their promising ideas for making prescription drugs more affordable: importing cheaper drugs from other countries and using Medicare's bargaining power to negotiate lower prices for seniors.

In fact, when Senator Byron Dorgan tried to amend the Senate health care bill to allow lower-cost, FDA-approved versions of drugs to be imported from other countries, the Senate defeated it, even though his measure had bipartisan support.[1] This measure has been a Democratic priority for years, but it also has the support of notable Republicans, including John McCain and Olympia Snowe. And it is sure to make prescription drugs cheaper for most Americans. The deal with PhRMA probably was necessary, in this round, to turn a potentially dangerous opponent into an ally. But now that reform has been signed into law, nothing should stop the administration and Congress from pursuing these good ideas for reducing drug costs on the next round.

Even on helping Americans get health coverage, the law does not go as far as it should. Instead of a national exchange—the structure that would have been the most consumer-friendly and would have had the lowest administrative costs—we have to deal with the uncertainties of fifty different state exchanges, some of which will be run better than others. And, of course, the public option is not in the law, even in a compromise form. Over time, the idea is bound to return, as Americans become more confident in the law and less scared of a "government takeover" of health care. In fact, it seems inevitable that we will have a public option someday, especially if the private health insurance market does not give people more affordable and stable coverage on its own.

Still, there will be many new insurance protections for all Americans, and that is a major accomplishment in itself. By the end of 2010, children will have to be accepted for coverage even if they have preexisting conditions. There will be no more lifetime limits on what health plans cover. Rescissions—canceling individuals' health coverage when they get sick—will be a thing of the past. And starting in 2014, health plans will have to accept everyone for coverage, even if they have preexisting conditions. They will not be able to charge you higher premiums because of your health status or your gender. They will not be able to limit what they will pay for your coverage in a given year. Important categories of benefits will have to be available in all health plans offered through the new exchanges. And there will be new limits on what you will have to pay out of your own pocket.

Even on the cost side, the law makes a serious effort to try the most promising reform ideas. Just about all of the leading ideas for paying providers differently, and for delivering care more efficiently, will be tried over the next ten years. None of this will be radical. We still will have a health care market—not a system. Most industrialized countries have a system, with universal financing and a centralized management infrastructure to administer health care delivery and payment. We still will have a market that delivers the best care to those that can afford it, with a big role for private insurers that still will have to answer to their shareholders.

But at least now, we will have a chance to make it more rational—and to protect millions of vulnerable Americans from falling through the cracks.

As we move forward, there are five goals the administration, Congress, and all of the health care stakeholders should keep in mind as they try to make the future of health care as successful as it should be. They may take years to achieve, but thanks to the passage of reform, all are now within our reach.

The first goal is to embrace the use of health information technology at every opportunity. It can save money, but it also has the potential to prevent many of the common errors in our medical care, such as physicians prescribing drugs a patient should not take, ordering tests or procedures the patient has already received, or not providing preventive care the patient should get. E-prescribing can take care of the age-old problem of pharmacies not being able to read your doctor's handwriting. And the data from secure electronic medical records can help us advance the research that will tell us what services truly work the best. Now that the reform law, and the stimulus bill before it, both advance the cause of health information technology, we have the opportunity to turn our 19th-century administrative rooms into 21st-century administrative rooms once and for all.

The second goal is to make our health care more transparent. For the first time, hospitals will have to post the prices of their services—but over time, all health care providers should have to do the same. There should be more Web sites to help people research the quality rankings of health care providers in all settings. And HHS and the states should give the strongest possible enforcement to the new transparency requirements for health insurance companies, including the disclosure of how much of their revenues go to actual health care—rather than administrative expenses—and the more detailed descriptions of what is covered and what is not.

Third, we must also do everything possible to reduce unnecessary medical care. That effort can take several forms. The law will test new ways of paying providers for the value of their care, not the volume of it. But we also need to find ways to discourage proprietary medicine, in which physicians see themselves as running a business rather than a practice—and therefore order tests that are good for the business, not the patients. We have to fight back against market-driven care, in which patients ask for some new drug that was advertised on television and the physician gives it to them, whether they need it or not. And we should keep looking for new ways to reduce defensive medicine, moving past the tired ideological debate over Republicans' proposals to limit medical malpractice lawsuits.

Fourth, we should take a new look at the health care pyramid, in which primary care is at the bottom and the most advanced procedures and technologies are at the top. Unlike other countries, we have been starting at the top and working our way down until the money runs out, leaving millions of Americans without the basic health care they need. If we make the most of the opportunity to eliminate unnecessary care, and save money in the process, we may have the resources for the first time to cover the entire pyramid. If we can do that, we will take a giant step toward giving everyone the health care he or she deserves.

And finally, we must embrace the use of best practices. There will be new penalties in the coming years for hospitals that have unnecessarily high readmission rates and infections that we know how to prevent. But the trick will be to spread the word about the best practices that can help the hospitals avoid those penalties. Readmissions and infection rates are still way too high. The Center for Quality Improvement and Patient Safety will have the responsibility for identifying and promoting the best practices used by the most successful health care providers, such as checklists and proper planning for discharging patients from hospitals. But as we learn more about these best practices, all providers must put them into use.

It took Obama two years to set the stage for reform in his presidential campaign, and it took Congress more than a year to write the legislation and pass it. But now, it will take 10 years to implement it. That work is only beginning, and there will be much hard work ahead by everyone involved. We will have to be honest about what works and what does not. There will have to be a lot of fine-tuning along the way. And there may even be issues that Congress has to revisit in the coming years. The law is not everything it should have been, but there will be chances to make it better.

We may not agree on the verdict right now, but over time, the verdict will become clear: This was a risk worth taking.

2 | LAYING THE GROUNDWORK: 2010–13

The transformation of our health care will take place over several years, not all at once. That was the wisest way to structure the law, because we need time to avoid big disruptions and give everyone a chance to prepare. But there is widespread agreement on the goals we need to achieve: better access to medical care for everyone who needs it, lower costs so everyone can afford it, and higher quality so everyone can be more confident in his or her care. By the time all of the changes are in place, we will have our best chance ever to achieve all three.

The new health care law is one of the most ambitious social changes our government has ever attempted. It ranks with the creation of Social Security in 1935 and the Medicare and Medicaid programs in 1965. In terms of creating new economic structures, it is one of the most significant advances since the creation of the Federal Reserve in 1913. It does not build an entire new federal program, the way Medicare did. But it does set up significant new responsibilities to be shared by the federal government and the states, just as Medicaid did for low-income health care. It also sets us on a course toward new ways of paying for and delivering health care in a way that Medicaid never did. And it sets new expectations for businesses, and for our own responsibility for our health care, that go well beyond anything our nation has attempted before.

This does not mean people's lives will be upended by the law. In fact, Congress went about as far as it could reasonably go to protect the health care arrangements people have now. Most workplace health plans, for example, will not have to change to comply with all of the new rules, such as the minimum benefit requirements that will take effect in 2014 and the rules that will limit how much they can vary their premiums. As long as they do not change their own coverage too much, they will be considered "grandfathered" health plans, meaning that they are exempt from a lot of the new rules—though they will have to comply with some of the most popular protections, such as covering people with preexisting conditions.

And despite all of the charges that everyone's premiums will go up, there is little risk of that if the main pieces of the law are allowed to work together. Health insurance premiums will continue to go up anyway, so it is unrealistic to expect that none of us will see any increases. But the Congressional Budget Office predicted that premiums for most people who have coverage through the workplace would either stay the same or even drop slightly, compared to what would have happened without the new law. The premiums would go up for people who get health insurance on their own, largely because the benefits and protections would be better than they are now. But even then, more than half of those people would get tax credits and subsidies in the new exchanges, and these would be more than enough to cover the difference.[1]

There will be changes that all of us will see along the way. Most of us will have more dependable health insurance, and there will be much better market-places to find coverage for individuals and small businesses. There will be experiments to find smarter ways to pay for health care and more efficient ways for us to get it, and while those will start in the Medicare and Medicaid programs, they may expand so more of us will see the changes.

But a lot of things have to go right for these changes to work. We can only achieve all of the goals—better coverage, better care, and lower costs—if the steps in the new law happen the way they are supposed to. If they are blocked by court challenges, political resistance, or even poor implementation, we will not achieve the goals in the law. But there is enormous potential to achieve them if all of the steps go well. All of us—government officials, insurance officials, providers, employers, patients, and everyone else with a stake in health care—must do our best to make sure that happens.

2010

The first year of the new law strengthens private health insurance so there are fewer cracks to fall through. By the end of this year, many of the "early deliverables" should be in place. These are the benefits Congress wanted to put in place, temporarily in some cases, so consumers would be able to get some help right away while the federal government and the states lay the groundwork for the bigger changes.

Under the old rules of health insurance, people with preexisting conditions were some of the most vulnerable people in the country. That was especially true of children, who could be denied coverage for something as common as asthma. A big change you will notice this year is that if your child has a preexisting condition, health insurance companies no longer will be able to reject him or her for coverage. Adults with preexisting conditions are not guaranteed coverage until 2014, but children are protected as of September.[2]

The new rules will start to phase out other industry practices that deny coverage to people in need. Health insurance companies will not be able to place lifetime limits on your benefits anymore, and the practice of rescission, canceling your coverage retroactively if you get sick, will end.[3] Most people never would have reached the lifetime limit, but the ban on this practice should give you peace of mind if you ever suffer a devastating illness or injury. And anyone with individual health insurance would have been vulnerable to rescissions, in which the insurance company looks for any excuse to cancel your coverage—any bit of information you might have left off of your application.

There will also be a new option to help young adults, who often don't have a good way to get health insurance. If you are under age twenty-six and can't get insurance on your own, you can be covered as a dependent on your parents' insurance (if their insurance allows dependent coverage).[4] Thanks to some skillful persuasion by the Department of Health and Human Services, a lot of health insurers started this change early. This new rule could help as many as 1.2 million young adults, according to HHS, including roughly 650,000 who are uninsured and about 600,000 who have their own insurance and might save money through their parents' plans.[5]

Because small businesses are so vulnerable to rising health care costs and big shifts in their premiums, the first phase of the new tax credit to help them buy coverage will begin this year. From now until 2013, if you own a business with up to twenty-five full-time employees and average wages of up to $50,000 a year, you can get a tax credit that will help you pay up to 35 percent of the premiums for health coverage. The full credit is only available to the smallest businesses, with up to ten full-time employees and average wages of up to $25,000 a year, but others can get at least partial credits. In the second phase, which starts in 2014, the credit will expand to 50 percent of the premiums.[6]

There are two temporary programs that should help vulnerable people until the full protections begin in 2014. Until then, health insurance companies can still turn down adults with preexisting conditions. But if you are one of those adults, you should be able to get coverage through a temporary high-risk pool program that will be available in all of the states.[7] And for early retirees between the ages of fifty-five and sixty-four, who can be vulnerable if their former employers decide to cut back on their retiree health coverage, there will be a "reinsurance" program to help them cover big expenses. Between now and 2014, this program will cover 80 percent of their retiree health costs for any expenses between $15,000 and $90,000.[8]

It is important to realize that the temporary risk pool program is not a great solution for people with preexisting conditions. It is only supposed to tide people over until the better solution—using the exchanges to bring together healthy people and those with health problems—is available in 2014. In the states that have high-risk pools now, people often have to pay high premiums because everyone in the pools has health problems, and the states often have to stop taking new people because they run out of money. The new program will have to do better than that. The success of this program will also depend on how much responsibility HHS can take on. While many of the states will run their own high-risk pools under the new program, twenty-one have asked HHS to run the pools for them.[9] Certainly, the people at HHS will do their best, but that is a lot to ask with all of the other new duties they will have.

We may also see the beginning of the new strategy for covering low-income people. Over the coming years, the law will expand Medicaid to provide health coverage to millions of people just above the poverty line. The first phase will come this year, when states can start expanding Medicaid coverage, voluntarily, to low-income adults without children and parents who haven't been eligible under the program's patchwork rules.[10] In 2014, they will have to do this—with generous help from the federal government.

For seniors on Medicare, this will be the first year of a gradual improvement in their benefits. They will get a down payment on the closing of the infamous drug coverage gap, the donut hole, with a $250 rebate on any prescription drug costs while they're in the gap.[11] Year by year, the gap will slowly disappear as Medicare adds other discounts and subsidies to fill in the coverage seniors need.

In the private insurance market, we will see the beginnings of a new commitment to preventive care, giving people better screenings and tests early on so they do not get sick later. All private health insurance plans, as of September, will have to cover recommended preventive services without making you share the costs. They will have to be services that are endorsed by official panels, such as the U.S. Preventive Services Task Force, so you should be able to get services such as screenings for high blood pressure, annual flu shots, and nutrition counseling.[12]

And we will see the first step in our new commitment to learning what kinds of medical care work better than others. The expansion of comparative effectiveness research will begin with the appointment of the board of governors of the Patient-Centered Outcomes Research Institute, the nonprofit that will oversee the research.[13] It will take years to see the benefits of the research, but when people see that it is not leading to the rationing of their medical care, we should be able to focus more attention on how it can actually make our medical care better.

2011

In the second year, we will see more reforms of private insurance and the beginning of a new, voluntary program to help people pay for long-term care. But we will also see the first measures to help pay for reform, and if there are any consequences, they will become obvious quickly. And a new center will be launched to help us find the path toward better, less costly medical care.

One new health insurance reform will try to respond to the public concern that insurance companies pay more attention to their shareholders than their customers. Every year, health insurance companies will have to start reporting to HHS how much they have paid for their customers' medical care compared to the amount they have collected in premiums. This is called the "medical loss ratio," but what it really tells you is how much of your money is going to actual health care and how much is going to administration and profits. Starting in 2011, if insurance companies spend less than 85 percent of their revenues on health care for large-group coverage, or 80 percent for small-group or individual coverage, they have to give you a rebate.[14]

The other benefit will be the new long-term-care coverage program. If your employer participates, you will be able to sign up through the workplace and pay your premiums through payroll deductions. HHS will come up with another way to sign up if you're not at a participating workplace. After you have paid into the program for five years, you would be fully vested, and you would be able to receive up to $50 a day in benefits if you became too severely limited to perform at least two or three "activities of daily living"—such as feeding or dressing yourself—or too mentally impaired to take care of yourself without help. The program is supposed to pay for itself over seventy-five years, without any help from the taxpayers. So HHS will have to design a way for it to sustain itself and adjust the premiums accordingly.[15]

If you are on Medicare, you will notice the donut hole in your prescription drug coverage closing more rapidly, with the start of the 50 percent discount on brand-name drugs. You will also begin to see some subsidies for generic drugs, which will gradually increase over time.[16] And there will be another important shift in your coverage, as the law's commitment to keeping people healthy—rather than just treating them when they get sick—extends to Medicare. You will get new coverage of recommended preventive services without having to share the costs. And you will be able to get a free wellness visit with your physician once a year, including a personalized prevention plan that could identify some of your risk factors and help you set up a health screening schedule.[17]

However, the tighter Medicare spending will also begin—the changes the Republicans warned would be so cruel to seniors. The payments to Medicare Advantage plans, the private plans that provide Medicare coverage, will be frozen.[18] And the program will start to increase provider payments more slowly as it becomes official policy to expect the providers to be more efficient.[19] If you are in a Medicare Advantage plan, you may get fewer "extras," but you will not lose your standard Medicare benefits. However, we will have to keep a close eye on the Medicare provider payment reductions to make sure they do not make it harder for seniors to get the care they need. The warnings that doctors would stop seeing Medicare patients were certainly overblown, but it is not unreasonable for seniors to expect Congress and the administration to watch out for problems.

Another change that should bring more money into the Medicare program is aimed at high-income seniors—those who earn more than $85,000 a year, or couples that earn more than $170,000 a year. They already pay higher premiums than other seniors for Medicare Part B coverage of physician and outpatient services. Starting this year, however, Medicare will stop increasing those thresholds to keep up with inflation.[20] So over time, more seniors will be drawn into the income level where they have to pay higher premiums. These seniors will also get less of a subsidy for their prescription drug coverage. If you are close to this income level, you might be affected. If not, though, you will feel no impact at all.

The other important marker this year will be the start-up of the Center for Medicare and Medicaid Innovation. Over the coming years, the center will run experiments on a wide variety of different ways to deliver and pay for health care in these programs—including medical homes, paying physicians salaries instead of paying them for each service, new ways to coordinate the care of people with several chronic conditions, and using telecommunications technology to improve health care in rural areas.[21] If any of the experiments are successful, the center will be able to expand them nationally. The center will have to monitor these experiments carefully to watch for problems, but if they are done right, they could lead to more health care savings and better care.

2012

Even though this is an election year, and Obama will be trying to win a second term, there will be some significant health care events this year that are not politically safe. The effort to tighten Medicare spending to pay for reform will increase. And we will start to see the first experiments in paying for medical care more effectively as we start down the long road toward paying for value, not volume.

In the Medicare program, the savings from Medicare Advantage plans will increase as the payments to those plans are reduced, not just frozen.[22] In addition, this is the year when the Independent Payment Advisory Board, which will recommend ways to tighten Medicare spending even more, will be put in place. The president will have to nominate the fifteen voting members, all of whom will have to be confirmed by the Senate.[23] The first report will not be due for another two years, but in an election year, the appointment of the board is sure to lead to a new round of overheated charges about what the board might do to seniors' care.

This will also be the year that some of the experiments in new payment policies begin. We will see the start of the new incentives for accountable care organizations—the provider partnerships that would take care of their patients' care
across all settings—including hospitals, doctors' offices, and postacute care. If
they save money, and they can demonstrate that their patients have gotten good
care, they will get to keep some of the money they save for Medicare.[24] We will
also see the first pilot program on "bundled" payments—in which providers
receive a single payment to cover an "episode" of care, such as surgery and the
follow-up care—in the Medicaid program in as many as eight states.[25]

And starting in October, we will see the start of the value-based purchasing
program in hospitals, in which Medicare will give them reward payments for
skillful treatment of difficult conditions such as heart attacks or pneumonia.[26]
We will also see the first penalties for hospitals that have high rates of readmissions for conditions we know how to treat successfully.[27] This new policy on
readmissions will be important to watch closely, since there is always some risk
that hospitals could try to steer away patients in poor health—thinking they
are more likely to be readmitted—or that safety-net hospitals already on the
financial edge would have to close. But it is also important to send a message
that there are consequences for providing poor medical care.

One new development that should help all consumers, meanwhile, will be the
introduction of better descriptions of health plans. By March of this year, all
private health plans should be putting out clear, understandable descriptions of
what is covered and what is not, what share of the services you will have to pay,
and what you might have to pay under the scenario of a typical expensive illness.
And they will have to point you to a Web site where you can find the "evidence
of coverage"—the plan document that gives you the most detailed description of
what is covered and specific services that are not covered.[28]

2013

In the last year before the biggest changes take effect, we will see more improvements in benefits and the transparency of our medical care. But it will also
be the year that new ways of raising money for reform go into effect, which are
bound to make some people unhappy—even though they are needed so reform
can truly pay for itself.

On the benefits side, the donut hole in Medicare's prescription drug coverage will continue to close, with the beginning of more subsidies for brand-name drugs and increased help with generic drugs. By 2020, the hole should be completely closed.[29] If you are on Medicare, you still will have to pay 25 percent of the costs of both brand-name and generic drugs. But you no longer will have the enormous gap in coverage that can boost your costs well beyond that.

There will also be an improvement to the Medicaid program that should make it easier for low-income people to get the care they need. Starting this year, payments to primary care physicians will increase for two years so they get the same rate they would get under Medicare.[30] This may ease some of the problems low-income people have with access to doctors. It is too bad this only lasts for two years, though, because a permanent fix is badly needed.

And a new Web site, called Physician Compare, will help make our medical care more transparent than it has been in the past. It will be modeled on the Nursing Home Compare Web site, which is run by HHS and allows you to look up quality rankings, inspection reports, and other valuable information on nursing homes. The Physician Compare site is supposed to launch in 2011, but by 2013, HHS is supposed to have it fully developed. It will have critical information on how well patients did after treatment by these physicians, how well the physicians handled coordination and continuity of care, what kind of experience patients had with the physicians, and other measures of quality.[31] The site will focus on physicians who participate in Medicare, but it should also be useful to a broader consumer audience.

However, this is also the year when two new provisions begin to raise revenues for the coming expansion of coverage. High-income taxpayers—individuals who earn more than $200,000 a year and couples earning $250,000 a year—will have to pay a higher rate for Medicare's tax on wages. It is the Hospital Insurance tax—it shows up on your paycheck as the HI tax—and it will increase from 1.45 percent to 2.35 percent for these taxpayers.[32] There will also be a new, 3.8 percent tax on unearned income, such as investments, for these high-income taxpayers.[33]

The other provision applies to all taxpayers. If you deduct your medical expenses, you currently can do that once you have spent more than 7.5 percent of your annual income. Starting this year, though, most taxpayers will only be able to deduct them once they exceed 10 percent of their income. The exception, though, is that seniors will be able to keep deducting at the 7.5 percent level for four more years, until 2017.[34] This is because the Finance Committee was worried about how the tax change would affect seniors, who have higher medical expenses than the other age groups.

Finally, there will be one more step on the road to providing medical care as efficiently as possible. The national pilot program for bundled payments will begin in Medicare this year and run for five years. If it does well, and saves money while improving care, HHS can propose to expand the program throughout the country by 2016.[35] This will be an important test of our ability to change the incentives in our medical care. There is widespread agreement—in both parties—that the way we pay providers encourages them to provide more care, rather than better care. If bundled payments show even general signs of promoting better care, we should expand them sooner rather than later.

3 | A NEW ERA: 2014–18

By far, the most important year in the implementation of reform will be 2014, four years after the enactment of the law. The biggest changes to help Americans get health coverage will all begin this year: the exchanges, the rest of the rules to prevent people from being denied coverage, the requirement that everyone must have coverage, the fines for employers who do not provide insurance for their workers, and the expansion of Medicaid to help more low-income people. By the end of the year, we should have a better idea of how close we are to the goal of affordable health coverage for everyone who needs it.

This will be a pivotal time, because so much has to happen at once and it all has to go well. The exchanges—the new marketplaces for health insurance—will be based in the states, so one way or another, they will have to be up and running at the beginning of the year. But it is very possible that some states will choose not to create them. In that case, the Department of Health and Human Services will have to set up those exchanges so every state will have one. Everyone will need to have health insurance or pay a fine, unless he or she is granted an exemption—but if too many people choose to pay the fine, it will be harder to keep premiums stable. And if too many employers decide to pay their own fines rather than cover their workers, the exchanges could get overloaded.

We all have a strong interest in preventing these worst-case scenarios, because this is our best chance to solve the problems that have prevented so many people from getting decent health coverage. But this is also our best chance to learn how to cut the wasted spending out of our health care, and there will be more chances to do this as reform moves into its later stages. If we can do both, we will be much closer to providing the smarter, more efficient, and more dependable health care everyone deserves.

2014

If you work for a small business or get health insurance on your own, there will be a health insurance exchange where you can go to a Web site, compare plans in four different categories, and pick the one that has the best balance of price and benefits for you.[1] There will be four standard categories: bronze plans, which will cover an average of 60 percent of the value of the benefits; silver plans, which will cover 70 percent of the benefits; gold plans, which will cover 80 percent; and platinum plans, which will cover 90 percent. They will also offer catastrophic coverage, with much more limited benefits, to people who are under thirty or cannot afford the standard plans.[2]

There would now be a set of "essential benefits" that all of the exchange plans would have to cover, as well as individual and small business plans outside the exchange. HHS would define the specifics, but in general each plan would have to cover such services as doctors' visits, hospital care, emergency services, maternity care, prescription drugs, mental health and substance abuse, pediatric care, and preventive services.[3] The states would have a lot of responsibility for the exchanges, however. They would have to police the health plans and make sure they comply with the rules, set up the Web sites and toll-free numbers to help people solve problems, and handle requests from individuals who want to be exempt from getting coverage because they cannot afford it.[4]

In general, the exchanges will be open only to individuals who cannot get coverage through the workplace and small businesses. However, if your employer offers coverage that would cost more than 9.5 percent of your income, or it would pay less than 60 percent of the cost of the benefits, you would be able to go to the exchange instead.[5] The idea is that if the coverage is too expensive or too limited through your employer, you should be able to go to the exchange to get a better deal.

The rest of the new insurance protections will begin this year, too. Health insurance companies will have to give you coverage even if you have a preexisting condition,[6] and they will not be able to use your health, or your gender, as a factor when they are setting your premiums. They will be able to charge you up to three times more based on your age, and they can vary your premiums based on where you live, how generous the coverage is, whether you are buying family or individual coverage, and whether you use tobacco.[7] But they will not be able to hike your premiums if you are sick. And there will be no more annual limits on what they will pay for your medical care.[8]

In return, however, you will have to get health coverage starting this year unless you have a strong financial reason why you should be exempt. In general, if your only health insurance options would force you to pay more than 8 percent of your income in premiums, you can get an exemption from the individual mandate. There is a handful other exemptions, such as people who have been uninsured for less than three months or those whose incomes are too low to owe any taxes.[9]

Otherwise, if you do not have either private health insurance or Medicaid coverage—or one of the other accepted forms of coverage, such as through TRICARE or the Veterans Administration—you will be charged a penalty of either a flat fee or a percentage of your income, whichever is greater. The penalties will be phased in, so this year, they will only be a $95 fee per person or 1 percent of your income. When the full penalties go into effect in 2016, you would pay $695 per person or 2.5 percent of your income.[10]

This is where the tax credits will be important, to help bring down the cost of coverage if you have a modest income. Starting this year, there will be a tax credit for your premiums, and a separate set of subsidies that would reduce your out-of-pocket costs. You will be able to get help if your income is up to four times the federal poverty line—$43,320 for an individual, or $88,200 for a family of four. But the amount of help will be biggest for the people with the lowest incomes, and it will phase out at the higher income levels. For example, people with incomes up to 133 percent of the poverty line—$14,404 for an individual, $29,327 for a family of four—will not have to pay more than 2 percent of their income for premiums. For people with incomes between three and four times the poverty line, however, the maximum premium will be 9.5 percent of their annual income.[11]

There will also be a cheaper option this year for the people with the lowest incomes. Starting this year, Medicaid will now be available to everyone with incomes up to 133 percent of the federal poverty line.[12] This should ease the financial hardship on the people who are struggling the hardest. We will find out quickly if this is truly a burden to the states, even with the federal government picking up all of the costs for the first three years. If you apply for coverage through your state's exchange, there will have to be a system that determines whether you are eligible for Medicaid. If you are, you should be enrolled automatically.

This also will be the year that employers, with the exception of small businesses, will face fines if they do not provide affordable health coverage and their workers have to get coverage through the exchange instead. If employers have more than fifty full-time workers and do not provide coverage at all, they will have to pay $2,000 for each worker. (The first thirty workers are not counted, to keep businesses from facing such a big hit when they grow to fifty-one workers.) If they provide coverage, but it is so expensive that the workers go to the exchange instead, the employer will pay $2,000 for each worker or $3,000 for each one that gets a tax credit—whichever penalty is less.[13] Small businesses are exempt from all of this, and this is the year that the full, 50 percent tax credit becomes available for two years if they provide health coverage.[14]

We will also get a better sense this year about how effective the new private, national health insurance plans are as an alternative to the public option. When the exchanges begin, the Office of Personnel Management should have at least two multistate plans available in each state, and one of them should be a nonprofit.[15] This was the compromise that the Senate Gang of 10 came up with when they got rid of the public option. The Office of Personnel Management does not have experience running health plans other than the one for federal workers, but if it does well, perhaps Jay Rockefeller will be right that the nonprofit plan can provide the private health insurance market with needed competition. We should also know whether the co-ops—Kent Conrad's other alternative to the public option—are establishing a successful market presence in the country.[16]

There will be one more important marker early this year—this time, dealing with our runaway health care costs. On January 15, if Medicare costs are still growing too fast, the Independent Payment Advisory Board will have to submit its first proposal to Congress on how to trim spending. The Centers for Medicare and Medicaid Services, which runs the Medicare program, will determine whether Medicare's spending has grown beyond the target rate.

If the board sends a proposal to Congress, its recommendations will take effect unless Congress comes up with other ways to get the same amount of savings. Congress would have to pass that bill under special fast-track procedures to limit the amount of time it could spend on debate.[17] This would be a big test of whether we have the political will to accept any reductions in health care spending—even when those decisions are outsourced to an independent board.

2015

By now, most of the biggest health care changes should be in place. However, one new experiment in paying providers for better care, rather than more care, will begin this year. The Medicare program will start phasing in a value-based purchasing program for physicians, in which they will get paid for delivering the best care compared to the cost of their services. HHS will have to decide how to measure quality, based on how healthy the physicians' patients are after their medical care, and how to keep track of the costs. The new payment policy will start for specific groups of doctors this year, to be chosen by HHS, and will expand to the rest of the physicians in 2017.[18]

This is also the year that the Independent Payment Advisory Board will have to submit its first recommendations on how to reduce national health spending, not just Medicare spending. The report, due January 15, will not be binding in the same way that the board's Medicare recommendations will be. But the board will have to point out which of its suggestions will need to be taken up by Congress, which ones HHS or other federal agencies can put into effect, and which ones the private sector would have to handle voluntarily. These reports will be due every two years.[19]

2016

This will be an important year for gauging people's reaction to the individual mandate, as the full penalties for not having insurance take effect for the first time. The penalties will be $695 per person or 2.5 percent of annual income, whichever is greater. The upper limit will be the national average premium for a bronze plan (the cheapest kind).[20] This will only take place, however, if the individual mandate survives the court challenges from the states.

And even if it does, the big unknown is how many people will choose to pay the fine rather than buy health insurance. Some may do that because they consider it in their best financial interests, and some will be granted exemptions from the fine because they truly cannot afford coverage. But some may simply want to protest what they consider to be an overreach of federal power. Most people in Massachusetts complied with the individual mandate there, since more than 97 percent of the state's residents had health insurance in 2009.[21] But conservatives have turned the individual mandate into a much bigger controversy nationally than they did in Massachusetts, and the penalties in the new law are relatively weak. If large numbers of people avoid coverage, the new insurance protections will become more expensive for everyone else, and the costs of treating uninsured people will continue to be passed on to the rest of us.

The other new development this year will be the beginning of "health care choice compacts"—special agreements that will allow health insurers to offer the same plan in different states, as long as they comply with each state's consumer protection laws. This was the Democrats' answer to the Republicans' suggestion of letting insurers sell across state lines. The problem with the Republican version, if you do not have minimum standards, is that insurers will put their headquarters in the states that have the least amount of rules. That way, they can sell skimpy insurance with just about no oversight. Instead, under these new agreements, health insurers would at least have a "floor" of standards and coverage. They not have to comply with every law and regulation in every state, but they would have to offer the same amount of coverage you would get through the exchange plans, without undermining state consumer protection laws.[22]

2017

This year marks the beginning of a partial handoff to the states. It will still be a national health care effort with national rules, but the states will have more ways to build upon it—or even depart from it, if they can come up with better ways to cover their residents. They also will have to start to pick up some of the costs of the Medicaid expansion, though even then, they will enjoy far more generous federal support than they ever had before.

The flexibility for states to try new coverage approaches will expand in a substantial way. They will be able to open up their exchanges to large employers with more than one hundred workers, potentially broadening the reach of the new exchange market.[23] But the states also will be able to go in very different directions. Starting this year, they will be able to apply for waivers for up to five years from much of the structure of the law—the exchanges, the individual mandate, the tax credits, the benefit requirements, and the employer fines—if they can convince HHS that they have a better way to cover the same number of people. They would also have to do it without increasing the federal deficit.[24]

This is a part of the law that has not received a lot of attention, and it is worth watching closely. For one thing, we do not know which party will be in power at this point. (If Obama wins a second term, his last year in office will be 2016.) If the Obama administration is succeeded by a Republican administration that is not committed to the success of the law, it could grant waivers too freely, with too little oversight, putting much of the law's progress in jeopardy. On the other hand, if the public considers the law a success by this point, the new administration will have to grant waivers carefully—with clear goals and expectations—no matter which party is in charge. And the states will have a greater incentive to propose good-faith ways to improve on the new structures, not tear them down.

This will also be the year that the federal government begins to cut back its funding of the expanded Medicaid coverage, slowly transferring some of the responsibility back to the states. The federal share of the funding for the newly covered people will drop from 100 percent to 95 percent. And it will gradually continue to fall in the coming years—to 94 percent in 2018, 93 percent in 2019, and 90 percent in 2020.[25] This will be a test of our commitment to keep offering low-cost Medicaid coverage to the people who need it. If the states cannot handle the extra financial burden, Congress could face new pressure to continue to pick up the full cost. And both Congress and the new administration will have to watch closely to make sure states do not try to cut their Medicaid costs in harmful ways.

2018

In the final new development, the Cadillac tax will begin this year, at a rate sharply reduced from the original idea. It will apply to health plans that are worth $10,200 a year for individual coverage or $27,500 a year for family coverage.[26] That is far more than the average value of the health insurance most people have: $4,824 for single coverage and $13,375 for family coverage.[27] And it would raise only about 20 percent of the amount the Senate bill would have raised, since the House insisted on cutting it way back in the final version.

The tax will be worth 40 percent of the amount that goes over those limits. If, for example, you have a family health plan that is worth $29,000, the tax would apply to the $1,500 that is over the limit. The tax, therefore, would be $600. The law tries to focus on health coverage that is truly excessive, but the Democrats also recognized that some of these plans are expensive because they cover people in dangerous professions, not because the benefits themselves are over the top. So the limits will be substantially higher for people in high-risk careers, such as law enforcement officers, emergency medical technicians, fire-fighters, longshoremen, and construction workers.[28]

There could still be a backlash when this tax begins, but Congress did a reasonable job of minimizing the impact. For example, by delaying the tax until 2018, Congress gave employers and unions plenty of time to get ready. In fact, many might be able to avoid the tax completely by trimming back the costs of their health plans so they are within the limits.

If so, the tax will have served a useful purpose. We do need to pay more attention to the costs of our health coverage. Where there are legitimate reasons to have generous coverage, people should continue to have it. But when these plans simply contribute to the "third party" mentality—where there is no reason to question the cost of our medical care, because someone always pays the bills—we need to become less shielded from our decisions. Over the long run, the law will only work if we can all learn to look at the costs of our health care in a new way.

4 │ NEW RESPONSIBILITIES

To make sure all of these changes happen smoothly in the coming years, the federal government will have to watch over them closely and define a lot of the details that were too technical for Congress to write into the law. The Department of Health and Human Services, in particular, will have a heavy load of new responsibilities, from helping states set up the health insurance exchanges to running the experiments that could change how we deliver and pay for health care. It may even have to set up some of the exchanges itself, since some state leaders have decided it is better politics to fight the law than to make it work.

We have to make sure that the federal bureaucracies do their jobs right, because the health of millions of Americans depends on it—and because this is an enormous opportunity to prove, once again, that the federal government can make people's lives better. But we should not overstate how strong the federal role will be. It will not be, as the opponents continue to charge, a "government takeover" of our health care. If anything, the federal role got scaled back during the debate in Congress to win enough moderate votes to pass the bill. Instead, the responsibility within government for making the law work will be shared with the states.

It will be the states' job to set up the exchanges by the beginning of 2014. They will have to enforce the new health insurance protections, which will work much better if the exchanges are well designed and well run. And they will have to expand their Medicaid programs and make them a more reliable safety net for low-income people. All of this will happen at a time when the states are, admittedly, facing tough fiscal challenges. Many are struggling to maintain the services they already provide. Some are cutting back on their Medicaid programs, their State Children's Health Insurance Program coverage, or important medical services for the elderly and people with disabilities.[1]

It may be that the states will need more federal aid in the coming years. But this is not the time for them to argue that their burden is too much. This is the time to prove they are up to the job. After all, there has always been a strong state role in health care. It has been their role to regulate health insurance, and they have shared the responsibility with the federal government for important safety-net programs like Medicaid and the State Children's Health Insurance Program. And Congress went to great pains to preserve their power.

By setting the right priorities within their limited resources, the states have a tremendous opportunity to show that they can use their authority, within a broad federal framework, to make health care work better for millions of Americans. If the federal government has to set up exchanges for some of the states—just as it will have to set up high-risk pools for some of them—it will not be because of a federal "takeover." It will be because the states have willingly passed the buck.

It is also the time for the private sector to prove it can handle its responsibilities well. Remember, Congress took out the public option because so many health insurers argued that it would be unfair competition, and many lawmakers believed them. So now, the insurance companies must prove they can live responsibly within their new rules, not just look for all the loopholes they can find. And it will be crucial for physicians, hospitals, and other health care providers to become more efficient in their own spending, so they do not simply send larger and larger bills to the insurance companies. The new law sets us on a course to pay them for value, not volume. They should accept that new course and adopt it as their own.

In the short term, the Department of Health and Human Services will be busy setting the stage for the broader reforms to come. It will oversee the temporary high-risk pool program, which will help adults with preexisting conditions get coverage until regular private insurance plans have to accept them in 2014. In addition, it will have to launch the temporary "reinsurance" program for early retirees, which will help them keep their retiree health coverage by reimbursing a lot of their biggest expenses. It lasts until 2014, when early retirees will be able to get coverage through the exchanges.

And all of the early, new protections from health insurance problems will need rules from the department to explain exactly how they are to be carried out. In a very short time, HHS has had to write detailed rules on how to guarantee coverage to children with preexisting conditions, how to make sure that young adults under age twenty-six can stay on their parents' health plans, and how to get rid of lifetime coverage limits and restrict annual limits. It also has had to explain how to keep health plans from canceling sick people's coverage and how to make sure the plans cover preventive services. As this book went to press, HHS had yet to issue the rules to determine how much of each health insurance dollar spent must be allocated to health benefits. And because of the executive order Obama issued to win the votes of Bart Stupak and his allies, HHS will have to tell state insurance commissioners how to keep the money for abortion coverage walled off from any federal funds.

This is a lot for the department to take on so quickly, and it will all have to happen within the first year or so. In many cases, it will have to coordinate with the Department of Labor and the Internal Revenue Service, which adds the potential for delays and complications. The states will have to enforce these new protections, but first they will need HHS to fill in the kinds of details that can make the difference between success and failure.

Here is an example: How strict should we be in limiting health plans' profits? The law says they will have to spend at least 85 percent of their premium revenues on actual medical care, not administrative expenses or profits. (For small group and individual health plans, it only has to be 80 percent.) This was one of the concessions the Senate Gang of 10 made to please progressive Democrats. What you can count toward the 85 percent or the 80 percent, however, makes all the difference in the world.

For example, health plans will be able to count "quality improvement" activities. So what are legitimate quality improvement activities? Should they be able to count the expenses of setting up health information technology, which can help them compile the quality data they will need? Naturally, health insurance companies would like the definition to be as broad as possible. But Democrats want it to be tight so health insurers cannot charge high premiums for expenses that have little to do with medical care. And the hospital groups share their concern.[2]

This is a case where a well-intentioned measure can backfire. Yes, health insurers can pad their premiums with unnecessary expenses, and Congress was right to try to address the problem. But if HHS writes such a tight definition that it becomes too difficult for health insurers to comply with it, they could also raise their premiums and blame it on the high cost of complying with the new rules. Some insurers might even pull out of critical markets. The best approach would be less rigidity and greater practicality, with a more flexible definition that we could tighten over time. That way, we would be less likely to cause too much disruption early on, and we would be less likely to threaten health care quality initiatives that we will need in the long run.

The temporary high-risk pool program will be another initiative that has to be handled well. For adults with preexisting conditions, it will be their only hope if they do not have health insurance through the workplace, or if they have lost a job that gave them secure coverage. Unfortunately, because of all the pressure to keep costs down, Congress did not set aside a lot of money for it. The law provides $5 billion between now and 2014 for the high-risk pool program. That is not much more than the states have spent on their old risk pools, which only covered about 200,000 people.[3] A risk pool has to be well funded to cover the costs, because everyone in it has a health issue of some kind.

So HHS will have to find wise ways to use the limited resources. It will have to suggest ways to keep premiums as low as possible, since many of the existing state high-risk pools set premiums so high that people cannot afford them. And for twenty-one states, as of this writing, HHS will have to run a national program because the states declined to run their own. But this program, as limited as it is, will help to set the tone for the rest of the effort. It must be a success. If we can prove to vulnerable people that we can look out for their interests, Americans will have much more confidence in the bigger changes that will come next.

Those changes will come in 2014, with the launching of the health insurance exchanges and the rest of the rules to protect people's health coverage. HHS will have to define the minimum benefits that health plans in the exchanges must offer, and it will have to keep a close eye on what insurance companies do once they have to accept everyone for insurance. And if the experience with the high-risk pool is any indication, HHS will have to be prepared for the possibility that some states will choose not to set up exchanges. If so, HHS will have to do the job for them. For the states that do run their own exchanges, HHS will have to set ground rules so the exchanges do what they are supposed to do: give individuals and small businesses the rational, easy-to-use health insurance marketplace they deserve.

Since much of this will depend on which health plans will be offered through the exchanges, and the states have to certify the plans, HHS will have to make sure the states hold these plans to the highest standards. Most states will rise to the challenge, because it is a tremendous opportunity to offer people better health care through a competitive marketplace. The danger, though, is that states that do not support the new law will not try very hard to make it work.

For example, states are supposed to look out for health plans that raise their premiums too much and shut the worst offenders out of the exchanges. But it would be easy for the states to decide they do not have the time or resources to do that kind of monitoring. In addition, HHS is supposed to write rules on how to make sure the exchange health plans do not try to steer away people with health problems, how to make sure they have enough providers in their network, and how to rate the plans on their quality and their price.[4] In states that are hostile to the new law, however, it would be easy for them not to work very hard at any of these things.

There are also lots of intangibles. States that are not committed to the law's success could design their exchange Web sites poorly, so people have a hard time finding the information they need. If you look at the Medicaid Web sites of different states, for example, you can tell which states are trying to make enrollment easy and which ones are not. Or the states could simply do a poor job of advertising the exchange itself, so people who need it will not know where to find it and might not even know it exists. This is why strong federal oversight of the exchanges will be so important—not as a "government takeover," but to make sure the new health insurance marketplaces work the way they should.

While HHS works on making it easier to get coverage, the federal government also will have to enforce the new requirement, unpopular as it may be, that everyone must have coverage. Otherwise, the newly strengthened coverage will be too expensive. That job will fall primarily to the Internal Revenue Service. It will have to manage the new tax credits to help people pay their premiums, the subsidies to reduce people's out-of-pocket costs, and the separate tax credits that will help small businesses cover their workers. This means that, among other things, it will have to set up a good system for people to get advance payments of their tax credits if they need them. But it also will have to verify who has health coverage and who does not, and it will have to collect the tax penalties for those who do not—unless they have been granted an exemption.

There have been a lot of scare tactics about how much power the IRS will have once the individual mandate kicks in. The worst has been the claim, repeated over and over on Fox News, that people who do not get health insurance and do not pay the penalty will go to jail.[5] Here is how it will actually work: Whoever provides your health insurance—your insurance company or, if your company insures itself, your employer—will report to the IRS that you have health insurance. It will send you a copy of that statement.[6] IRS Commissioner Douglas Schulman has compared it to a bank sending a 1099 form to the IRS, reporting your interest income. It is not something the IRS generally checks; it simply accepts the information.[7]

There is always the chance of a paperwork hassle if your insurance company or employer does not report your health insurance—just as there would be if your bank did not send your 1099. You do not want to be wrongly charged a penalty, so it will be a good idea to watch for that statement to make sure they report your coverage. But that is a different issue from what happens if you owe the penalty and do not pay it. If anything, the IRS will have a hard time coming after you, because it cannot use the kinds of liens and levies it usually uses to collect unpaid taxes.[8] It might be able to withhold your tax refund, but it cannot use its usual collection tools.[9] And it cannot send you to jail.

All of this will help us expand and improve health coverage, but just as important, in the long run, will be our success in finding smarter ways to pay for health care and better ways to deliver it. HHS will be running these experiments in the coming years, and it will have a lot of latitude to expand the ones that work well. The Center for Medicare and Medicaid Innovation, in particular, will be able to expand its experiments with new models such as medical homes—where teams of providers give people a consistent starting point for all of their care—and paying providers salaries rather than paying them for each service. And HHS is already supposed to plan for an expansion of the pilot program on bundled payments, where providers get one overall payment for treatment and follow-up care, if it is successful.

The key, though, is that we must make sure that the best new models actually do become used more widely. As Drew Altman, president and CEO of the Henry J. Kaiser Family Foundation, points out, pilot programs often take so long that by the time they are finished, everyone has moved on to newer ideas.[10] The law creates so many experiments for a good reason: We need to learn more about what will actually bring our costs down and make our medical care better. Once we know, however, we must commit ourselves to these new methods. The culture of health care will not change overnight, but it certainly will not change if we do not keep up the pressure over the long term.

There are two major political challenges hanging over the entire effort. One is the critical need for resources. Now that the federal agencies—particularly HHS and the IRS—will have so many new responsibilities, lawmakers must give them the funding they need to do their jobs well. Congress has an unfortunate habit of establishing new programs and then shortchanging them over the years, especially as power shifts from one party to the other. That is a particular danger in the coming years if Republicans gain strength in Congress. It would be all too easy to kill the reform effort not by repealing it, but by starving it. The law gives HHS $1 billion in implementation funding, but lawmakers must sustain that commitment over the years, especially if some of the states decline to run their own exchanges.[11]

The other is the need to avoid bureaucratic turf wars. It would be a mistake if HHS and the White House spent precious energy wrestling for control of the implementation of reform—which could happen easily, since each has its own political stake in the success of the effort. It would also be a shame if the various departments and agencies that share responsibility for different parts of the effort—including HHS, Treasury, the Department of Labor, and the Office of Personnel Management—did not work well together. This is an effort that will need a spirit of shared responsibility, because everyone in the administration will benefit if reform is a success. And more importantly, everyone in America will benefit if it is a success. No one will win if it collapses because of bureaucratic infighting.

As much as the federal government will have to do in the coming years, the states will play an enormous role in determining how well the new law achieves its goals. They will be responsible for creating the exchanges and getting them going by 2014. Their insurance departments will have to enforce the new federal rules on how to make private health insurance more dependable. And they will have to not only expand Medicaid, but also make it easy for people to enroll in it, and in the State Children's Health Insurance Program, through the exchanges.

The exchanges will be the most visible and transformational undertaking, since the states will have to create entire new health insurance marketplaces from scratch. These marketplaces will give the states a lot of control over the fate of the reform, since they are so central to the effort. The states will decide which health insurance companies get to offer their plans through the exchanges. They are supposed to watch those health insurers' rate increases closely over the next few years, looking for insurers that hike their premiums too much between now and the start of the exchanges. They will design the exchange Web sites and rate the plans. They will decide whether to run a separate exchange for small businesses, which is allowed under the law, or put small businesses and individuals together in one exchange. And they will determine who is exempt from the requirement to get health coverage, usually because they have no affordable coverage options, and make sure the IRS knows who is off the hook.[12]

If the states run the exchanges well, there could be as many as 24 million people who use them. In addition, however, the states will have to open Medicaid and the State Children's Health Insurance Program to as many as 16 million new low-income people.[13] Many of them will be just above the poverty line, but many will be low-income adults without children or even parents below the poverty line—groups the states have not had to reach before. This is why outreach will be so important. The states can make the exchanges and the Medicaid expansion well-known to their residents, or they can make them the best-kept secrets in the world.

Realistically, we are likely to see examples of both. "There will be pacesetting states that perform brilliantly, and there will be states that perform badly and are laggards, and there will be a lot that are somewhere in the middle," says

Altman. He points out one important lesson we can learn from welfare reform in the 1990s: Some states became models of how to run the new programs in creative and humane ways, and the other states later learned from them.[14] It will be important for states to learn from each other in health reform, too, and to adopt the best approaches to the exchanges and Medicaid expansion as quickly as possible.

It would be a lot to ask, even in the best of times, for the states to take on a project as ambitious as launching new health care marketplaces. Add new insurance rules to the mix plus the integration of completely different coverage choices—private health insurance, Medicaid, and the State Children's Health Insurance Program—and you have a challenge as great as any the states have taken on. Yet they will have to do it at a time when they barely have enough staff to handle their current obligations, as the recession dries up their revenues. And even though there will be federal grants available to help the states start their exchanges, the law does not say how much.[15]

The states can see their new responsibilities as either an opportunity or a burden. For their own good, as well as the good of millions of Americans, they should see it as an opportunity. By covering more uninsured people through well-run exchanges, and providing better and more easily comparable coverage to those who cannot get it through the workplace, the states can save themselves billions of dollars in uncompensated care costs.[16] And the Medicaid expansion is a chance to cover 16 million low-income children and adults at very little extra cost to the states, since the law guarantees that the federal government will cover all of the costs for the first few years and most of the costs after that.[17] It will also make it easier to determine which low-income people are eligible: everyone under 133 percent of the federal poverty line, rather than only those who fit specific, narrow categories.

The states can also distinguish themselves by becoming the trailblazers of health reform. It will be a new task for most of the states to review the rates set by individual health insurers, but if they do it well, they can protect their residents from getting gouged by unnecessary premium hikes. If they enforce the new insurance rules quickly and efficiently, they can have a successful launch of the new exchanges, which will depend on the new rules being in place. If they plan ahead, they can have smooth enrollment of newly insured people, including the low-income people who will be eligible for Medicaid for the first time. (They could get overwhelmed if they do not plan ahead, however, which is why a paper by the National Governors Association suggested that states expand Medicaid early so they do not get hit by a rush of people applying all at once.)[18]

And the states do have options on how to design the exchanges. They can set them up as nonprofits or as government agencies. They can serve small businesses and individuals separately, or all together in one exchange. They can work with other states to set up regional exchanges, or set up more than one exchange within a state to serve different areas.[19] All of these choices introduce an element of uncertainty, since some of these options are bound to work better than others. But since Congress gave the states this much flexibility, they should see it as an opportunity to experiment and find the solution that fits their values. If their residents are worried about expanding government, for example, a nonprofit exchange may be a better choice than one run by an agency. But states with more progressive residents might prefer the government approach.

There should be other opportunities for the states to take advantage of the flexibility they have. For example, Kansas insurance commissioner Sandy Praeger, who heads the health insurance and managed care committee of the National Association of Insurance Commissioners, believes the states will have a fair amount of discretion on how to review insurance rates. They may, for example, be able to help define what spending should count as medical expenses and what should not. And the states can look for ways to go beyond the federal guidelines, she says, such as posting additional information on the exchange Web sites about complaints against insurance companies.[20]

There will be more opportunities for states to try different approaches in the years ahead. In 2016, they will be able to join the interstate health care compacts that will offer health plans, within reasonable guidelines, across state lines. This might give their residents access to cheaper health plans, as long as they do not erode the states' consumer protection laws. And in 2017, the states will be able to apply for waivers to provide the same level of health coverage through different means. It will be important for HHS to approve only proposals that will not unravel health reform, but the waivers could also be an opportunity to improve on the law. If the most creative states can come up with innovative approaches that would cover people more effectively, they should be encouraged to do so.

The bottom line, however, is that it is in the states' interests to make reform a success—not to undermine it. Praeger is a Republican, but she does not buy into the idea that our health care will be better if reform falls apart. "To say we want it to fail is to go back to the existing system, which we know is not working," she said. "At least now we are talking about how to make this better, not whether we should do anything at all."

5 | NEXT STEPS

No country that has attempted health care reform has gotten it exactly right on the first try. So it is unrealistic to think that we will be the first. There are important problems that the new law did not address well enough, and in some cases, did not address at all. There are solutions that will not work as well as intended. And there are some that might even cause their own problems.

Getting health care reform right will be an ongoing process. It did not end with the enactment of the law, and it will not end when all of the parts of the law are implemented. We will have to evaluate our progress constantly, fixing the parts that do not work well and adding new measures along the way. This is not the last time Congress will have to address health care reform. Lawmakers may hope they do not have to deal with it again for a long time, but somewhere down the road, they will have to.

We almost certainly will have to do more to get health care costs under control. The law will try a lot of things, but we do not know yet if the most effective measures will actually be expanded. There are significant cost issues that the law does not even consider. And Congress put so many restrictions on the most promising device—the Independent Payment Advisory Board—that it may have to remove some of them in future years. We are also likely to be struggling with the quality of our medical care for a long time. There will be steps to try to improve quality, but we will still have a fragmented approach, full of different public programs and private market offerings that make medical care unnecessarily complicated for providers and patients.

And even though the law is strongest on expanding health coverage, there is potential for trouble serious enough that Congress will have to make fixes down the road. Ironically, given the uproar over the individual mandate, one of the most likely scenarios is that the penalties for people who do not get health coverage will be too weak. If they are, and too many healthy people decide to pay the fine rather than getting coverage, the newly strengthened health benefits could become too expensive for everyone else. Congress might have to make the penalties tougher, and that is the last thing lawmakers would want to do now, with so many states and conservative groups questioning whether the individual mandate is even constitutional.

We should not be surprised that so many major issues may remain unresolved. Other countries that gave all of their citizens health coverage decades ago, including France and Germany, are still making changes to get their own costs under control. Some nations have gone too far and drawn complaints from doctors and hospitals. Many Americans may be understandably worried if the law does more to expand coverage than to reduce costs, but that may be the natural evolution of health care reform. As long as we keep up our efforts to get costs right, we can still consider ourselves on the way to better health care if expanded coverage comes first.

The good news, however, is that the law gives us a real opportunity to do better at covering the right priorities. Remember the illustration of the health care pyramid, with primary care at the base and the most sophisticated technologies and procedures at the top. Unlike most countries, which start at the bottom and work their way to the top until the money runs out, we start at the top and work our way down. And the money always has run out. The new law probably will not stop us from starting at the top and working our way down. But if we do well enough at bringing down costs and providing medical care, we have a real chance, for the first time, to have enough money to cover the entire pyramid. That, in itself, would be a tremendous achievement.

It may take us years to get health care costs under control. Perhaps it will not even be done in the first ten years of the new law. One way or another, however, it must be done. We cannot simply add 32 million more Americans to the expensive medical care we already have. We do need to learn more about how to control costs without hurting patients, and we can build on the law to add more cost-control measures later. But this is a goal we cannot let out of our sight—even if it means taking steps Congress considered too politically risky on this round.

I still believe the Federal Health Board I proposed in *Critical* is the best model for giving us high-value medical care that brings down costs. The administration and Congress did not pursue it, and given all of the hysteria we saw over "government making medical decisions," it is hard to see how the board could have gotten a fair hearing in this debate. However, it is still the "gold standard" by which all of our cost and quality efforts should be judged. A board of experts that is accountable to politicians—but able to make the kinds of technical, policy, and regulatory decisions they cannot make—would be able to cut through the kinds of distortions we saw in this debate and make our medical care more rational than it is now.

Although the board is not a part of the law, some of its most important functions would be addressed in other ways. For example, comparative effectiveness research will add to our knowledge of which treatments are the most valuable and cost-effective. And the new Medicare value-based purchasing program for hospitals and physicians, together with the penalties for hospitals that have to readmit too many patients, can help to achieve the board's goal of paying providers for the best health outcomes, not just the number of services they perform.

It is the new Independent Payment Advisory Board, however, that will come closest to the functions of the Federal Health Board. It will not have the same range of decision-making authority, but it will give medical experts a way to recommend Medicare savings—and, in the process, influence overall health care spending—with more power than the typical board. By allowing the board's Medicare recommendations to take effect unless Congress comes up with a better way to save the same amount of money, the law ensures that the board's ideas will take effect in some form, not just gather dust on a shelf.

But with so many limitations on the board, it is not clear how much it can accomplish. Because of the deal with the hospitals, the board cannot make any recommendations that would cut their payments until 2019. The same is true of hospices. And to protect themselves from charges that the board's cuts would hurt vulnerable seniors, members of Congress took one category after another off the table. Under the law, the board will not be able to "ration health care," raise Medicare premiums or revenues, increase the amount that seniors on Medicare would have to contribute to their health care, tighten benefits, narrow the eligibility for Medicare benefits, or reduce the amount of help low-income seniors get with their premiums.[1]

These are all politically sensitive areas, and it is not surprising that Congress would want to rule them out. No one, for example, wants the board to "ration health care"—even though that term is more of a scare tactic than a serious threat—or to control Medicare spending on the backs of low-income seniors. When you add them all up, however, it is hard to see what tools the board will have left to reduce Medicare spending. That is why Paul Ginsburg, president of the Center for Studying Health System Change, wonders if the board will simply become a mechanism for cutting provider payments more deeply than Congress could do on its own.[2] Since Congress has a long history of turning to provider payment cuts as the quickest fix for Medicare spending growth, and then canceling the cuts when the providers complain, we can only hope that the Independent Payment Advisory Board will be able to find more creative solutions.

There is also a danger that the board's cuts will simply shift the costs to other patients. After all, if Medicare pays less to doctors, hospitals and other providers, it is all too easy for them to make up the difference by charging more to people with private insurance—just as the costs of treating uninsured people currently get passed on to the rest of us. This is why our cost control efforts would be more likely to succeed if the payment decisions were made by a board with authority over a wide range of health programs, not just Medicare.

There is real promise in the experiments and pilot programs that will take place in the coming years. The law will test just about all of the most promising approaches in one form or another: value-based purchasing, bundled payments, accountable care organizations, medical homes, and penalizing hospitals that have too many readmissions. These experiments will send providers a clear message: In the future, they will get paid for providing the best and most cost-effective care, not for doing things as they have always been done.

But this is no guarantee that we will apply the lessons we learn more broadly, beyond the pilot programs. One of the frustrations of public policy research in general, including pilot programs, is that it often produces mixed results. Even when the results seem solid enough to political leaders, they may be complex enough to keep researchers arguing for years over what they really mean. We do not have that kind of time on health care costs. To make real progress in bringing costs down, we will need a constant stream of up-to-date information on how the experiments are going, so HHS can make changes quickly if anything goes wrong. But if they seem to be going reasonably well, HHS should be flexible enough to expand them quickly, without waiting for the definitive, final report that convinces every last holdout in the health policy community.

We will also need more transparency in all areas of medical care, so patients know what a given service is likely to cost and do not just let their insurance company worry about it. The law will require all hospitals to disclose their standard charges for their services, but that is not enough. What we need is full disclosure by all health care providers and other businesses—including hospitals, physicians, pharmacies, drug manufacturers, and dentists—of the prices of all their services. Representative Steve Kagen, the allergy specialist from Wisconsin who held one of the raucous town hall meetings in August 2009, has been trying to get Congress to pass a bill requiring this kind of disclosure so you can check the price of a service before you get it.[3] If we had this kind of transparency, we would be less likely to be blindsided by high costs, and more likely—at least in nonemergency situations—to ask the kinds of questions that might make providers a bit more careful about their prices.

Clearly, we will have to take another run at drug costs. The White House may have felt constrained to keep the Pharmaceutical Research and Manufacturers of America on its side in this round, to keep the group from launching well-funded advertising campaigns against reform. But sooner or later, we need to allow Americans to import safe prescription drugs, an idea that can serve as an effective and needed correction to the lack of price discipline in our pharmaceutical market. We will also have to take steps to discourage market-driven medicine, in which people demand drugs they have seen on television even though cheaper and better alternatives are available. The law does not really address the issue, but it is an obvious factor in our rising costs.

Finally, we are not finished debating the role of defensive medicine in our rising health care costs. The law gives federal grants to the states to let them test alternatives to medical malpractice lawsuits, focusing on full disclosure of mistakes made by health care providers and early resolution of the disputes.[4] These demonstrations are not likely to satisfy Republicans, who have held out for strict limits on lawsuits. But they might show us some ways to get past the stale debate over tort reform, as long as we actually expand the alternatives that work. Democrats cannot simply pretend that defensive medicine is not a problem.

We can address the issue by giving doctors a "safe harbor" against malpractice lawsuits as long as they follow the established best practices in medical care—ordering tests or procedures when we know they're useful, or not ordering them when we know they have little benefit. And there would have to be a compensation fund to help people who were truly the victims of medical mistakes. In return, doctors would have to agree to complete transparency about what happened, and there would have to be a way to discipline physicians who are the subject of numerous complaints. But this might be a way to get past the usual arguments about medical malpractice and reduce whatever role defensive medicine is playing in our escalating health care costs.

In the everyday practice of medicine, cost problems and quality problems are frequently connected to each other. Sandy Praeger, the Kansas insurance commissioner, often talks about a situation her husband, Mark, a surgeon, faced one day when three patients came into the hospital showing clear signs of appendicitis. The hospital wanted to run CAT scans on all three of them because it was standard procedure. You don't need to do that, he told the hospital officials, because they won't change what I'm going to do. He operated on all three, and sure enough, all three had appendicitis. Only one CAT scan got done that day. It came back normal—a result that, if Mark Praeger had waited for it, would have delayed the medical care the patient needed.[5]

Unnecessary tests and procedures can drive up the cost of our medical care, but they can also make our care worse. They carry their own risks—not just because of a wrong or misleading test result, but because there are more chances for things to go badly. The law will take some actions to reduce unnecessary care and make our medical care better coordinated than it is now. But even if they all go well, we will still have a lot of work to do.

The expanded comparative effectiveness research, to be run by the new Patient-Centered Outcomes Research Institute, will take years to show results. But little by little, it will add to our knowledge of what medical procedures and treatments have real value in most situations, and which ones are likely to work better than others. The real test, however, is whether it will be able to have a real impact on the practice of medical care. Anxious to avoid the emotional charges that they were trying to "ration" health care, the Democrats put so many restrictions in the law—declaring that the research could not be used as "practice guidelines, coverage recommendations, payment, or policy recommendations"— that it could almost become irrelevant.[6] The key is to make sure that patients know about the research and use it to its full potential—not as "rationing," but as a way to have better-informed discussions with their physicians about what medical care is likely to be the best use of money.

One big question we may have to decide in future years is whether people should have financial incentives to go to the best, most efficient health care providers. New measures of health care quality will be developed across the industry in the coming years, but these can only do so much good if people continue to go to the inefficient places. Not everyone has a choice of providers, of course, especially in rural and underserved areas. But as Paul Ginsburg points out, if people do have a choice, there are ways to encourage them to go to the best ones—such as offering them a lower deductible if they go to the local hospital with the highest quality ratings. Providers are sure to fight any such incentives, so it is no surprise that Congress steered away from them on this round. But in the future, when the entire fate of reform does not hang in the balance, Congress may need to take the risk.

There will be steps to address the lack of coordination in our medical care—when we end up with duplicate tests, or drugs that should not be taken together, because the providers we see in different settings do not talk to each other. This should become less of a problem as physicians and other providers gradually expand their use of health information technology, which can tell them more about your recent medical treatments—through the use of electronic medical records—and flag issues that need their attention. And the technology will make it easier for them to report the kind of quality data we will need for patients to make meaningful comparisons between providers.

But this does not mean everything will go smoothly. There is good health information technology software and there is bad software. The kind that is most likely to work well for doctors and hospitals, as Phillip Longman of the New America Foundation has rightly pointed out, is "open source" software, which can be modified by anyone—so health care professionals can improve it over the years to fit their needs. The kind that has caused problems is proprietary software, which cannot be modified and often is designed by people who do not know what medical professionals need to do their jobs.[7] There may be cases where proprietary software is more appropriate, but as we work to bring the health care industry into the 21st century, open-source software should be the dominant approach.

We can also gain an important vehicle for coordinating people's care if medical homes become more widespread. By bringing together "community health teams" such as medical specialists, nurses, and pharmacists to coordinate their patients' medical care, medical homes may give people a more consistent "home base" and prevent the kinds of mistakes that happen when they have to go from one provider to another. But there are potential problems with this approach, too. If the medical homes simply put up roadblocks when their patients need to see a specialist or go to the hospital, for example, they could become just another source of bureaucratic hassles rather than a place for people to get more efficient medical care. So we will need to watch the medical home experiments closely to make sure they fulfill their potential.

These are good short-term steps, but in the long run, we should decide if we want our health care to become more of a system, not just a market. Remember that the other developed nations have true systems, with central decision-making and a rational structure for coverage and payment. Instead of a system, we have so many different "silos" with different coverage and payment rules—private health insurance, Medicare, Medicaid, the Veterans Administration, the Indian Health Service—that it makes life unnecessarily complicated for providers and patients.

Even under the new law, we will have a health care market, with generous and high-quality care for the luckiest Americans and lesser care for everyone else. Instead of a market, we could have a smoothly functioning system, with a central decision-making authority for coverage and payment decisions. It would not have to be a single-payer system. It could be a public-private system that simply consolidates different programs so everyone can get the same quality of care, rather than giving the best care to the luckiest people.

This was not the time to have that debate. The hysteria over "government-run health care" would not have allowed it. As people get used to the new law and see its potential, we should have a broader debate over how to streamline our health care so it works well for everyone. After all, we all want the same thing, and it is not complicated. We just want to be healthy.

If all goes well, we will make the biggest advances in health care coverage that we have made since the creation of Medicare and Medicaid. This is the most well-developed area of the law, and Congress and the administration deserve great credit for delivering a package that could allow us to make tremendous strides. But there is still the potential for serious problems down the road, so we should be prepared to make changes to the law—including changes that might be deeply unpopular—to shut down those problems if they do occur.

One possibility, for example, is that too many people will skip health coverage because the penalties for avoiding coverage are not strong enough. Congress did not want to make the fines too harsh, because the cost of health insurance could be a real burden for some people. And some people will get hardship exemptions if they truly cannot afford insurance. But if too many people avoid the new requirement to get health insurance, the exchanges could become more expensive because most of the people left in them would have health problems. And health insurers could refuse to participate in the exchanges because the customers would be too expensive to cover.

Remember that state high-risk pools have always struggled to offer affordable coverage because they draw customers who need more medical care than most people. The last thing the exchanges need is to become bigger, more elaborate versions of high-risk pools. They need a good mix of customers to keep their costs stable. But it may be too easy for others to sign up for coverage when they need it—since they can no longer be rejected for preexisting conditions—and drop the coverage when they do not need it. If so, Congress may have to consider other steps to make it harder for people to skip coverage. It could increase the fines, for example, or simply make people pay greater fines if they do not sign up for coverage by a deadline. This is a critical area where lawmakers will have to watch developments closely and be prepared to make changes to head off serious problems.

We will also have to watch to make sure employers do not simply drop health coverage and tell their employees to get it through the exchanges. There are fines for businesses with more than 50 workers who do not offer coverage, but just as the penalties for uninsured individuals may be too small, the fines for businesses may be too light as well compared to the cost of providing health insurance. It would not be easy for Congress to increase the fines on either individuals or employers. Lawmakers would be sure to face protests if they did either one. But if either the viability of the exchanges or the stability of employment-based health coverage is in jeopardy, Congress may have to take tougher measures to get the problems under control.

Most important of all, however, we will have to make sure that we have made health coverage more affordable for most people. If we have not, lawmakers will face great pressure from their constituents to do something about it. The tax credits and cost-sharing subsidies may not be generous enough to help people with modest incomes, and businesses may continue to struggle with costs. If so, Congress may have to look for ways to cut the costs of the exchange health plans, such as taking another look at how many benefits they should be required to cover. The states, or even the federal government, may need stronger powers to review insurance companies' rate increases. But in the long run, the best answer is to get costs under control. Health insurance companies have plenty of problems, but if providers continue to spend too much and bill too much for their services, the insurance companies can only do so much to keep their premiums down.

Unfortunately, Congress removed the biggest single tool for bringing down costs, improving quality, and expanding coverage when it took the public option off the table. Down the road, we probably will have to consider it again. Republicans and moderate Democrats became way too stubborn about fighting an idea that, more than anything else, was about competition. Obama was right to conclude that there might be other ways to achieve the same goals, and the law is now written in a way that will test those other ways. But if they do not work, and the public sees that private health insurance companies need more competition, Congress should pass the public option. There will be no more excuses for avoiding it simply because of the overblown fears of "government-run health care."

Finally, we should remember how far we still will have to go to achieve universal coverage. If everything goes well, according to the Congressional Budget Office, we will expand health coverage to 32 million new people—meaning that 94 percent of all Americans under age sixty-five will be insured. That would be an enormous step forward, and we should all feel great pride if it happens. But

94 percent is not universal coverage. It would leave 23 million people uninsured, according to the Congressional Budget Office. And of that total, about one-third would be undocumented immigrants.[8]

The immigration debate is as raw and emotional as any political debate of our time. It was deeply unfortunate that Congress, in order to win enough moderate Democratic votes in the Senate, banned immigrants from coverage in the exchanges even if they paid the entire premium themselves. We can debate what other penalties people should face for entering the country illegally, but denial of health coverage should not be one of them. It is shortsighted because it simply shifts costs to the states and local communities that have to pay for their uncompensated care. And it is not moral to argue that they should not receive medical care when they need it.

We may have to wait until the politics of immigration are shifting in a more humane direction, when people on both sides are prepared to discuss rational solutions. But when the moment is right, we should search for a fair, widely acceptable way to make basic health coverage available to undocumented immigrants. As long as we continue to leave entire groups of people without coverage, we will not put an end to the serious health care problems we have worked so hard to solve.

Conclusion

In the first election after Social Security was created, Franklin D. Roosevelt's opponents were determined to make him pay a price for it. As he ran for a second term in 1936, his Republican rival, Alf Landon, promised to repeal the new program. Landon charged that Social Security was "unjust, unworkable, stupidly drafted, and wastefully financed."[1] He went on to lose every state except Maine and Vermont.

Medicare quickly won acceptance with the public. For all of the cries of "socialized medicine" when Congress was debating it, it was not an issue in the next elections once it was the law of the land.[2] The civil rights legislation of the 1960s, however, was a different story. The backlash against the Civil Rights Act of 1964 and the Voting Rights Act of 1965, along with other initiatives to help African-Americans, was slow to build. But there were hints of it even in 1964, when Barry Goldwater, despite his landslide loss, outpolled Lyndon B. Johnson among white Southerners.[3]

Then came the Democratic losses in the 1966 election, along with the election of a new California governor, Ronald Reagan, who had called the civil rights and voting rights acts unconstitutional.[4] Reagan is now revered by millions of Americans who know him for his eloquent, optimistic presidency, but his opposition to civil rights in the 1960s was an unfortunate part of his political record. And the realignment of the South—the shift of white Southerners, starting in the 1980s, to become overwhelmingly Republican rather than Democratic— had subtle, but unmistakable, undertones of a civil rights backlash.[5] As historian Taylor Branch wrote, "A slow incoming tide was mistaken for an ebbing ripple."[6]

But today, everyone accepts the civil rights laws and the contributions they have made to our society. Their legitimacy is so completely settled that when Kentucky Senate candidate Rand Paul tried to revisit the debate over the 1964 act, the rest of the country shouted him down. No one debates the need for Social Security, and even the most vocal opponents of "government-run health care" do not suggest we should repeal Medicare. Major social change sometimes takes years to win acceptance. But now, Social Security, Medicare, and the civil rights laws are politically untouchable.

The new health care law deserves the same chance. There is so much potential for good in every aspect of the law, and people will begin to see the good once the biggest reforms take effect. But this will only happen if we give the law enough time to show its full potential. It is not at all certain, however, that the law will get this chance. Republicans are running on promises to repeal the law. States are suing to declare the individual mandate and other central parts of the law unconstitutional.

Even though the odds are against both efforts, they can still do real damage to the cause of reform. By constantly suggesting to the public that the law is illegitimate, they could encourage large groups of Americans to give up on the law, or even fight it, before it has had a chance to prove itself. The biggest threat to the cause of reform is no longer the decades of deadlock in Congress. Thankfully, we have finally overcome that barrier. Now, the danger is that the critics of reform will kill it before it ever has a chance to take hold.

Opponents in state governments could undermine it at every turn, or simply say they cannot do what the law requires. Providers and health insurance companies could resist it. Congress could fail to give it the ongoing support it needs. And large parts of the country could simply give up on it. Democrats could become discouraged because they think too many progressive reforms were missing. Independents could remain skeptical because they think we cannot afford it. And Republicans could pay too much attention to the ideologues who still want them to believe it is a "government takeover" of health care.

We cannot allow this to happen. To allow the cause of reform to fail now, after all of the obstacles Obama and Congress overcame, would be a waste of their hard-fought efforts. It would leave us with nothing to show for the many long months our nation spent on the health care debate, or for the two years Obama spent setting the stage for it on the campaign trail. And it would be a betrayal of the millions of Americans who need relief from the rising costs of medical care, who cannot get health coverage at all, or who find themselves on the edge of bankruptcy when they do get it.

Many Americans listened to this debate and concluded that there was nothing in the new law for them. It was all about other people, they decided, and they were the ones who would get stuck with the check. In reality, though, this law has many good things to offer all of us. We will be better protected from trouble, and over time, we have a very good chance of seeing our health care become better and cheaper.

If we already have good health insurance through the workplace, there will be fewer gaps that we find out about the hard way. If we lose our health insurance—a fate that can happen to anyone who loses a job—we will have a much better chance of finding new coverage. It will be easier to leave a job to start a business, since we will not have to worry so much about health coverage. And if we get sick or hurt, there will be less of a chance that the medical bills will ruin us.

Our health insurance premiums will keep rising, but as we learn more about how to cut the waste out of medical care, we should be able to get those premium increases under control. As we start to pay providers for value rather than volume, they will have stronger reasons to give us the best possible care. We are all vulnerable to medical mistakes, but the new quality initiatives should make us less vulnerable over time. As we learn more about new models of health care, we may be able to cut out a lot of the problems that arise when our providers do not talk to each other.

And there will be benefits that most people never heard about during the debate. We will get better coverage of preventive services, as a new incentive to get the tests and exams we need to stay healthy. There will be a new source of long-term care coverage for people who become disabled. Nursing homes will be held to higher standards. There will be more adoption of electronic medical records and other technology that can improve our medical care. We will see, little by little, more transparency in an industry that desperately needs it.

There are plenty of things that can go wrong with these reforms, and we will have to watch for them and be prepared to correct them. But there are many things that will go right, and when they do, we will all see how much progress we have made toward better coverage, improved care, and lower costs. And we will not want to go back to the way our medical care used to be.

It will not be all about benefits. We will have new responsibilities, too. We will have to get coverage and stay insured. We will have to work harder to stay healthy—a sure way to bring health care costs down for everyone. And we will have to become more serious about seeking out the best, most cost-effective care. Even now, many people believe more care is automatically better, and that the more expensive the care is, the better it is likely to be.[7] This is not true, and it may take many more years of public debate before people realize that smarter choices will bring costs down for all of us.

But the biggest challenge of all—the great divide over the role of government—does not need to stand in our way any longer. It can still cause trouble in the years ahead, and it may even limit our progress. But it does not have to stop us from solving big problems. If we see the divide for what it is, we can overcome it.

Nelson Mandela once said, "It always seems impossible until it is done." For decades, the challenge we faced was to make comprehensive health care reform the law of the land. It seemed impossible, and then it was done. Now, we must turn the promise of the law into reality.

It will take many years, and there is no guarantee of success. But now that we have taken the biggest step, we know we can take the next ones. We can join the rest of the industrialized world in creating the health care safety net all of our people deserve. We can rise to the economic and moral challenge of our time.

And when we do, we will live up to the promise the ailing Ted Kennedy held out for all of us that night in the Denver convention hall: that our political differences will not stop us from rising to the challenge of our time, and that "every American—north, south, east, west, young, old—will have decent, quality health care as a fundamental right and not a privilege."

The dream lives on.

Acknowledgments

Over these past two years, I have confidently used the word *transformational* to describe the historic and extraordinarily consequential passage of comprehensive health reform. It will rank among the most important accomplishments in social policy in the United States and will have meaningful ramifications for every citizen of our country, perhaps in all perpetuity.

It has also been a transformational chapter of my life. The past two years have been tumultuous, painful, exhilarating, and life-changing. I faced several crossroads over these past twenty-four months, and I am reasonably confident that I have made the best decisions given my circumstances with each of these developments along the way. Regardless, I am very grateful to have had the remarkable opportunity to be both a spectator and a participant in this transformational moment in the creation of a new health care infrastructure.

My primary purpose in writing this book was to share this incredibly fascinating account of history in the making as honestly and as completely as I can.

I could not have accomplished my goals for this project were it not for the incredible help and support that I generously received from family, friends, and a number of colleagues.

I must thank my wife, Linda, for her constant support and encouragement. For nearly thirty years, she has shared her life, her love, and her strength in good times and in bad. This book is yet another illustration of that commitment.

I am deeply grateful to my coauthor, David Nather, for his partnership and extraordinary efforts to make this book all that it is. I simply could not have done it without him. His professionalism, competence, and character made this one of the most enjoyable projects on which I have ever worked. I simply cannot be more appreciative of his efforts.

I want to thank Thomas Dunne and St. Martin's Press for their support and the freedom to write this account in the manner that I have. No writer could be more fortunate to have such backing. We have also immensely enjoyed working with Karyn Marcus, our book editor. She has been patient and helpful, with a careful editing touch and a great sense of humor.

That is also true of Victoria Skurnick, my agent and constant advocate. She was there from the beginning, once again, and for that I am eternally grateful.

I have also been blessed by terrific staff, for whom I am deeply grateful. Jody Bennett, who recently left to join the Obama administration, Tim Hogan, and Lindsey Wagner have gone above and beyond what would be expected of professionals in support of a project of this kind.

Senate Majority Leader Harry Reid and Speaker Nancy Pelosi deserve extraordinary credit for providing the leadership in Congress to make this incredible accomplishment possible. History will note their remarkable achievements. I am deeply grateful to both of these special friends, not only for their leadership, but for their willingness to share their invaluable insights and experiences with me along the way during this historic journey.

Two valued friends and former members of my Senate staff were of great assistance to me in ensuring the highest degree of accuracy. Pete Rouse and Mark Childress were most helpful in reviewing my account of these historic months. They provided an important perspective for which I am especially indebted.

I am grateful to John Podesta, Judy Feder, and Karen Davenport of the Center for American Progress (CAP). They are good friends and consummate professionals. It has been my good fortune to work with them on health care for many years. They were pivotal in the success of this project. I must also thank Emma Sandoe, formerly of CAP, who provided a tremendous amount of research and fact-checking help. She offered very useful suggestions on many key questions. Finally, I deeply appreciate the most helpful contributions from Lesley Russell, another member of the superb CAP staff.

The same can be said for Chris Jennings. His guidance, counsel, and friendship have been important to me for many, many years. He was the guiding light in our efforts to reach a successful conclusion on the Bipartisan Policy Center project on health reform. And he was vitally important in the writing of this book.

I am also indebted to Jason Grumet, the president of the Bipartisan Policy Center. His vision for the center and his commitment to engage the organization in the health reform debate was a critical factor in our success.

I am especially grateful for Dr. Larry Horowitz's assistance. He and I spent many hours together, largely in coast-to-coast telephone calls, over the course of the past two years. His assistance in coordinating help for my brother, along with his partnership in our work on health reform, is one of my life's treasured gifts.

My greatest admiration goes to Dr. Allan Friedman and Dr. Henry Friedman, who have directed and provided the care for my brother Greg for nearly two years. There are simply no words to adequately describe the gratitude and affection my family and I have for both of them. They are doctors who happen to be the best in the world. And they are now special friends.

I am most grateful to Judy Hodges and Barry Keene for sharing their health care experiences in Part One. And I wish to thank the Patient Advocate Foundation for putting us in touch with Judy.

Karen Pollitz was of great assistance in explaining the individual market problems for the access chapter of Part One. I am very appreciative of her thoughtful insights. The same can be said for Cathy Schoen of the Commonwealth Fund, Tsung-Mei Cheng of Princeton University, and Victor Rodwin of New York University, each of whom deserve heartfelt thanks for checking parts of the chapter on "Lessons from Other Countries."

Several of my former colleagues were gracious enough to give us some of their valuable time for interviews and to provide their critical insights. Henry Waxman, Olympia Snowe, Sherrod Brown, Jay Rockefeller, Ron Wyden, Rob Andrews, and Bart Stupak were especially generous with their time. I couldn't be more grateful.

Drew Altman at the Kaiser Family Foundation, Paul Ginsburg at the Center for Studying Health System Change, and Kansas insurance commissioner Sandy Praeger provided invaluable guidance on critical issues to the success of health care reform implementation. I am deeply appreciative of their thoughtful assistance.

Yeats once wrote, "Think where man's glory begins and ends, and say my glory is that I had such friends."

My glory is to have had such friends, colleagues, and contributors who have been so generous in their support and assistance on a project about which I care so deeply.

Notes

Part One: The Stakes

1. THE GREAT DIVIDE

1. Gene Green town hall meeting, August 3, 2009, YouTube video (accessed September 29, 2009).
2. Maggie Fox, "Medical bills underlie 60 percent of bankrupts: study," Reuters, June 4, 2009.
3. Christopher T. Robertson, Richard Egelhof, and Michael Hoke, "Get Sick, Get Out: The Medical Causes of Home Mortgage Foreclosures," *Health Matrix: Journal of Law-Medicine* 18, no. 65 (2008).
4. M. M. Doty, S. R. Collins, J. L. Nicholson, and S. D. Rustgi, "Failure to Protect: Why the Individual Insurance Market Is Not a Viable Option for Most U.S. Families," Commonwealth Fund, July 2009.
5. "Growth in National Health Expenditures Expected to Slow by 2009 as a Result of Recession," Centers for Medicare and Medicaid Services, February 24, 2009.
6. Interview on CNN, September 19, 2009, CQ Transcripts.
7. "The 60 Second Update with Senator Jim DeMint," 60secondupdates.com (accessed September 8, 2009).
8. Interview on Fox News, September 22, 2009, CQ Transcripts.
9. Donna Miles, "VA Outranks Private Sector in Health Care Patient Satisfaction," DefenseLink, January 20, 2006.
10. "Wilson Health Information Finds TRICARE #1 Health Insurance Carrier in Member Satisfaction for Sixth Consecutive Year," Reuters, January 16, 2009.
11. Theodore R. Marmor, *The Politics of Medicare* (New York: Aldine Publishing Company, 1973), 8.
12. "Doctors Condemn Health Insurance," *The New York Times,* June 12, 1934.
13. Marmor, *Politics of Medicare,* 13.
14. J. James Rohack, inaugural address, AMA House of Delegates annual meeting (Chicago, IL, June 16, 2009).

15. "Independents Take Center Stage in Obama Era," Pew Research Center for the People and the Press, May 21, 2009.
16. Andrew Kohut, "Would Americans Welcome Medicare If It Were Being Proposed in 2009?" Pew Research Center for the People and the Press, August 19, 2009.
17. "Independents Take Center Stage," Pew Research Center.
18. Phone interview, October 16, 2009.

2. "LET ME TELL YOU WHAT YOU WANT TO HEAR"

1. Haynes Johnson and David S. Broder, *The System: The American Way of Politics at the Breaking Point* (Boston: Little, Brown and Company, 1996), 192–93.
2. Ibid., 274.
3. Ibid., 264.
4. "Support for Health Care Overhaul, But It's Not 1993," Pew Research Center for the People and the Press, March 19, 2009.
5. NBC News–Wall Street Journal Poll, February 26–March 1, 2009.
6. Kaiser Health Tracking Poll, Henry J. Kaiser Family Foundation, September 2009.
7. ABC News–Washington Post Poll, September 10–12, 2009.
8. Kaiser Health Tracking Poll, Henry J. Kaiser Family Foundation, January 2010.
9. "Seniors Lean Against New Healthcare Law," Gallup, September 24, 2009.
10. USA Today–Gallup Poll, September 11–13, 2009.
11. Kaiser Health Tracking Poll, September 2009.

3. THE COST PROBLEM

1. "Health Care Costs: A Primer," Henry J. Kaiser Family Foundation, March 2009.
2. Ibid.
3. Ibid.
4. David M. Cutler, "Health System Modernization Will Reduce the Deficit," Center for American Progress Action Fund, May 2009.
5. "Growth in Health Care Costs," Congressional Budget Office, testimony before the Senate Budget Committee, January 31, 2008.
6. "Health care takes its toll on Starbucks," Associated Press, September 14, 2005.
7. Sarah Goodell and Paul B. Ginsburg, "High and rising health care costs: Demystifying U.S. health care spending," Robert Wood Johnson Foundation, Synthesis Project, Policy Brief no. 16, October 2008.
8. Mark Pearson, Organisation for Economic Cooperation and Development, written statement to the Senate Special Committee on Aging, September 30, 2009.
9. "Employer Health Benefits 2009 Annual Survey," Henry J. Kaiser Family Foundation, September 2009.
10. "Income, Poverty, and Health Insurance Coverage in the United States: 2008," U.S. Census Bureau, September 2009.
11. "Accounting for the cost of U.S. health care: A new look at why Americans spend more," McKinsey Global Institute, December 2008.
12. "Employer Health Benefits 2009 Annual Survey," Kaiser Family Foundation.
13. Katherine Baicker and Amitabh Chandra, "The Labor Market Effects of Rising Health Insurance Premiums," *Journal of Labor Economics* 24 (July 3, 2006): 609–34.

14. "Employer Health Benefits 2009 Annual Survey," Kaiser Family Foundation.
15. Kaiser Health Tracking Poll, Henry J. Kaiser Family Foundation, February 2009.
16. Christina D. Romer, Council of Economic Advisers, "The Economic Case for Health Care Reform," testimony before the House Budget Committee, June 19, 2009.
17. Goodell and Ginsburg, "High and rising health care costs."
18. Peter R. Orszag testimony to Senate Budget Committee Congressional Budget Office, January 31, 2008. Also see Cutler, "Health System Modernization."
19. David M. Cutler, "Technology, Health Care Costs, and the NIH," Harvard University and National Bureau of Economic Research, September 1995.
20. "Accounting for the cost," McKinsey Global Institute.
21. Goodell and Ginsburg, "High and rising health care costs."
22. "Health Care Costs," Kaiser Family Foundation.
23. Cutler, "Health System Modernization."
24. "Accounting for the cost," McKinsey Global Institute.
25. Jon Leibowitz, Federal Trade Commission, testimony before the House Energy and Commerce Subcommitte on Commerce, Trade, and Consumer Protection, May 2, 2007.
26. Atul Gawande, "The Cost Conundrum: What a Texas Town Can Teach Us About Health Care," *The New Yorker,* June 1, 2009.
27. Goodell and Ginsburg, "High and rising health care costs."

4. THE QUALITY PROBLEM

1. Carolyn M. Clancy, "What Is Health Care Quality and Who Decides?" Testimony before the Senate Finance Subcommittee on Health Care, March 18, 2009.
2. Nicholas Bakalar, "U.S. Still Struggling with Infant Mortality," *The New York Times,* April 6, 2009.
3. World Health Organization, *The World Health Report 2000: Health Systems: Improving Performance,* 155. The organization measured performance by the nations' overall score on several issues, including responsiveness, fairness of financial contribution, overall level of health, and distribution of health throughout the population. The United States scored better on some measures than others. It ranked ahead of all other countries in responsiveness, for example, but below more than fifty other countries in fairness of financial contributions. It scored twenty-fourth on level of health and thirty-second on distribution of health throughout the population.
4. Karen Davis, testimony before Senate Health, Education, Labor, and Pensions Committee, January 29, 2009.
5. Commonwealth Fund Commission on a High Performance Health System, "Why Not the Best? Results from the National Scorecard on U.S. Health System Performance, 2008," Commonwealth Fund, July 2008.
6. Ibid.
7. Peter R. Orszag, "A View from the Institute of Medicine," Office of Management and Budget blog, October 5, 2009.
8. "To Err Is Human: Building a Safer Health System," Institute of Medicine, September 1999.
9. Commonwealth Fund, "Why Not the Best?"
10. Dr. Marjorie Kanof, Government Accountability Office, "Health-Care-Associated Infections in Hospitals," testimony before Senate Finance Subcommittee on Health Care, March 18, 2009.
11. "Preventing Medication Errors," Institute of Medicine, July 2006.

12. Mark R. Chassin, "Assessing Strategies for Quality Improvement," *Health Affairs*, May/June 1997, 151–61.

13. E. A. McGlynn et al., "The Quality of Health Care Delivered to Adults in the United States," *New England Journal of Medicine* 348 (2003): 2635–45.

14. "National Healthcare Disparities Report 2008," Agency for Healthcare Research and Quality, March 2009.

15. Ellen-Marie Whelan and Sonia Sekhar, "Better Health Through Better Information: Comparative Effectiveness Research Will Help Deliver Better Medical Care," Center for American Progress, September 29, 2009. Also see Uwe E. Reinhardt, "How Appropriate Is Your Medical Care?" *The New York Times,* March 6, 2009.

16. Whelan and Sekhar, "Better Health Through Better Information."

17. Atul Gawande, "The Cost Conundrum: What a Texas Town Can Teach Us About Health Care," *The New Yorker,* June 1, 2009.

18. R. A. Paulus, K. Davis, and G. D. Steele, "Continuous Innovation in Health Care: Implications of the Geisinger Experience," *Health Affairs* 27, no. 5 (September/October 2008): 1235–45.

5. THE ACCESS PROBLEM

1. Phone interview, October 9, 2009.

2. "Income, Poverty, and Health Insurance Coverage in the United States: 2008," U.S. Census Bureau, September 2009.

3. "Data Spotlight: Unemployment's Impact on Uninsured and Medicaid," Henry J. Kaiser Family Foundation.

4. C. Schoen, S. R. Collins, J. L. Kriss, and M. M. Doty, "How Many Are Underinsured? Trends Among U.S. Adults, 2003 and 2007," Health Affairs Web Exclusive, June 10, 2008, w298–w309.

5. Ibid.

6. Phone interview, October 9, 2009.

7. Schoen et al., "How Many Are Underinsured?"

8. Phone interview, October 12, 2009.

9. "More Small Businesses Stop Providing Health Insurance to Employees," Robert Wood Johnson Foundation, May 26, 2009.

10. M. M. Doty, S. R. Collins, J. L. Nicholson, and S. D. Rustgi, "Failure to Protect: Why the Individual Insurance Market Is Not a Viable Option for Most U.S. Families," Commonwealth Fund, July 2009.

11. M. M. Doty, S. D. Rustgi, C. Schoen, and S. R. Collins, "Maintaining Health Insurance During a Recession: Likely COBRA Eligibility," Commonwealth Fund, January 2009.

12. Karen Pollitz, Richard Sorian, and Kathy Thomas, "How Accessible Is Individual Health Insurance for Consumers in Less-Than-Perfect Health?" Henry J. Kaiser Family Foundation, June 2001.

13. Phone interview, October 8, 2009. This interview was conducted before Pollitz joined the Department of Health and Human Services in spring 2010 to help oversee the implementation of the new law.

14. Pollitz, Sorian, and Thomas, "How Accessible Is Individual."

15. Memorandum by House Energy and Commerce Committee staff, "Supplemental Information Regarding the Individual Health Insurance Market," June 16, 2009.

16. J. M. Colwill, J. M. Cultice, and R. L. Kruse, "Will Generalist Physician Supply Meet

Demands of an Increasing and Aging Population?" *Health Affairs* 27, no. 3 (2008): w232–w241.
17. "New International Survey: More Than Half of U.S. Chronically Ill Adults Skip Needed Care Due to Costs," Commonwealth Fund, November 13, 2008.
18. "The Uninsured: A Primer," Henry J. Kaiser Family Foundation, October 2008.
19. S. Zuckerman, J. McFeeters, P. Cunningham, and L. Nichols, "Changes in Medicaid Physician Fees, 1998–2003: Implications for Physician Participation," Health Affairs Web Exclusive, June 23, 2004.

6. OUR HEALTH CARE PYRAMID

1. "Accounting for the cost of U.S. health care: A new look at why Americans spend more," McKinsey Global Institute, December 2008.
2. Cathy Schoen et al., "Taking the Pulse of Health Care Systems: Experiences of Patients with Health Problems in Six Countries," Health Affairs Web Exclusive, November 3, 2005.
3. Jeanne M. Lambrew and John D. Podesta, "Promoting Prevention and Preempting Costs: A New Wellness Trust for the United States," Center for American Progress, October 5, 2006.
4. Ibid.
5. "F as in Fat 2009: How Obesity Policies Are Failing in America," Trust for America's Health, July 2009.
6. "Diabetes and Obesity 2025: Four Future Scenarios for the Twin Health Epidemics," Institute for Alternative Futures, June 2006.
7. Melissa Healy, "Growing obesity swells healthcare costs," *Los Angeles Times*, July 27, 2009.

7. KEEPING WHAT PEOPLE LIKE

1. Robert J. Blendon, Mollyann Brodie, and John Benson, "What Happened to Americans' Support for the Clinton Health Plan?" *Health Affairs*, Summer 1995, 7–23.
2. Haynes Johnson and David S. Broder, *The System: The American Way of Politics at the Breaking Point* (Boston: Little, Brown and Company, 1996), 205.
3. "Senate Minority Leader Bob Dole, Republican Response to President Bill Clinton's State of the Union Address, January 25, 1994," Federal News Service transcript, published in *CQ Weekly*, January 29, 1994.
4. Theda Skocpol, *Boomerang: Health Care Reform and the Turn Against Government* (New York: W. W. Norton & Company, 1996), 148–49.
5. Blendon, Brodie, and Benson, "What Happened to Americans' Support."
6. Presidential debate, Hempstead, New York, October 15, 2008, CQ Transcripts.
7. Douglas W. Elmendorf, director, Congressional Budget Office, "Additional Information Regarding the Effects of Specifications in the America's Affordable Health Choices Act Pertaining to Health Insurance Coverage," letter to Representative Dave Camp, July 26, 2009.
8. Neera Tanden interview, October 22, 2009.
9. "President Obama Delivers Remarks Before Joint Session of Congress," CQ Transcripts, September 9, 2009.
10. David Cutler interview, October 29, 2009.
11. Frank I. Luntz, "The Language of Healthcare 2009," obtained by ThinkProgress.org's "The Wonk Room" blog (accessed October 15, 2009).

8. LESSONS FROM OTHER COUNTRIES

1. World Health Organization, *The World Health Report 2000: Health Systems: Improving Performance*, 153.
2. T. R. Reid, *The Healing of America: A Global Quest for Better, Cheaper, and Fairer Health Care* (New York: Penguin Press, 2009).
3. Victor G. Rodwin, "The Health Care System Under French National Health Insurance: Lessons for Health Reform in the United States," *American Journal of Public Health* 93, no. 1 (January 2003): 31–57.
4. Joseph Shapiro, "Health Care Lessons from France," National Public Radio, July 11, 2008.
5. Reid, *Healing of America*.
6. Richard Knox, "History of Tinkering Helps German System Endure," National Public Radio, July 3, 2008.
7. Reid, *Healing of America*.
8. Kyle James, "German Health Care Reform: Mission Impossible?" Deutsche Welle, March 8, 2006.
9. Cathy Schoen, David Helms, and Amanda Folsom, "Harnessing Health Care Markets for the Public Interest: German and Dutch Approaches to Multi-Payer Systems with Insights for U.S. Reforms," Commonwealth Fund, November 2009.
10. Panos Kanavos and Uwe Reinhardt, "Reference Pricing for Drugs: Is It Compatible with U.S. Health Care?" *Health Affairs* 22, no. 3 (May/June 2003): 16–30.
11. Stuart Altman and Terri Jackson, "Health Care in Australia: Lessons from Down Under," *Health Affairs*, Fall 1991, 129–46.
12. Commonwealth Fund, "The Health Care System and Health Policy in Australia."
13. Sharon Wilcox, "Promoting Private Health Insurance in Australia," *Health Affairs* 20, no. 3 (May/June 2001): 152–61; Commonwealth Fund, "Health Care System and Health Policy in Australia."
14. Ian McAuley, "Private Health Insurance: Still Muddling Through," *Agenda* 12, no. 2 (2005): 159–78.
15. Tsung-Mei Cheng, "Taiwan's New Health Insurance Program: Genesis and Experience So Far," *Health Affairs* 22, no. 3 (2003): 61–76; and "Sick Around the World," transcript, *Frontline*, Public Broadcasting System, April 15, 2008.
16. Reid, *Healing of America*.
17. "Sick Around the World," PBS.
18. Ibid.
19. Cheng, "Taiwan's New Health Insurance Program."
20. Jui-Fen Rachel Lu and William C. Hsaio, "Does Universal Health Insurance Make Health Care Unaffordable? Lesson from Taiwan," *Health Affairs* 22, no. 3 (2003): 77–88.
21. Rodwin, "Health Care System Under French."

Part Two: The Plan

2. THE MAKING OF THE OBAMA PLAN

1. Heather Higginbottom interview, November 6, 2009.
2. Barack Obama, *The Audacity of Hope: Thoughts on Reclaiming the American Dream* (New York: Crown Publishers, 2006), 184–85.
3. CQ Transcripts, May 29, 2007.

4. "Barack Obama's Plan for a Healthy America," May 29, 2007.
5. Blumenthal, Cutler, and Liebman memo, "Obama Health Care Plan," May 2007.
6. CQ Transcripts, May 29, 2007.
7. "Barack Obama's Plan for a Healthy America."
8. Ibid.
9. Higginbottom interview.
10. "Massachusetts Health Care Reform: Three Years Later," Henry J. Kaiser Family Foundation, September 2009.
11. Dora Hughes interview, October 27, 2009.
12. Higginbottom interview.
13. Ibid.
14. Health Connector Web site; Amy M. Lischko, Sara S. Bachman, and Alyssa Vangeli, "The Massachusetts Commonwealth Health Insurance Connector: Structure and Functions," Commonwealth Fund, May 2009; and "Massachusetts Health Care Reform," Kaiser Family Foundation.
15. Jon Kingsdale, executive director, Commonwealth Health Insurance Connector Authority, testimony before the Senate Health, Education, Labor, and Pensions Committee, April 28, 2009.
16. Certificate of Exemption Application, Commonwealth Health Insurance Connector Authority.
17. Jacob S. Hacker, "Medicare Plus: Increasing Health Coverage by Expanding Medicare," Robert Wood Johnson Foundation, October 31, 2003.
18. "Universal Health Care Through Shared Responsibility," Edwards campaign, February 2007.

3. THE PRIMARIES

1. David Plouffe, *The Audacity to Win: The Inside Story and Lessons of Barack Obama's Historic Victory* (New York: Viking, 2009), 47.
2. "New Leadership on Health Care: A Presidential Forum" (transcript, Las Vegas, NV, March 24, 2007).
3. Ibid. Video at Health08.org, Henry J. Kaiser Family Foundation (accessed November 16, 2009).
4. "New Leadership on Health Care."
5. Ibid.
6. "Sen. Clinton Holds Online News Conference on Health Care," CQ Transcripts, September 18, 2007.
7. "American Health Choices Plan," September 2007.
8. Ibid.
9. Neera Tanden interview, Oct. 22, 2009.
10. Ben Smith, "More on Obamacare," *Politico,* May 29, 2007.
11. David Cutler interview, October 29, 2009.
12. "Clinton vs. Obama: Who's right on health care, Social Security?" FactCheck.org, November 16, 2007.
13. "New Hampshire Democratic Presidential Candidates Debate," CNN.com transcript, June 3, 2007.
14. "Democratic Presidential Candidates Participate in a Debate Sponsored by CNN," CQ Transcripts, November 15, 2007.

15. Ibid.
16. "Democratic Presidential Candidates Participate in a Debate Sponsored by CNN," CQ Transcripts, January 31, 2008.
17. "Harry & Louise Again? Obama mailer on Clinton health care plan lacks context," Fact-Check.org, February 4, 2008.
18. "Misleading Pennsylvania Voters," FactCheck.org, April 21, 2008.
19. Ibid.
20. Ibid.
21. "Sen. Clinton Delivers Remarks at the Democratic National Convention," CQ Transcripts, August 26, 2008.
22. "Sen. Obama Delivers Remarks at the Democratic National Convention," CQ Transcripts, August 28, 2008.

4. THE STAKEHOLDERS

1. "A Vision for Reform," America's Health Insurance Plans, November 2006.
2. "Now Is the Time for Health Care Reform: A Proposal to Achieve Universal Coverage, Affordability, Quality Improvement and Market Reform," America's Health Insurance Plans, December 2008.
3. Phone interview, October 29, 2009.
4. Mary Agnes Carey, "Hidden Costs of the Uninsured," CQ Weekly, August 8, 2005, 2178.
5. "Health Care Reform in America: A Business Roundtable Plan," Business Roundtable, September 2008.
6. "Expanding Health Care Coverage in the United States: Background Information on a Historic Agreement," Health Coverage Coalition for the Uninsured, January 18, 2007.
7. "The Divided We Fail Platform," DividedWeFail.org, January 2007.
8. John B. Judis, "Abandoned Surgery: Business and the Failure of Health Reform," American Prospect, March 21, 1995.
9. Ibid.
10. Interview with Health08.org, Henry J. Kaiser Family Foundation, May 21, 2008.
11. Phone interview, November 5, 2009.

5. OBAMA vs. McCAIN

1. "Republican Presidential Candidates Participate in a Debate Sponsored by ABC," CQ Transcripts, January 5, 2008.
2. "Republican Presidential Candidates Participate in Debate Sponsored by Fox," CQ Transcripts, October 21, 2007.
3. "Republican Presidential Candidates . . . Sponsored by ABC."
4. "McCain's Oct. 11, 2007, speech on health care" (Des Moines, IA), CNN.com transcript.
5. "2008 Presidential Candidate Health Care Proposals: Side-by-Side Summary," Health08.org, Henry J. Kaiser Family Foundation.
6. Ibid.
7. "McCain's Oct. 11, 2007, speech."
8. Jeanne Lambrew, "McCain's Health Plan Puts at Least 56 Million People with Chronic Disease at Risk of Losing Health Coverage," Center for American Progress Action Fund, April 29, 2008.

9. Barack Obama, *The Audacity of Hope: Thoughts on Reclaiming the American Dream* (New York: Crown Publishers, 2006), 185.

10. Heather Higginbottom interview, November 6, 2009.

11. Domenico Montanaro, "Obama Ad Pushes Health Care," "First Read," MSNBC.com, October 4, 2008.

12. "Prescription" ad, YouTube, October 1, 2008.

13. "Health Care Hyperbole," FactCheck.org, September 9, 2008.

14. Angie Drobnic Holan, "Health care ad is right—until the end," PolitiFact, October 3, 2008.

15. "Sen. Obama and Sen. McCain Participate in a Presidential Candidates Debate," CQ Transcripts, October 15, 2008.

16. "Sen. McCain Delivers Remarks at the Republican National Convention," CQ Transcripts, September 4, 2008.

17. "Sen. McCain and Sen. Obama Participate in a Presidential Candidates Debate," CQ Transcripts, October 7, 2008.

18. "Barack Obama and Joe Biden's Plan to Lower Health Care Costs and Ensure Affordable, Accessible Health Coverage for All," archived on Barackobama.com.

19. "Sen. McCain and Sen. Obama . . . Presidential Candidates Debate," October 7, 2008.

20. Higginbottom interview.

21. "Transcript: 'This is your victory,' says Obama," CNN.com transcript, November 4, 2008.

6. PREPARING THE ROAD MAP

1. Health policy team memo to the president-elect, December 10, 2008.

2. "Call to Action: Health Reform 2009," Senate Finance Committee, November 12, 2008.

3. Health policy team memo.

4. Ibid.

5. Ibid.

6. Conference report, S Con Res 13, fiscal year 2010 budget resolution.

7. Tony Blankley, "Obama's Health Care Czar," *Washington Times,* November 26, 2008.

8. Edwin Chen and Julianna Goldman, "Daschle Said to Accept Offer as Health Secretary," Bloomberg, November 19, 2008.

9. Kevin Freking, "Obama hopes to avoid Clinton health care missteps," Associated Press, December 6, 2008.

10. "President-elect Obama Holds News Conference," CQ Transcripts, December 11, 2008.

11. Health policy team memo.

7. OPENING THE DOORS

1. The video and the comments are archived at http://change.gov/page/content/discusshealth-care.

2. "Health Care Community Discussion: Host and Moderator Guide," Obama-Biden Transition Project, Change.gov, December 2008.

3. "Americans Speak on Health Reform: Report on Health Care Community Discussions," Department of Health and Human Services, March 2009, 5.

4. Ibid., 5, 9–10.

5. Memo from the health policy team to the transition team, December 5, 2008.

8. HEALTH CARE VS. THE ECONOMY

1. "President-elect Obama Holds News Conference," CQ Transcripts, December 11, 2008.
2. Conference report, American Recovery and Reinvestment Act of 2009, House Report 111–016; and "Federal Coordinating Council for Comparative Effectiveness Research Membership," HHS.gov.
3. Confirmation hearing, Senate Health, Education, Labor, and Pensions Committee, CQ Transcripts, January 8, 2009.
4. Health policy team memo to the president-elect, December 10, 2008.
5. "Full Transcript: President Barack Obama's Inaugural Address," ABCNews.com, January 20, 2009.

9. MELTDOWN

1. "Baucus Comment Regarding Daschle Nomination," Senate Finance Committee release, February 2, 2009.

Part Three: No Margin for Error

1. THE WHITE HOUSE STRATEGY

1. Obama remarks before joint session of Congress, CQ Transcripts, February 24, 2009.
2. Henry Waxman phone interview, April 16, 2010.
3. Chip Kahn phone interview, March 5, 2010.
4. Office of Management and Budget, "A New Era of Responsibility: Renewing America's Promise," fiscal year 2010 budget proposal, February 26, 2009, 27.
5. Senate Finance Committee hearing on the fiscal 2010 budget, CQ Transcripts, March 4, 2009.
6. "Independent Sector Statement on Changes to Tax Incentives for Charitable Giving and Health Care Reform," March 26, 2009.
7. Opening remarks at the White House Forum on Health Reform, CQ Transcripts, March 5, 2009.
8. Closing session, White House Forum on Health Reform, CQ Transcripts, March 5, 2009.
9. Waxman interview.
10. Closing session, White House Forum on Health Reform, CQ Transcripts, March 5, 2009.
11. Fiscal year 2010 budget resolution (S Con Res 13), Sec. 301.
12. Ibid., Secs. 201–2.
13. Letter to President Obama, May 11, 2009.
14. Robert Pear, "Health Care Leaders Say Obama Overstated Their Promise to Control Costs," *The New York Times,* May 15, 2009.
15. Committees on Energy and Commerce, Ways and Means, and Education and Labor, "Section-by-Section Analysis, the Affordable Health Care for America Act (HR 3962)," Sec. 1182, November 1, 2009.
16. "Barack Obama and Joe Biden's Plan to Lower Health Care Costs and Ensure Affordable, Accessible Health Coverage for All," 5.
17. David D. Kirkpatrick, "White House Affirms Deal on Drug Costs," *The New York Times,* August 5, 2009.
18. Manu Raju, "Reid Says He's Not Bound by Drug Deal," *Politico,* August 29, 2009.

2. THE SENATE

1. Sherrod Brown interview, March 12, 2010.
2. "Obama's Deal," *Frontline,* PBS, April 13, 2010.
3. Bipartisan health care summit, CQ Transcripts, February 25, 2010.
4. Ron Wyden phone interview, May 28, 2010.
5. Ibid.
6. David Catanese, "Sen. Bennett loses Republican nomination," *Politico,* May 10, 2010.
7. Senate Finance Committee, "Prepare for Launch: Health Reform Summit 2008," June 16, 2008. Information comes from agenda, prepared remarks, and archived webcasts of panel discussions.
8. Senate Finance Committee Chairman Max Baucus, "Call to Action: Health Reform 2009," November 12, 2008.
9. Senate Finance Committee, "Roundtable to Discuss Reforming America's Health Care Delivery System," April 21, 2009; "Roundtable Discussion on Expanding Health Care Coverage," May 5, 2009; and "Roundtable Discussion on Financing Comprehensive Health Care Reform," May 12, 2009.
10. Letter to President Obama, February 5, 2009.
11. Election Center 2008, CNN.com. McCain won 59 percent of the vote in Arkansas, while Obama took 39 percent.
12. David Nather, "Bipartisanship Isn't the Main Goal on Health Care, Dodd Says," CQPolitics.com, June 18, 2009.
13. Robert Pear and Sheryl Gay Stolberg, "Obama Urges Quick Action on Insurance," *The New York Times,* June 2, 2009.
14. Congressional Budget Office, "Preliminary Analysis of Major Provisions Related to Health Insurance Coverage Under the Affordable Health Choices Act," June 15, 2009.
15. Senator Mike Enzi, "Health Care Markup, Day 1: Republicans Sharpen Focus on Kennedy Bill Costing Too Much, Covering Too Few," June 17, 2009.
16. David Nather, "Riding the Eye of a Legislative Storm," *CQ Weekly,* June 22, 2009, 1424.
17. Douglas W. Elmendorf letter to the Honorable Edward M. Kennedy, Congressional Budget Office, July 2, 2009.
18. Ceci Connolly and Lori Montgomery, "Senate Health Markup Off to a Rocky Start," *The Washington Post,* June 17, 2009.
19. Senator Orrin Hatch, "Hatch Statement on Need for Financially Responsible and Truly Bipartisan Healthcare Reform," July 22, 2009.
20. Rick Umbdenstock, Sister Carol Keehan, and Chip Kahn, "Statement About Agreement with White House and Senate Finance Committee on Health Reform," July 8, 2009.
21. Chip Kahn phone interview, March 5, 2009.
22. Senator Judd Gregg, "Gregg Eliminates $2 Trillion in Future Debt," July 7, 2009.
23. Congressional Budget Office, "Affordable Health Choices Act," July 2, 2009.
24. Robert Pear and David M. Herszenhorn, "Health Care Vote Illustrates Partisan Divide," *The New York Times,* July 15, 2009.

3. THE HOUSE

1. Henry Waxman with Joshua Green, *The Waxman Report: How Congress Really Works* (New York: Twelve, Hatchette Book Group, 2009), 79.
2. Beth Donovan, "Leaders to Forge New Bill from Committee Efforts," *CQ Weekly,* July 2, 1994.

3. Rob Andrews phone interview, March 4, 2010.
4. Henry Waxman phone interview, April 16, 2010.
5. Andrews interview.
6. Ibid.
7. Waxman interview.
8. Blue Dog Coalition, letter to Speaker Pelosi and Majority Leader Hoyer, July 9, 2009.
9. Steven T. Dennis and Tory Newmyer, "Blue Dogs' Objections Could Delay Release of Health Care Bill," *Roll Call,* July 9, 2009.
10. Mike Ross phone interview, March 4, 2010.
11. House tricommittee discussion draft, June 19, 2009, Sec. 312.
12. Blue Dog Coalition, letter to Speaker Pelosi and Majority Leader Hoyer.
13. House Speaker Nancy Pelosi press conference, CQ Transcripts, July 9, 2009.
14. House Democrats press conference on health care, CQ Transcripts, July 14, 2009.
15. Ross interview.
16. Richard Rubin, "Panel Tackles Health Care Tax Issues," CQ.com, July 16, 2009; and Karoun Demirjian and Adjoa Adofo, "After Marathon Markup, Panel Approves Health Overhaul Bill," CQ.com, July 17, 2009.
17. Blue Dog Coalition, "Blue Dogs: 'We are committed to passing health care reform that lowers costs and improves quality for all Americans,'" July 16, 2009.
18. Committee on Energy and Commerce, roll call vote, July 17, 2009.
19. Ross interview.

4. HOLDING DOWN COSTS

1. America's Healthy Future Act (S 1796), Sec. 3023.
2. Ibid., Sec. 3001.
3. Kelly Devers and Robert Berenson, "Can Accountable Care Organizations Improve the Value of Health Care by Solving the Cost and Quality Quandaries?" Robert Wood Johnson Foundation/Urban Institute, October 2009.
4. Paul B. Ginsburg et al., "Making Medical Homes Work: Moving from Concept to Practice," Center for Studying Health System Change, December 2008. Also see "Understanding the Medical Home," National Partnership for Women & Families.
5. Adjoa Adofo, "Senate Panel Continues Working Through Health Care Amendments," CQ.com Committee Coverage, June 23, 2009. Also see Office of Senator Tom Harkin, "Harkin's Prevention and Wellness Investments Included in Landmark Health Reform Bill," July 15, 2009.
6. America's Affordable Health Choices Act (HR 3200), Sec. 122(c); and America's Healthy Future Act, Sec. 2243.
7. America's Affordable Health Choices Act, Sec. 1305; and America's Healthy Future Act, Secs. 2001, 2002.
8. Sara Rosenbaum presentation, "Health Information Technology and Its Future: More Than the Money" (transcript Alliance for Health Reform and Robert Wood Johnson Foundation, George Washington University, June 20, 2008).
9. House Ways and Means Committee, "Health Information Technology for Economic and Clinical Health Act or HITECH Act," January 2009; and conference report, American Recovery and Reinvestment Act of 2009, House Report 111-016, Secs. 4101, 13001.
10. Patient Protection and Affordable Care Act (HR 3590), Secs. 1561 and 6114.

5. IMPROVING QUALITY

1. America's Healthy Future Act (S 1796), Sec. 3501.
2. Medicare Payment Advisory Commission, "Report to the Congress: Reforming the Delivery System," June 2008, 107–37.
3. Patient Protection and Affordable Care Act (HR 3590), Sec. 3501.
4. America's Affordable Health Choices Act (HR 3200), Sec. 1151.
5. America's Healthy Future Act, Sec. 3008.
6. National Conference of State Legislatures, "Medicare Nonpayment for Hospital Acquired Conditions."
7. John Lumpkin presentation, "Health Information Technology and Its Future: More Than the Money" (Alliance for Health Reform, June 20, 2008).
8. Patient Protection and Affordable Care Act, Secs. 2718, 6002, 10331, and 2715.
9. Michelle M. Mello and Troyen A. Brennan, "The Controversy over High-Dose Chemotherapy with Autologous Bone Marrow Transplant for Breast Cancer," *Health Affairs* 20, no. 5 (September/October 2001): 101–17.
10. Medicare Payment Advisory Commission, "Report to the Congress," 113–14.
11. House Energy and Commerce Committee markup, CQ Transcripts, July 30, 2009.
12. Fox News interview, CQ Transcripts, June 16, 2009.
13. America's Healthy Future Act, Sec. 3501.
14. Medicare Payment Advisory Commission, "Report to the Congress," 116.

6. REACHING (NEARLY) EVERYONE

1. America's Affordable Health Choices Act (HR 3200), Secs. 111–12; Affordable Health Choices Act (S 1679), Secs. 2702–3, 2705; and America's Healthy Future Act (S 1796), Secs. 2202–3.
2. America's Affordable Health Choices Act, Sec. 113; Affordable Health Choices Act, Sec. 2701; and America's Healthy Future Act, Sec. 2204.
3. America's Affordable Health Choices Act, Sec. 122; Affordable Health Choices Act, Sec. 2711; America's Healthy Future Act, Sec. 2242.
4. Ricardo Alonso-Zaldivar, "Health care loophole would allow coverage limits," Associated Press, December 11, 2009; and Ezra Klein, "Senate bill allows insurers to establish annual limits," Washingtonpost.com, December 11, 2009.
5. Senate managers amendment, Sec. 2711.
6. "The Uninsured: A Primer," Henry J. Kaiser Family Foundation, October 2009.
7. Finance Committee, "Baucus Introduces Landmark Plan to Lower Health Care Costs, Provide Quality, Affordable Coverage," September 16, 2009; and Finance Committee markup, America's Healthy Future Act, CQ Transcripts, October 1, 2009.
8. America's Affordable Health Choices Act, Sec. 401.
9. Finance Committee markup, America's Healthy Future Act, CQ Transcripts, September 22 and October 1, 2009.
10. America's Affordable Health Choices Act, Sec. 1701.
11. Ibid., Sec. 201.
12. America's Healthy Future Act, Secs. 2235–37.
13. "Health Insurance Exchanges: House or Senate Style?" Alliance for Health Reform, January 8, 2010.
14. Senate Finance Committee summary, "America's Healthy Future Act," October 13, 2009.

15. America's Healthy Future Act, Sec. 2242; and America's Affordable Health Choices Act, Sec. 122.
16. America's Healthy Future Act, Sec. 2235(e)(2)(B).
17. "The Medicare Prescription Drug Benefit," Henry J. Kaiser Family Foundation, November 2009.
18. America's Affordable Health Choices Act, Sec. 1181.

7. THE PUBLIC OPTION

1. America's Affordable Health Choices Act (HR 3200), Sec. 224.
2. John Holahan and Linda Blumberg, "Can a Public Insurance Plan Increase Competition and Lower the Costs of Health Reform?" Urban Institute, 2008.
3. White House Forum on Health Reform, CQ Transcripts, March 5, 2009.
4. Letter to the president, June 5, 2009.
5. John G. Black and Gary A. Delaney, South Carolina Medical Association, June 5, 2009.
6. "Contact lawmakers to oppose House proposal," Medical Association of Georgia alert, July 2, 2009.
7. Susan Eckerly, "Letter Opposing America's Affordable Health Choices Act of 2009 (HR 3200)," National Federation of Independent Business, July 15, 2009.
8. Hannity, Fox News, August 18, 2009. Video clip posted by Media Matters for America, August 19, 2009.
9. David Nather, "A Liberal Dose of Disappointment," CQ Weekly, September 7, 2009, 1946–55.
10. David Nather, "Liberal Democrats Can Make Threats, Too," CQPolitics.com, July 30, 2009.
11. David Nather, "Obama's Warning: Yes, We Have to Cut Health Care Costs," CQPolitics .com, March 5, 2009.
12. Ezra Klein, "Has Kent Conrad Solved the Public Plan Problem? An Interview," Washingtonpost.com, June 11, 2009.
13. Congressional Budget Office, "Preliminary Analysis of Specifications for the Chairman's Mark of the America's Healthy Future Act," September 16, 2009.

8. PAYING FOR IT

1. Senate Finance Committee, "Financing Comprehensive Health Care Reform: Proposed Health System Savings and Revenue Options," May 20, 2009, 3.
2. "Employer Health Benefits: 2009 Summary of Findings," Henry J. Kaiser Family Foundation and Health Research & Educational Trust, September 2009.
3. Representative Jared Polis letter to House Speaker Nancy Pelosi, July 16, 2009.
4. Joint Committee on Taxation, "Estimated Revenue Effects of the Revenue Provisions Contained in H.R. 3962, the 'Affordable Health Care for America Act,' as Amended," November 6, 2009, JCX-48–09.
5. Congressional Budget Office, "Preliminary Analysis of Specifications for the Chairman's Mark of the America's Healthy Future Act," letter to the Honorable Max Baucus, September 16, 2009.
6. Statement of Glenn M. Hackbarth, chairman, Medicare Payment Advisory Commission, to the House Ways and Means Subcommittee on Health, March 17, 2009.

7. Brian Biles and Grace Arnold, "Medicare Advantage Reforms: Comparing House and Senate Bills," Commonwealth Fund, December 2009.
8. Weekly Republican radio address, CQ Transcripts, July 18, 2009.
9. Viveca Novak and Brooks Jackson, "More 'Senior Scare': A TV ad's false claims about Democratic Medicare proposals," FactCheck.org, August 18, 2009.

9. ONE BIPARTISAN SOLUTION

1. Howard Baker, Tom Daschle, and Bob Dole, "Crossing Our Lines: Working Together to Reform the U.S. Health Care System," Bipartisan Policy Center, June 2009, 41–46.
2. Ibid., 32–41.
3. Ibid., 46–49.
4. Congressional Budget Office Director's Blog, "CBO's Analysis of the Effects of Proposals to Limit Costs Related to Medical Malpractice ('Tort Reform')," October 9, 2009.
5. Baker, Daschle, and Dole, "Crossing Our Lines," 40.
6. Sam Stein, "Daschle Urges Obama to Drop Federal Public Health Plan," HuffingtonPost.com, June 18, 2009.
7. Baker, Daschle, and Dole, "Crossing Our Lines," 43–44.

10. ROADBLOCKS

1. Henry Waxman phone interview, April 16, 2010.
2. Mike Ross phone interview, March 4, 2009.
3. Waxman interview.
4. Patrick O'Connor, "Health care talks fall apart," *Politico,* July 24, 2009; and Steven T. Dennis, "Waxman Convenes Emergency Meeting to Save Health Bill," *Roll Call,* July 24, 2009.
5. Waxman interview.
6. Ross interview.
7. America's Affordable Health Choices Act (HR 3200), Sec. 412; Blue Dog Coalition summary of agreement.
8. Blue Dog Coalition summary of agreement.
9. Representative Mike Ross amendment, House Energy and Commerce Committee Web site.
10. Waxman interview.
11. Representative Jan Schakowsky amendment, House Energy and Commerce Committee Web site; and Alex Wayne, "Energy and Commerce Panel Approves Health Overhaul," CQ.com, Aug. 31, 2009.
12. David D. Kirkpatrick, "White House Affirms Deal on Drug Cost," *The New York Times,* August 5, 2009.
13. Duff Wilson, "Waxman Takes on Drug Makers over Medicare," *The New York Times,* August 26, 2009.
14. Sherrod Brown interview, March 12, 2010.
15. Olympia Snowe phone interview, March 16, 2010.
16. David Nather, "Reid Doesn't Mind Busting Health Care Deadline," CQPolitics.com, July 23, 2009.

17. Shailagh Murray and Paul Kane, "Senators Close to Health Accord," *The Washington Post,* July 29, 2009.

18. Grassley interview transcript, *NPR News Morning Edition,* July 29, 2009.

19. Russ Sullivan e-mail, July 29, 2009.

20. Grassley news conference call, CQ Transcripts, July 29, 2009.

21. Snowe interview.

22. Brown interview.

11. AUGUST

1. Austin Tea Party video, August 1, 2009 (accessed March 16, 2010).

2. Lloyd Doggett town hall meeting, August 1, 2009, YouTube video (accessed March 16, 2010); and Jenny Hoff, "Austinites protest health care reform," KXAN.com, August 3, 2009.

3. Travis County Clerk Elections Division Web site.

4. W. Gardner Selby, "Critics of health care reform say demonstration reflects unease over health care reform," *Austin American-Statesman,* August 4, 2009.

5. Rosemary Edwards, "Tell Doggett what you think about Health Care Reform," July 31, 2009.

6. Austinreteaparty.com (accessed March 16, 2010); and David M. Herszenhorn and Sheryl Gay Stolberg, "Health Plan Opponents Make Voices Heard," *The New York Times,* August 3, 2009.

7. Patients United Now Web site (accessed March 17, 2010).

8. Ian Urbina, "Beyond Beltway, Health Debate Turns Hostile," *The New York Times,* August 7, 2009.

9. Specter and Sebelius health care forum in Philadelphia, August 2, 2009, YouTube video (accessed March 17, 2010); and Specter town hall meeting in Lebanon, PA, August 11, 2009, CNN Video (accessed March 17, 2010).

10. Dingell town hall meeting in Romulus, MI, August 6, 2009, YouTube video (accessed March 17, 2010).

11. Lansing, Michigan, Tea Party, "Action Alert: Health Care Town Hall with Congressman John Dingell," August 4, 2009.

12. Tim Phillips, "Visit Your Representatives and Senators!" Americans for Prosperity blog, August 3, 2009; and Tim Phillips, "We 'Greeted' Obama Today in Bristol!' Americans for Prosperity blog, July 29, 2009.

13. FreedomWorks, "Turn Up the Heat in August: Help Defeat Obamacare and Cap-and-Trade," August 5, 2009; and FreedomWorks "August Recess Action Kit."

14. Bob MacGuffie, "Rocking the Town Halls—Best Practices," posted on ThinkProgress, July 31, 2009.

15. Kagen phone interview, March 15, 2010.

16. Russ Keen and Scott Waltman, "No simple health care solutions," *Aberdeen News,* August 19, 2009.

17. "HCAN and AFSCME Launch Ads Against Republicans Opposing Health Insurance Reform," Health Care for America Now, August 17, 2009.

18. Sherrod Brown interview, March 12, 2010.

19. Sarah Palin Facebook post, "Statement on the Current Health Care Debate," August 7, 2009; and "A Much-Debated Health Care Proposal," *The New York Times,* August 14, 2009.

20. America's Affordable Health Choices Act (HR 3200), Sec. 1233.
21. Affordable Health Care for America Act (HR 3962), Sec. 1233.
22. Olympia Snowe phone interview, March 16, 2010.
23. Obama speech to joint session of Congress, CQ Transcripts, September 9, 2009.
24. Snowe interview.
25. Jason Hancock, "Grassley: Government shouldn't 'decide when to pull the plug on grandma,'" *Iowa Independent,* August 12, 2009.
26. Ezra Klein, "Chuck Grassley Fundraises Against Health-Care Reform," *The Washington Post,* August 31, 2009.
27. Jamie Johnson, "Grassley May Have Primary Opponent," *Iowa Republican,* April 10, 2009.
28. Enzi weekly Republican address, August 29, 2009, YouTube clip (accessed March 17, 2010).
29. Drew Armstrong, "Lawmakers Look to Address Affordability of Mandated Health Coverage," CQ.com, September 18, 2009.
30. Senate Finance Committee, "Baucus Modifies Chairman's Mark to Improve Health Care Affordability, Maintain Deficit Reductions," September 22, 2009.
31. Carrie Budoff Brown, "Public option fate in Obama's hands," *Politico,* September 29, 2009.
32. Schumer-Snowe Amendment C3—Financing (Modified), Senate Finance Committee Web site.
33. Snowe interview.
34. Snowe Finance Committee markup closing statement, October 13, 2009.
35. Snowe interview.

12. BREAKTHROUGH

1. Bart Stupak interview, April 27, 2010.
2. Committee on Energy and Commerce, HR 3200, America's Affordable Health Choices Act of 2009 Markup, Day 5, July 31, 2009. Video and amendments available on committee Web site. Also see Lois Capps, "Stupak-Pitts goes beyond status quo," *Politico,* November 20, 2009.
3. Terence P. Jeffrey, "Bravest Congressman Is Calling Obama's Bluff," CNSNews.com, October 28, 2009.
4. Stupak interview.
5. House Democrats press conference, CQ Transcripts, October 29, 2009.
6. Mike Ross phone interview, March 4, 2010.
7. Herseth Sandlin Statement on House Health Care Bill, November 6, 2009.
8. Shailagh Murray and Lori Montgomery, "Democrats wary of health-bill defections," November 6, 2009.
9. House floor debate, November 7, 2009.
10. Douglas W. Elmendorf, Letter to the Hon. John A. Boehner, Congressional Budget Office, November 4, 2009; and "The Uninsured: A Primer," Henry J. Kaiser Family Foundation, October 2009.
11. Stupak interview.
12. David Clarke, "Moderate Democrats Resist Restrictive Rules for Spending Bills," CQ.com, July 16, 2009.
13. Stupak interview.
14. "The Stupak Amendment: A New Ban on Abortion Coverage for Millions of Women and an Assault on Women's Health," National Women's Law Center.

15. United States Conference of Catholic Bishops, "Bishops' Conference Blankets Parishes with Inserts Against Expansion of Abortion Through Health Care Reform," October 30, 2009.
16. Stupak interview.
17. Henry Waxman phone interview, April 16, 2010.
18. Rob Andrews phone interview, March 4, 2010.
19. House floor debate, November 7, 2009.
20. Ibid.

13. SIXTY VOTES

1. Olympia Snowe phone interview, March 16, 2010.
2. McConnell remarks on Senate floor, October 22, 2009.
3. January Angeles and Judith Solomon, "Changes in Senate Health Bill Make Coverage More Affordable for Millions of Moderate-Income Families, Although Not for Those on Low End of Subsidy Scale," Center on Budget and Policy Priorities, November 19, 2009.
4. Joint Committee on Taxation, "Estimated Revenue Effects of the Revenue Provisions Contained in the 'Patient Protection and Affordable Care Act,'" November 18, 2009, JCX-55-09.
5. Patient Protection and Affordable Care Act (HR 3590), Sec. 4002.
6. Reid news conference, CQ Transcripts, October 26, 2009.
7. Nelson Statement on Health Care Motion to Proceed, November 18, 2009.
8. Landrieu Floor Statement on Motion to Proceed to Senate Health Care Bill, November 21, 2009.
9. Shailagh Murray, "Public option at center of debate," *Washington Post,* November 23, 2009.
10. Chris Frates and Carrie Budoff Brown, "Daschle draws health care fire," *Politico,* December 2, 2009; and Jennifer Haberkorn, "Daschle, as private adviser, wields clout in health care debate," *Washington Times,* December 3, 2009.
11. Drew Armstrong and Alex Wayne, "Nelson Might Hold Up Health Bill," CQ.com, December 16, 2009.
12. McCain remarks, Senate floor debate, December 3, 2009.
13. Jay Rockefeller phone interview, April 30, 2010.
14. CBS News, *Face the Nation* transcript, December 13, 2009.
15. Michael Scherer, "Re Re Re Re: Joe Lieberman," Time.com, Swampland blog, December 14, 2009.
16. Sherrod Brown interview, March 12, 2010.
17. Governor Dave Heineman letter to the Honorable E. Benjamin Nelson, December 16, 2009.
18. Rockefeller interview.

14. THE RESCUE PLAN

1. Public Policy Polling, "Toss-up in Massachusetts," January 9, 2010.
2. Rasmussen Reports, "Election 2010: Massachusetts Special Senate Election," January 12, 2010.
3. Brown for U.S. Senate Web site, "On Jobs Tour, Brown Opposes National Health Care Legislation," December 31, 2009.

4. Hannity, January 8, 2010, YouTube video (accessed May 3, 2010).
5. Henry Waxman phone interview, April 16, 2010.
6. Lori Montgomery and Michael D. Shear, "White House nears deal on health care," *Washington Post,* January 15, 2010.
7. Matt Viser and Andrea Estes, "Big Win for Brown," *Boston Globe,* January 20, 2010.
8. Robert Pear and David M. Herszenhorn, "A New Search for Consensus on Health Care Bill," *The New York Times,* January 22, 2010.
9. ABC News interview transcript, January 20, 2010.
10. Carl Hulse and Sheryl Gay Stolberg, "His Health Bill Stalled, Obama Juggles an Altered Agenda," *The New York Times,* January 29, 2010.
11. Joint Committee on Taxation, "Estimated Revenue Effects of the Manager's Amendment to the Revenue Provisions Contained in the 'Patient Protection and Affordable Care Act,'" December 19, 2009, JCX-61-09.
12. Waxman interview.
13. Obama remarks at House Republican retreat, CQ Transcripts, January 29, 2010.
14. Kathleen Sebelius letter to Leslie Margolin, President, Anthem Blue Cross, February 8, 2010.
15. Duke Helfand, "Anthem Blue Cross withdraws request for rate hikes," *Los Angeles Times,* April 30, 2010.
16. Erica Werner, "HHS Secretary asks insurer to justify rate hike," Associated Press, February 8, 2010.
17. Rahm Emanuel and Kathleen Sebelius letter to Speaker Pelosi, Senator Reid, Senator McConnell, and Representative Boehner, February 12, 2009.
18. "The President's Proposal," Whitehouse.gov, February 22, 2010.
19. Bipartisan summit on health care, CQ Transcripts, February 25, 2010; and Obama letter to Speaker Pelosi, Senator Reid, Senator McConnell, and Representative Boehner, March 2, 2010.
20. Bipartisan summit on health care, CQ Transcripts.
21. Douglas W. Elmendorf, Congressional Budget Office, letter to the Honorable John A. Boehner, November 4, 2009; and Patient Protection and Affordable Care Act (HR 3590), Sec. 1101.

15. THE FINAL PUSH

1. Sheryl Gay Stolberg and Robert Pear, "Obama Takes Health Care Deadline to Democrats," *The New York Times,* March 4, 2010; and Alex Wayne, Edward Epstein, and Kathleen Hunter, "White House Whips for Health Care," CQ.com, March 4, 2010.
2. "Health Reform Bill Needs More Work Despite New Language on Abortion, Say Catholic Bishops," United States Conference of Catholic Bishops, December 19, 2009.
3. Bart Stupak interview, April 27, 2010.
4. Patrick Healy and Robin Toner, "Wary of Past, Clinton Unveils a Health Plan," *The New York Times,* September 18, 2007.
5. Patient Protection and Affordable Care Act (HR 3590), December 24, 2009.
6. Mike Ross phone interview, March 4, 2009.
7. James Hohmann, "Hoyer: Dems still working on the votes," *Politico,* March 16, 2010.
8. Lori Montgomery and Paul Kane, "House may try to pass Senate health-care bill without voting on it," *The Washington Post,* March 16, 2010.
9. "Kucinich Remarks on Health Care Vote," March 17, 2010; and Michael Muskal, "Obama's Uneasy Passenger: Kucinich," *Chicago Tribune,* March 15, 2010.

10. "Gutierrez to Vote 'Yes' for Health Care Legislation," March 18, 2010.
11. Matt Viser, "In shift, Lynch will vote no on health bill," *Boston Globe,* March 19, 2010.
12. Douglas W. Elmendorf, Congressional Budget Office, letter to the Honorable Nancy Pelosi, March 20, 2010.
13. "Congressman Bart Gordon: The Status Quo Is No Longer Affordable," March 18, 2010.
14. Alex Leary, "Allen Boyd, Suzanne Kosmas, flip from 'no' to 'yes' on health care vote," *St. Petersburg Times,* March 19, 2010; David M. Herszenhorn, "Boccieri to Vote Yes," *New York Times,* March 19, 2010; "Congressman Murphy Announces Intention to Vote Yes on Health Care Reform," March 19, 2010; and Mark Matthews, "Kosmas to back healthcare reform," *Orlando Sentinel,* March 19, 2010.
15. Jared Allen, Jeffrey Young, and Molly K. Hooper, "Pro-Choice Caucus livid at talk of deal with Stupak on abortion," *The Hill,* March 19, 2010.
16. Stupak interview.
17. Ibid.
18. Coauthor's notes from Capitol protests, March 21, 2010.
19. Stupak interview.
20. Dan Pfeiffer, "One More Step Towards Health Insurance Reform," March 21, 2010.
21. Stupak press conference, March 21, 2010.
22. Todd J. Gillman, "Rep. Pete Sessions' balcony cameo in 'Kill the Bill,'" *The Dallas Morning News,* Trail Blazers blog, March 22, 2010.
23. House debate on the Patient Protection and Affordable Care Act (HR 3590), March 21, 2010.
24. Ibid.
25. Stupak interview.
26. House debate.
27. "Neugebauer Statement on Health Care Floor Debate," March 22, 2010.
28. Monica Guzman, "Marcelas Owens' big day: Seattle boy spent it with Obama," *Seattle Post-Intelligencer,* "The Big Blog," March 23, 2010.
29. Remarks by the President and Vice President at Signing of Health Insurance Reform Bill, White House, March 23, 2010.

Part Four: The Road from Here

1. HOW CLOSE DID WE COME?

1. Senate Roll Call Vote 377, 111th Congress, 1st sess., December 15, 2009.

2. LAYING THE GROUNDWORK: 2010–13

1. Douglas W. Elmendorf, Congressional Budget Office, letter to the Honorable Evan Bayh, November 30, 2009.
2. Patient Protection and Affordable Care Act (PL 111–148), Sec. 10103.
3. Ibid., Secs. 2711 and 2712.
4. Ibid., Sec. 2714.
5. Department of the Treasury, Department of Labor, and Department of Health and Human Services, "Interim Final Rules for Group Health Plans and Health Insurance Issuers

Relating to Dependent Coverage of Children to Age 26 under the Patient Protection and Affordable Care Act."

6. Patient Protection and Affordable Care Act, Sec. 1421.
7. Ibid., Sec. 1101.
8. Ibid., Sec. 1102.
9. National Conference of State Legislatures, "Coverage of High-Risk Uninsurables: State and Federal High-Risk Pools," updated May 27, 2010.
10. Patient Protection and Affordable Care Act, Sec. 10201.
11. Health Care and Education Reconciliation Act of 2010 (PL 111–152), Sec. 1101.
12. Patient Protection and Affordable Care Act, Sec. 2713.
13. Ibid., Sec. 6301.
14. Ibid., Sec. 10101.
15. Ibid., Sec. 8002.
16. Health Care and Education Reconciliation Act, Sec. 1101.
17. Patient Protection and Affordable Care Act, Secs. 4103 and 4104.
18. Health Care and Education Reconciliation Act, Sec. 1102.
19. Patient Protection and Affordable Care Act, Sec. 3401.
20. Ibid., Sec. 3402.
21. Ibid., Sec. 3021.
22. Health Care and Education Reconciliation Act, Sec. 1102.
23. Patient Protection and Affordable Care Act, Sec. 3403.
24. Ibid., Sec. 3022.
25. Ibid., Sec. 2704.
26. Ibid., Sec. 3001.
27. Ibid., Sec. 3025.
28. Ibid., Sec. 2715.
29. Health Care and Education Reconciliation Act, Sec. 1101.
30. Ibid., Sec. 1202.
31. Patient Protection and Affordable Care Act, Sec. 10331.
32. Ibid., Sec. 9015.
33. Health Care and Education Reconciliation Act, Sec. 1402.
34. Patient Protection and Affordable Care Act, Sec. 9013.
35. Ibid., Sec. 3023.

3. A NEW ERA: 2014–18

1. Patient Protection and Affordable Care Act (PL 111–148), Sec. 1311.
2. Ibid., Sec. 1302.
3. Ibid.
4. Ibid., Sec. 1311.
5. Ibid., Sec. 1401.
6. Ibid., Sec. 2704.
7. Ibid., Sec. 2701.
8. Ibid., Sec. 2711.
9. Ibid., Sec. 1501.
10. Health Care and Education Reconciliation Act of 2010 (PL 111–152), Sec. 1002.
11. Ibid., Sec. 1001.

12. Patient Protection and Affordable Care Act, Sec. 2001.
13. Health Care and Education Reconciliation Act, Sec. 1003.
14. Patient Protection and Affordable Care Act, Sec. 1421.
15. Ibid., Sec. 1334.
16. Ibid., Sec. 1322.
17. Ibid., Sec. 3403.
18. Ibid., Sec. 3007.
19. Ibid., Sec. 10320.
20. Health Care and Education Reconciliation Act, Sec. 1002; and Joint Committee on Taxation, "Technical Explanation of the Revenue Provisions of the 'Reconciliation Act of 2010,' as Amended, in Combination with the 'Patient Protection and Affordable Care Act'" (JCX-18–10), March 21, 2010, 31–34.
21. Massachusetts Division of Health Care Finance and Policy, "Study Reveals Health Insurance Coverage Rates in Massachusetts Holding Steady at 97 percent," October 14, 2009.
22. Patient Protection and Affordable Care Act, Sec. 1333.
23. Ibid., Sec. 1312.
24. Ibid., Sec. 1332.
25. Health Care and Education Reconciliation Act, Sec. 1201.
26. Ibid., Sec. 1401.
27. "Employer Health Benefits: 2009 Summary of Findings," Henry J. Kaiser Family Foundation and Health Research & Educational Trust, September 2009.
28. Health Care and Education Reconciliation Act, Sec. 1401; and Joint Committee on Taxation, "Technical Explanation," 57–66.

4. NEW RESPONSIBILITIES

1. Nicholas Johnson, Phil Oliff, and Erica Williams, "An Update on State Budget Cuts," Center on Budget and Policy Priorities, April 19, 2010.
2. Senator John D. Rockefeller IV, letter to the Honorable Kathleen Sebelius, May 7, 2010; and Robert Pear, "Health Insurance Companies Try to Shape Rules," *The New York Times*, May 15, 2010.
3. Karen Pollitz, "Issues for Structuring Interim High-Risk Pools," Henry J. Kaiser Family Foundation, January 2010.
4. Patient Protection and Affordable Care Act (PL 111–148), Sec. 1311.
5. Kate Pickert, "Jail Time for Insurance Evaders? Yes, Said Fox News," Time.com, Swampland blog, April 14, 2010.
6. Joint Committee on Taxation, "Technical Explanation of the Revenue Provisions of the 'Reconciliation Act of 2010,' as Amended, in Combination with the 'Patient Protection and Affordable Care Act,'" JCX-18-10, March 21, 2010, 35–36.
7. Schulman testimony, House Ways and Means Oversight Subcommittee, March 25, 2010.
8. Joint Committee on Taxation, "Technical Explanation," 33.
9. Martin Vaughan, "IRS May Withhold Tax Refunds to Enforce Health-Care Law," *Wall Street Journal*, April 15, 2010.
10. Drew Altman phone interview, May 24, 2010.
11. Health Care and Education Reconciliation Act of 2010 (PL 111–152), Sec. 1005.
12. Patient Protection and Affordable Care Act, Sec. 1311.
13. Congressional Budget Office cost estimate, HR 4872, Reconciliation Act of 2010 (Final Health Care Legislation), March 20, 2010.

14. Altman interview.
15. Patient Protection and Affordable Care Act, Sec. 1311.
16. For a good breakdown of uncompensated care costs, see Jack Hadley and John Holahan, "The Cost of Care for the Uninsured: What Do We Spend, Who Pays, and What Would Full Coverage Add to Medical Spending?" Henry J. Kaiser Family Foundation, 2004.
17. January Angeles, "Health Reform Is a Good Deal for States," Center on Budget and Policy Priorities, April 26, 2010.
18. "State Decision-Making in Implementing National Health Reform," National Governors Association working paper, March 15, 2010.
19. Patient Protection and Affordable Care Act, Sec. 1311.
20. Sandy Praeger phone interview, May 28, 2010.

5. NEXT STEPS

1. Patient Protection and Affordable Care Act (PL 111–148), Secs. 3403, 10320.
2. Paul Ginsburg phone interview, May 24, 2010.
3. Transparency in All Health Care Pricing Act of 2010 (HR 4700).
4. Patient Protection and Affordable Care Act, Sec. 10607.
5. Sandy Praeger phone interview, May 28, 2010.
6. Patient Protection and Affordable Care Act, Sec. 6301.
7. Phillip Longman, "Code Red: How software companies could screw up Obama's health care reform," The Washington Monthly, July/August 2009.
8. Congressional Budget Office cost estimate, HR 4872, Reconciliation Act of 2010 (Final Health Care Legislation), March 20, 2010.

CONCLUSION

1. Charles Merz, "Issues the Campaign Has Brought to the Fore," The New York Times, November 1, 1936.
2. "The Voters' Mood: Most Issues Fail to Stir Public; Apathy Likely to Benefit Incumbents," Wall Street Journal, November 7, 1966; Max Frankel, "Humphrey and Nixon: Substance and Styles," The New York Times, September 30, 1968; and Howard A. Rusk, "Health as Election Issue: Humphrey Would Extend Medicare, but His Rivals Say Little on Subject," The New York Times, November 3, 1968.
3. Earl Black and Merle Black, The Rise of Southern Republicans (Cambridge, MA: Belknap Press of Harvard University Press, 2002), 205.
4. David S. Broder, "Reagan Victory Aids G.O.P. Right," The New York Times, June 9, 1966.
5. Black and Black, Rise of Southern Republicans, 215–18.
6. Taylor Branch, Pillar of Fire (New York: Simon & Schuster, 1998), 523.
7. Kristin L. Carman et al., "Evidence That Consumers Are Skeptical About Evidence-Based Health Care," Health Affairs 29, no. 7 (July 2010).

Index